NOT QUITE PARADISE

The author on the southern beaches of the island.

Not Quite Paradise

An American Sojourn in Sri Lanka

ADELE BARKER

Beacon Press
BOSTON

Beacon Press
25 Beacon Street
Boston, Massachusetts 02108-2892
www.beacon.org

Beacon Press books
are published under the auspices of
the Unitarian Universalist Association of Congregations.

13 12 11 10   8 7 6 5 4 3 2 1

This book is printed on acid-free paper that meets the uncoated paper
ANSI/NISO specifications for permanence as revised in 1992.

Composition by Wilsted & Taylor Publishing Services

Library of Congress Cataloging-in-Publication Data
Barker, Adele Marie.
  Not quite paradise : an American sojourn in Sri Lanka / Adele Barker.
     p. cm.
  ISBN 978-0-8070-0061-8 (hardcover : alk. paper) 1. Barker, Adele Marie,
1946–Travel—Sri Lanka. 2. Sri Lanka—Description and travel. 3. Sri Lanka—
Ethnic relations. 4. Ethnic conflict—Sri Lanka. 5. War and society—Sri Lanka.
6. Sri Lanka—History—Civil War, 1983– 7. Tsunamis—Sri Lanka. 8. Indian
Ocean Tsunami, 2004. 9. Teachers—Sri Lanka—Biography. I. Title.
  DS489.B26 2009
  954.9303'2092—dc22   2009013015

An excerpt from the poem "April 1971" is reprinted here with permission.

Many names and identifying characteristics of people mentioned in this work
have been changed to protect their identities.

For Jon

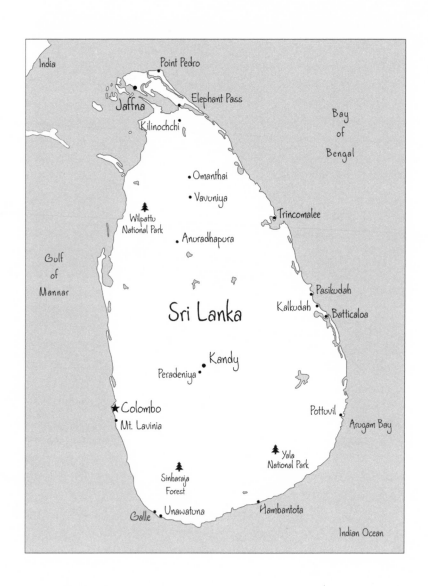

India

Point Pedro

Jaffna
Elephant Pass

Kilinochchi

Bay
of
Bengal

Omanthai

Vavuniya

Wilpattu
National Park

Trincomalee

Anuradhapura

Gulf
of
Mannar

Pasikudah
Kalkudah
Batticaloa

Sri Lanka

Kandy

Peradeniya

Colombo
Mt. Lavinia

Pottuvil

Arugam Bay

Yala
National Park

Sinharaja
Forest

Galle   Unawatuna

Hambantota

Indian Ocean

CONTENTS

PART I

Peradeniya, where I went to teach.

CHAPTER I

Going and Coming I

A voyage in time of peace, especially when it is to the East, has always,
more or less the same general characteristics. When the voyage is taken in
time of war, the whole aspect changes. . . . then a voyage, no matter
where, is of a very different class altogether.

—Frederick Lewis, *Sixty Years in Ceylon*

An Italian named Marignolli was the first European tourist to be
robbed in Ceylon. In the mid-fourteenth century, he was on his
way back to Florence from China with the various treasures he had
amassed. Blown off course, his ship landed in Seyllan (Ceylon), where
it fell into the hands of a devious Saracen robber who proceeded to
strip him of all the finery he was bringing back from China. Apart
from that incident, Marignolli found the island quite to his liking.
Judging by his accounts, he decided that the isle was, if not Paradise
itself, very close to it in a literal sense. Using some imaginative math-
ematical calculations, he calibrated the distance between the two
places and arrived at the figure of a mere forty Italian miles, so close
that "the sound of the waters falling from the fountain of Paradise"
could be heard in Seyllan. Reason enough to want to come back.

And come back many did over the centuries before and after:
travelers from Europe, Asia, Africa, and, more recently, America.
Some were blown off course; some came for the spices; some to
conquer and rule; some, much later, simply to sunbathe. Fa-Hien,
from China in the late fourth century AD, was one of the first to

lead the brigade, followed by a Greek merchant named Cosmas in the mid-sixth century. Marco Polo briefly made port here, as did Ibn Batuta, a traveling Moor from Tangier. Dutch admirals, Portuguese soldiers, French envoys, German mercenaries, and (more recently) European sun worshippers shaking winter off their backs—all have come to the island.

I came to teach.

Over the centuries visitors invented wonderful, magical names for this small place in the Indian Ocean. As they drew maps, the island looked to them like a teardrop hanging off the coast of India. Some saw it rather as a pearl. Those with a more scientific bent considered the island a geological fragment broken off from the Indian subcontinent when the earth was still forming. The Greeks and Romans called it Taprobane (a corruption of the word *tambapanni,* meaning copper-colored palms); the Arab traders, Serendib, their version of Sihaladipa, the island of the Sinhala. The Portuguese, arriving in search of spice, called it Ceilao; the Dutch tweaked it to Ceylan; and the British, who moved in in 1815 and then out again in 1948, modified it to Ceylon, the name retained today by tea purveyors the world over. In 1972, the people who actually live on this island reclaimed the name Sri Lanka, which in Pali means "resplendent isle," a name that the Sinhalese majority of the population had used throughout even as foreign powers came and went. The Tamils knew the island as Ilankai, the Tamil translation of Lanka.

"Going and coming?" the man at passport control asked me at 3:00 in the morning as my son Noah and I stood rooted in line at Colombo International Airport after two and a half days of flying.

"Pardon?" was all I could muster at that hour.

"Going and coming, madam? And how long will you be staying?"

"No, not a tourist. One year. Resident visa."

"Very well, madam. And you will be living, madam?"

"Kandy," I answered, "but working in Peradeniya. I will be teaching there."

Half an hour later Noah and I stood in silence with a hundred or so other people, rendered stupid by sleeplessness, and listened to the grinding of a baggage carousel badly in need of oiling as it disgorged boxes carrying TVs, electrical appliances, baby carriages, oversized suitcases, and furniture wrapped in bubble wrap. We grabbed what was ours, wended our way through customs, down hallways, passed stores asleep for the night, and at 3:30 in the morning walked out into South Asia. And into a crowd of five hundred people on the walkway and street.

"Quite a welcoming committee," I remarked to Noah.

"I don't think they're here for us, Mom."

As we made our way through the crowd, I noticed signs up everywhere with pictures on them of something that looked like a cross between a pineapple and a small melon announcing in English and two indecipherable languages that under no circumstance was durian to be brought on board an airplane.

I looked at Noah. "Do you know what durian is?"

"Very smelly fruit, madam," a man nearby with his own load of luggage told us. "Very sweet taste, very bad odor."

I asked him if he knew anything about the crowd that had stationed itself here.

"They're waiting, madam. We didn't have this problem formerly. People could come and go into the airport. They could accompany whoever was leaving all the way to passport control. But we had this unfortunate incident this past summer and now only the people who are actually traveling and can produce a ticket are allowed in. Excuse me, but I believe you are American. We are very, very sorry." He put his hands together and bowed.

I thanked him and put Noah and myself into a cab.

"First time Sri Lanka?" our driver asked.

"Yes, first time."

"Madam, your country?"

"America," I replied. I looked over at Noah, who was already dozing in the seat next to me.

"Very sorry, madam, for your problems. Very big problem just now in America."

I thanked him. It is three weeks since 9/11. Thirteen time zones removed from where I am registered to vote, six degrees north of the equator, latitudinally level with the Republic of Central Africa,

Colombia, and Baker Island, there is not a person here who does not know about 9/11.

Things do not work quite the same the other way around. We have come to a country that has been at war with itself for close to twenty years. And yet it is a war that has gone underreported in the U.S. press. On July 24, 2001, two months prior to our arrival, the Liberation Tigers of Tamil Eelam (known as the LTTE) who, under the leadership of Vellupillai Prabhakaran, have been fighting for an independent homeland in the north for eighteen years, launched an attack on the Sri Lanka Air Force Base and the adjoining Colombo International Airport in the predawn hours. In the ensuing six-hour melee, twenty-six commercial and military airlines were destroyed or heavily damaged. All thirteen rebels were killed. The intervening weeks had done nothing to resolve the situation, as President Chandrika Kumaratunga proceeded to dissolve Parliament to avoid having her government toppled by the opposition. Subsequently two more car bombs had gone off, and two suicide bombers had detonated themselves in busy sections of Colombo.

By the time we arrived in 2001, the civil war had claimed forty thousand lives.

"You are going where for a year?" asked the woman at the company that handles my car insurance in Tucson, Arizona. "Did you say Sierra Vista?"

Our taxi took us through unlit, rain-soaked streets and deposited us into a time capsule approximately one hundred years back in the heyday of British colonialism at the Galle Face Hotel. We were greeted in our predawn haze by a Sri Lankan doorman with a handlebar moustache, dressed in a white uniform with gold braid, looking like something out of Kipling. We went immediately to our room and collapsed into sleep to the sound of waves fifty feet from us doing battle with the seawall.

Toward afternoon we roused ourselves and found our way down a carpeted staircase of nineteenth-century elegance. Ever so slightly the worse for wear, our hotel still retained something of the grace it sported under the British Raj. Something was wrong here, though. We seemed to be the only guests. We were in a play with no people in it.

We walked out onto a portico with tables set up and a view of the Indian Ocean. We seated ourselves and looked around nervously until a lone waiter appeared from another room. Gracious and attentive, he ministered to our breakfast needs and stood over us should we need anything, just anything at all. And for the next five days we were watched over by a staff that catered to the slightest nod of the head or movement of the hand. We ate long, lingering breakfasts on the hotel veranda. Sometimes I would watch a bartender sitting lazily on a stool, pausing from his languor long enough to dust some glasses; I would order gin and tonics on the back porch; we dined by candlelight and sea spray on the patio. We walked through empty dining rooms and ballrooms.

An American named Jon Pearce came over to join us one evening for dinner, having learned from the Fulbright Commission that some new American Fulbrighters had just arrived. He had been teaching for four months at the University of Colombo. His family was still back in California, but his wife would be joining him shortly. He talked to us a little bit about being here on 9/11. I could tell we were getting only half the story. For our part I gave him the formal version of why we were here. It's a Senior Fulbright, I told him, but up in Kandy and for a year. That was the version the State Department got, but for me it had all come down to something Bruce Chatwin once said: "If it's a case of going or staying, always get the hell out."

And I did.

Jon's travels had taken him to Africa and Turkey. It was obviously Africa that he had absorbed. Sitting there alone, he seemed to be that part of his family that had been struck with wanderlust. I felt an instantaneous bond with this nomad with a shock of white hair.

Ironically, we who had come here to be anything but tourists *were* the tourists. We are the objects of everyone's day, the goal of what remains of the tourist trade in and out of our hotel. In the wake of 9/11, there is simply no one here. But we aren't very good tourists. We don't budge. We spend our first days in Sri Lanka in the United States, Noah in front of the television watching CNN and the BBC, me in front of the window or on the veranda of the old colonialist dowager, staring out to sea.

I spend a lot of time outside just looking at the sky. The young men who are doing repairs watch me watching the sky. Rain hangs heavy in the air as the gray sea creeps into a gray sky.

"Madam, you are watching our sea a lot, no?" asks one of the men who works here.

"Yes," I tell him. "I am from the desert, and I love the sea. I am trying to get to know Sri Lanka's waves."

"Our monsoon this year was late," he tells me. "But now it is finished almost. But when monsoon is finished, still we have a monsoon sea. That is why waves are very big just now."

He is quiet for a moment. The two of us just stand there and look.

"Madam," he says, "our monsoon is like our war. We know we can count on it, but we don't know when."

On our last day in Colombo I stood on the portico looking out onto Galle Face Green, assessing the possibility for rain that day. A Sri Lankan gentleman, perhaps guessing my nationality, came over to join me. We talked about the sea, the winds, the late monsoon this year and the drought in the south. And then:

"We are all very, very sorry."

I thanked him.

The next day Noah and I got ready to leave for our new home. We shut the windows, drew the curtains, packed up, and turned off the TV. We turned our back on the sea and headed inland up into the mountains.

CHAPTER 2

Student Life

In 1940 an Englishman named Ivor Jennings, dressed in the de ri-
gueur white drill suit and Panama hat worn by white men coming
to the tropics for the first time, arrived on the island that the English
called Ceylon. He brought with him several steamer trunks and a
vision. Even as World War II was moving into Asia, Jennings had
his sights set on founding a university, an oriental Cambridge nestled
at the foot of the Hantana range in the hill country of the island. By
1942 his dream began to take shape as the University of Ceylon was
founded in Colombo. It would take another twelve years of inordi-
nate delays, mind-numbing bureaucratic hassles, and the clearing of
scrub jungle and rubber and tea plantations that had been running at
a loss for some time before Jennings's pastoral vision would be realized. After the war the architects, gardeners, and landscapers moved
in, carving out of the brush, tea, and rubber a horticultural Eden
that would become the intellectual home for Ceylon's brightest and
best. Scrub was moved out; aloe plants were moved in. Finally, in
1954 a residential university came into being up at Peradeniya in the
hill country of Ceylon. Graced with greenery and laced with the
streams that fell from the upper reaches of the mountains, the place
was designed originally as an extension of the Peradeniya Botanical
Gardens, the beauties of the one spilling over into the other through
interlinking footpaths. Today if you hike up into the Hantana range
far enough, you will come across some of the remaining tea estates,
several of which are still being cultivated. Along the old road lead-

ing up there sit the campus Buddhist temple, the Hindu *kovil,* the campus chapel, and the mosque, each partially concealed behind a scrim of green.

I was late for the start of the school year by four months. I had been asked via e-mail the previous summer whether I could teach nineteenth- and twentieth-century Russian literature since the students in the English program need one foreign literature for their degree. I agreed since most of my training had been in Russian studies. And criticism. Could I do feminist literary theory? Yes, of course. What about a semester of early American literature? This was a little more complicated, but over the summer I was able to pull things together before we left the States.

"We've got two batches of students here," my colleague Thiru Kandiah had told me in one of a series of long e-mails we exchanged before I arrived. He told me about the student insurrections that started in the early 1970s and then resurfaced in the 1980s during the civil war. Some of the other university campuses were affected by them, but Peradeniya was the epicenter. The government closed the campus down. In the meantime, a new batch of students were accepted, causing difficulties when the university reopened. "We're still processing the backlog of students from the 1980s and 1990s who got accepted but couldn't attend because the university was shut down," Thiru told me. There are now two different tracks with two different sets of requirements as a result of all the closures. Thiru thinks they should be finished with the backlog by 2005 or 2006.

In this same e-mail he warned me, "Expect nothing to go smoothly."

We had come up to the town of Kandy where we would be living for the next year in and out of intermittent downpours. I rubbed the steam from the window of the van and could see young women alongside the road taking cover under their tarps. Next to them stood tables with bags of varying shapes and sizes all lined up.

"What are they selling?" I asked.

"These are the cashew ladies," came the answer from the driver. "You're in Pasyala. Each town here sells something different. Soon, madam, you will come to the wicker town and then the clay pots town."

As we inched up the mountain, the rain showed no signs of abating, and the driver pulled over at a tea *kade* to wait out the storm.

"Is it the monsoon?" I asked.

"Well, madam, we are calling it here pre-monsoon, so not exactly monsoon yet."

"So, is the monsoon worse?"

"No, not actually worse, madam."

"So, what is the difference then? How can I tell the difference between the two?" I pressed on.

"It is rain, madam," he said with a shrug of the shoulders and a smile.

As we waited for our tea I watched banana leaves torn from their trees lying drenched on the ground. Something rather grandiose, slimy and black and seemingly impervious to the rain, made its way across the street.

"Monitor lizard, madam," said the driver, seeing the look on my face. "Come madam, we are going now to Kandy Town."

We had taken a house for the first week up on a hill alongside the lake in Kandy. The place was a hand-me-down of sorts from an American family who had lived there briefly the year prior before moving up into the hills. I looked around me. No, we will not stay here, I thought to myself, but for now it was a place to lay our heads. I got Noah into school, the International School across the river, headed by a British master who, from what I could gather, was fed up with life in the Midlands, pulled up stakes, and ended up six degrees north of the equator with a new life.

With Noah at least marginally settled, I called the university and was told to show up the next morning prepared to start classes.

Food. Our bubble of colonialist privilege had suddenly burst the day we arrived in Kandy, as I realized somewhat belatedly that we were going to have to feed ourselves. But the bubble closed in around us once more as we walked into the one grocery store in town, clearly designed for foreigners and Kandy's upper crust, a place called Food City, where the door was held open for us by a man straight out of Kipling, looking suspiciously like the doorman at the Galle Face Hotel. The stuff on the shelves looked to be straight out of Kipling as well. Jacobs Biscuits. Scotch malt. Clearly, this couldn't be where people actually shop, but we had fetched up here somehow because we were new and foreign and white, and because I didn't know enough to know what I was doing yet. We emerged with enough to keep body and soul together for the next two days until I could start putting the pieces of our life together. And for now that was good enough. From one of the sellers on the street, I bought a big red plastic tub with a picture of a Chinese baby on the bottom. It was to be our laundry tub for the next year.

As we emerged from the store a short, stocky Sri Lankan wearing a Sea World T-shirt and a pair of jeans appeared with his hand outstretched. He smiled broadly and introduced himself as Champika. "Madam, I am your *tuk-tuk* driver. Other American will say you will be coming. I am here your driver all year."

Champika was way ahead of me. I was still dealing with the word *tuk-tuk,* and Noah was getting his first close-up look at something that looked like a cross between a bumper car and a rickshaw. There were at least fifty of these all parked in a one-block area around the food store, from which people were coming and going with packages filled with colonialism.

I was getting the sense that word of our arrival had indeed preceded us. A small group of young men in their twenties had already gathered round to listen in and smile. They were all sporting T-shirts with American logos on them and all were *tuk-tuk* drivers. We seemed to have inherited Champika and didn't have the strength or the wherewithal to have it any other way, at least not for now. By the end of the conversation, I'd gotten Noah to school and back for the rest of the year and me to the university, all of this at the local grocery store.

"No problem. We go and come to campus," he assured me, grabbing our sacks and ushering us in the direction of his *tuk-tuk*. And so, tucked in the back of a metal three-wheeler with a canvas roof over our heads, propelled by a small motor that sputtered tentatively, we wove with Champika in and out through traffic—stalled buses, moving buses, people attempting more or less successfully

to cross the street—and lurched around the lake to our temporary
quarters, bringing home the plastic tub with the Chinese baby on the
bottom of it. I had the feeling I didn't need to give Champika our
address as he headed up the hill to Mahamaya Mawatha, where we
were staying. I looked out at the hawkers on the street and the min-
iature school vans glutting the roadway around the lake. Champika
was singing to the accompaniment of horns.

"You call me when you will be finished."

"Yes, yes, I'll call," I assured Champika as I looked down the hill
onto the campus the next morning.

"Good luck," he said in perfect English.

In my straw hat I headed down the stairs alongside the theater
and threaded my way in and out of a sea of umbrellas that young
women were carrying to protect themselves from the sun. People
turned and smiled. Someone pointed me toward the English Faculty,
and I walked through an open-air atrium, passed groups of Muslim
women in their veils, passed doors with signs reading "Department
of Tamil Studies," "Anthropology," "Department of Sinhalese Studies," and into the secretary's office of the English department. Half
an hour later I was standing in a classroom facing my six students: all
female, all English majors, all about to graduate.

"You will have us all year, until June, madam," they told me.
"We are what you call third-year batch."

I spent that morning telling them a little about myself: where I
came from, that I was here with my son, and that I needed a break
from the life I was living.

"Are you married, madam?" came the inevitable question.

"No, I'm not married; it's just me and my son." Are they surprised, I wondered?

We all wanted to know more about each other than we were
asking and so the larger questions got subsumed into the more immediate ones of textbooks. There is no university bookstore, and the
bookstores in Kandy for the most part sell Sri Lankan literature and
the British classics. They order what they can, but not everything is
easily available. Thiru had warned me about this ahead of time, and
so I had multiple copies of the various works we were going to read

shipped over. All arrived in good order until the anthrax scare hit the diplomatic pouch of the State Department and boxes destined for half a world away began to pile up in Washington. Some things arrived four months late. I simply changed the syllabus. Having dispensed with the textbook problem for now, we embarked that first day on Russian literature. Classes ran in two-hour segments. At the end of an hour, I asked my six girls if they would like a break.

"No, madam, we are quite fine, thank you."

And when the first class ended, the second began in the same room with the same young women.

"And so I will see you tomorrow," I told them at the end of our first day together.

I had just said something wrong. There was a stilled silence broken finally by Kanchuka, who proceeded to initiate me into the finer mysteries of Sri Lankan holidays.

"Madam, we have *poya* tomorrow. It is our full moon. It is a Buddhist holiday. The Buddha was born, received enlightenment, and died all under a *poya*. And so on these days everything is closed."

It is lovely, enchanting, and I told them I wished we had something like it in the States. Sri Lanka, I was about to learn, has the well-earned distinction of having more holidays than any other country in the world. Sometimes I will have trouble getting anything taught because of all the holidays. And so began my year of teaching with our classes woven in and out of *poya* days, election days, election violence days, the religious holidays of four different religions, and university-induced holidays.

"Kanchuka, Nirosha, Rozmin, Sumudu, Tanya, and Vihara," I repeated to myself in Champika's *tuk-tuk* on the way back to try to sort out our domestic situation.

CHAPTER 3

Housekeeping

I wasn't sure if we were going to keep this house. It sat above the lake constructed under the last Kandyan king and above the tennis courts of the Kandy Garden Club constructed under the British Raj, both defunct yet ever-present phenomena. The house was way too big for the two of us and seemed almost cavernous. Made of stucco with greenery clinging to its outside walls, the place seemed hollow and uninviting with its three bedrooms, two baths, and a long hallway that led out into an area that was part storage room, part work area. As I walked through its spaces, I saw mementos from other years: other families' pieces of Sri Lankan folk art, something else that suggested that someone had been to Africa. Old furniture stood side by side with tables and bookcases of hastily thrown together particleboard. From the kitchen and dining room I could see out onto a small back patio where the washing and drying was done and where a steep hill sent down coconuts and rocks torn loose from the world above our house. Further on beyond the connecting work area were other houses, where the landlords lived and where guests came to visit. A portico between the houses was rimmed by a small grassy area that bordered a long hedge punctuated by trees whose leaves and branches were as unknown to me as the birds that nested in them. Our own house had been vacant for a year and a half and bore all the marks of a place left to its own devices. Bus traffic from around the lake sprang into action at 5:00 in the morning, sometimes earlier, creating fumes that rose from the street below, up over our hedge, and into our lives and laundry. But by week's end I stopped looking for other places partially, though not entirely, out of lethargy. Something kept us here. Perhaps it was my fantasy of having a porch, which I initially saw as a place of Buddhist contemplation. But as the months went by and the power outages increased, a lot of our domestic activity would get shifted outside to make use of the lingering daylight. We ate, talked, read, and observed bird life. Noah prepared schoolwork and listened to music on his CD player. I dug up some old pots that had partially disintegrated and merged with the foliage and sat on the porch steps, planting seedlings and flowers in them.

We kept the house for other reasons too. The life in our compound seemed a microcosm of at least part of the island. Kush and Nandana, our landlords, were upper-class Sinhalese. Kush ran the local Kandyan branch of the Alliance Française, while Nandana oversaw that part of our compound that served as a guesthouse for travelers, mainly from France. Latha, a Sinhalese woman with some English, was in charge of cleaning and cooking in the main guesthouse and prepared Kush and Nandana's meals everyday. From our first day here I had seen an older man of unclear age, perhaps in his sixties, and of slight build, pruning, cleaning, taking care of Kush and Nandana's dog, planting, and doing repairs. He worked in his *sarong,* that piece of colorful material wrapped around his waist and reaching almost to the ground, and . . . an off-white button-down shirt. He was introduced to us as Velu, the Tamil guardian of the property. He had no English, just a gentle smile and a tongue made red by the daily chewing of betel leaf.

"How do I communicate with him?" I asked Kush, whose English, like that of many upper-class Sinhalese, was the product of schooling in the language both on the island and abroad.

"His native language is Tamil. He's estate Tamil, but it will be better for you to learn Sinhalese and speak to him in it. He can get you bread from the bakery in the morning."

"How do you say 'bread'?"

"Simple. It's *pan.*'"

"*Pan,*" I said. Velu smiled.

Kush started with the numbers. "Tell him how many loaves you will want. *Eka, dekka, tunai, hatarai.*" We stopped at four.

"We will never eat that many," I told her, laughing.

"You will need a housekeeper and a cook," she told me. "There is a woman available who used to work for one of the former tenants. Shall we get a message to her?"

This is where I dug in my heels. I didn't do this at home. Why should I do it here? There was also a race thing that was getting in the way. I didn't want people who are darker than me fixing our meals and cleaning for us. I was not going to do colonialism. I was going to do this myself. And so I turned down the offer.

"She needs the work," Kush told me. "But you decide."

I took down the heavy brown curtains in the living room, stiff with age and dirt. Noah and I washed and scraped the walls. I stripped the couches of their thick, brown wool covers and bought some cheap, yellow material at the market that I had made into slip covers. We changed lightbulbs, dusted off lighting fixtures, brushed away cobwebs, and made periodic cleaning forays into the bathroom. I moved seven large pieces of furniture out to a storage shed with Nandana's help, and threw buckets of hot water at the outside walls of the house, blackened by diesel fumes from the road below. We never did get everything really clean, but we went through the process of claiming the place as our own, which was more important. Occupied dirt was the way I like to think of it. We spent our first days in our home announcing our presence to everything that had taken up residence in it since the past tenants had moved away. Footsteps on the floors, doors slamming, toilets flushing, and electricity switched on and off served as necessary reminders to the creatures inside the walls that henceforth this was shared space.

The street outside our house reverberates with the generally happy cacophony of life. It starts up in the morning as the buses and trishaws begin their daily forays around the lake to the accompaniment of the blasting of horns—the modus operandi for driving in South Asia. By 6:00 the noise has spilled up onto our street, which starts to come alive with the chatter of pigtailed girls in their school whites heading up the hill to Mahamaya Girls College. By 7:00 vans glutted with other schoolkids, delivery trucks, local traffic, people walking to work, more *tuk-tuks,* construction workers, people taking shortcuts to avoid the gridlock on the street below, and locals on their way to the communal bathing spot at the top of the hill are all vying for the same lane and a half outside our house. Like most of the homes on this street, ours has a high metal gate with a chain and lock designed to keep the boundaries drawn. Some houses seem to accomplish this more efficiently than ours. The area just outside the gate becomes a parking area for some of the hundreds of small, white, privately owned vans that take kids back and forth to school in and around Kandy and create gridlock early in the morning and at 2:00 in the afternoon. Our gate area is also a meeting place for couples, while the gate itself becomes a swing for twenty to thirty schoolchildren who use it as a kind of teeter-totter while waiting for their school vans.

People drift in and out of our compound all day, selling housewares and clothes, looking for rooms. One Sunday from my porch I watched a man—barefoot, clad only in his *sarong,* and holding a plastic bag—deftly scaling our frangipani tree. He saw me and made a sign that I was not to worry. I continued to stare at him as he picked flowers from the tree and put them in his plastic sack. Soon Velu emerged, also half clad, with coconut in hand to chase the fellow away. I asked Kush about this later, and she told me that the flower sellers outside the Dalada Maligawa, the Temple of the Tooth where the reliquary of the Buddha's tooth is housed, come frequently to pick the blossoms from the frangipani tree since only flowers that have not yet touched the ground can be offered to the Buddha.

Another time a woman and her small daughter arrived with her husband's death certificate, wondering if we could help the family. We did. The next week she arrived again. I gave less that time and for four months after still felt wrong about it. I never saw her again.

After our first few days of settling in, I came out one morning, tea in hand, to make my morning inspection of the flora and fauna. A slight, middle-aged woman was standing on the dirt path leading from the house to the main gate. She had on a worn *sari* and carried a large pocketbook and a plastic bag. Her hair, streaked with gray, was pulled back into a bun. We stood looking at each other until Velu arrived to sort out the situation. They bowed to each other; clearly, they were old friends. He turned to me. "Loku Menike," he said, and I knew the name. This was the woman whom Kush had offered me when we first moved in to do our cooking and cleaning and whom I had turned down. Somehow she had turned up anyway.

I had talked briefly in Colombo with a young American woman who had employed her. "Don't get confused," she said. "She's not your servant. She is your key to the culture. Don't mix the two. She is educated, she knows a bit of English. The only thing is that she didn't get through her A levels, and so now she is working in different capacities for people. Her husband died a few years ago. She needs the work."

Now Nandana joined the group to translate. Much bowing and greeting ensued.

"She wants to start today," he said.

I told him that I didn't even know if I wanted to hire her and that I didn't feel right about this. I took him aside. "I don't want to be British and colonial."

"A lot of people say that, and then because of their principles a lot of other people are left without work," he said, smiling. "It's our economy; it's the war. But it's your choice."

"What do I call her? Loku?"

"No," he laughed. "Loku means 'big.' You can't just call someone 'Big.' Besides, she's little. You call her Loku Menike. It means 'Big Gem.' Some women are called Podi Menike, or 'Little Gem.' It's from Buddhist tradition. We worship the triple gems."

I went back and bowed to her. Inside the plastic bag she had brought her work clothes.

Loku Menike started work that day.

The next day I arrived home from the university and walked into the house to find all the furniture rearranged—but in a way that seemed to defy reason. Loku Menike had been at work, waxing the floors that day with a red wax paste. And so began our biweekly waxing, as this very small woman over whom I towered took cloth to floor and with considerable strength turned the floors at 2 Mahamaya Mawatha into replicas of all other floors in all other homes in Sri Lanka. It was our house's entry card into respectability.

There still remained the unsolved problem, however, of the other creatures in the house sharing our living space, the ant population for one. Our first weeks in Kandy consisted of a personal ant vendetta on my part. I pulverized them with the bug spray that we brought with us from the United States. One morning I walked into the bathroom to find a discreet ring decorating the edge of every available surface—over the door, down the cabinet, around the sink, and along the towel rack—with no particular point of origin. They looked like tiny brown beads . . . until I put my glasses on. I embarked on a raid and naively claimed victory. Within hours they had reclaimed their territory. After several weeks of repeated failures on Loku Menike and my part to rid the house of its cohabitants, I made an uneasy truce with them. A few days later, I opened the door of the microwave, which hadn't been used for years, only to find a suspicious-looking black film inside. I prodded it and watched the floor of the microwave leap into motion as the film devolved into thousands of black ants. I slammed the door closed in revulsion, remembering the Greek poet Sappho's injunction not to prod the rubble on the beach if you're squeamish about what you're going to find there. Wise words.

That evening I put the dishes away after dinner. The next morning I opened the cupboard only to be greeted by two shelves of our old friends, who had advanced in the night and taken up stationary positions on all available surfaces. I remembered Sappho's injunction and let them be. Noah and I ate our breakfast that morning out of paper cups. An hour later Loku Menike arrived and uttered an "*Aiyo,*" an exclamation that turned out to be one of the most useful Sinhalese words I learned. It can be heard an infinite number of times throughout the day, cutting across class, caste, gender, and race lines. It is the classic linguistic response to the dizzying number of things that can go wrong. Example: I emerge from the house early in the morning with a cup of tea in my hand to see Velu holding something in the garden, shouting, "*Polanga, polanga.*" Nandana comes down from his room, awakened by the noise, and translates. Velu is proudly displaying a Russell's viper that he managed to snare and kill just as it was slithering into my bedroom at 6:00 in the morning. *Polanga* is the deadliest snake on the island. A possible response to this scenario would be "*Aiyo.*"

But to return to the ants, Loku Menike explained to me that we couldn't kill the ants on this particular day because it was *poya,* or full moon day. Once again at the university there were no classes. Kush and Nandana would observe *poya* today by going to temple, taking flowers and fruit to the Buddha. On such days particular respect is paid to the sanctity of life—one of the seven major precepts of Buddhism. And so we closed the cabinet and went on about our business.

The next morning we were barely out of bed when Loku Menike made an unannounced appearance. This was not her usual day to work. It took her forty-five minutes on the bus to get to Kandy from her village of Ratemulla, a place that sits almost untouched by time at the top of the Hantana range way beyond the town of Ampitiya. But she was here, and I looked at her and shook my head, uttering one of my ten new words, which I thought meant "Wednesday" (*Badaadaa*), to let her know that this wasn't her day to work. She embarked on a narrative not limited to my ten new words, while changing from her *sari* into her house clothes. I understood nothing, but I watched as she headed into the kitchen, made short shrift of the ants, changed back into her *sari* again, and left to go back up the hill to Ratemulla.

"*Poya* finish," she told me. I smiled.

Noah seems to be handling this better than I am. At home in the United States he is the neater of the two of us. I watch here as he cleans and creates a place for himself in his bedroom and bathroom. He doesn't recoil in quite the same way I do from what nature throws our way. Is it a male thing, or am I simply too squeamish? Perhaps I am just being too Western about all this, too sanitized. My students look at me patiently as I discourse about my household bug situation in Kandy, but it is simply what people live with here. Maybe I just need to relax about this. But if I can just draw some kind of boundary line . . .

In my own defense, I am not the first in this country to be challenged by the ant population. In 1660 a Scotsman named Robert Knox was taken prisoner and held in the Kandyan Kingdom for "19 years, 6 months, 14 days," by his own account. He was given comparative freedom to live among the people, build his own house, and engage in trade. In 1679 he escaped with several Englishmen by making his way through the central jungle down to the western coast, where he emerged sporting an eight-year growth of beard and wearing nothing but a loin cloth (to the horror of incredulous foreigners). Knox and his party were taken on board a vessel heading back to England. It was on this voyage that he began to pen his *Historical Relation of Ceylon,* published in 1681, a book that remains the definitive account of life in the Kandyan Kingdom in the central highlands during the nearly twenty years that Knox spent there. He also included descriptions of the island as a whole since his English-speaking readers had as yet little knowledge of these parts. Not surprisingly, living in these hills, Knox spent considerable time contemplating the local flora and fauna. He became both botanist and ethnographer of no small distinction, recording the life that he observed around him. In his notebooks he noted six different kinds of ants, from the harmless variety called Coumbias ("reddish Ants like ours in England," he called them) to the Tale-Coumbias, Dimbios, Coura-atch, Coddia, and Vaeos. The first book recommended to me by colleagues at the university was Knox's. Someone suggested I read Knox on ants. And so I did. After class one day I headed over to the Ceylon Room in the university library, a venerable old room stacked with antique bookcases, housing the private collections of former professors. On my way I passed the Periodical Room and took a quick look in, where I spotted a magazine called *Mosquito News* prominently displayed on one of the shelves. I explained to the librarian outside the Ceylon Room that I was here to read about ants. He looked up. "Robert Knox on ants," I prompted him, lending some legitimacy to my claim to be stalking news about ants. From one of the locked glass cabinets, the librarian retrieved Robert Knox's two-volume treatise on Ceylon. Later several of my students happened by and were very impressed that I was reading Knox.

"What part are you reading?" they asked.

"I'm reading the part on ants," I said with a shrug.

Robert Knox on ants:

> A fifth [type of ant] is the Codia. This ant is of excellent bright black and as large as any of the former. They dwell always in the ground; and their usual practice is to be traveling in great multitudes, but I do not know where they are going, nor what their business is; but they pass and repass, some forwards and some backwards in great haste, seemingly as full of employment as people that pass along the streets. These ants will bite desperately, as bad as if a man were burnt with a coal of fire. But they are of nobler nature: for they will not begin; and you may stand by them, if you do not tred up on them nor disturb them. The reason their bite is thus terribly painful is this; formerly these ants went to ask a wife of the noya (cobra), a venomous and noble kind of snake; and because they had such a high spirit to dare to offer to be related to such a generous creature, they had this virtue bestowed upon them, that they should sting after this manner. And if they had obtained a wife of the noya, they should have had the privilege to have stung full as bad as he.
>
> There is a sixth called Vaeos. These are more numerous than any of the former. All the whole earth does swarm with them. They are of middle size between the greatest and the least, the hinder part white, and the head red. They eat and devour all that they can come at; as beside food, cloth, wood, thatch of houses and every thing excepting iron and stone. So that the people cannot set anything upon the ground within their houses for them. They creep up the walls of their houses and build an arch made of dirt over themselves all the way as they climb, be it never so high. And if this arch or vault chance to be broken, they all, how high soever they were, come back again to mend up the breach, which being finished they proceed forwards again, eating everything they come at in their way. This vermin does exceedingly annoy the Sinhalese so much that they are continually looking upon anything they value to see if any of these Vaeos have been at it.

We began life in this house with very small, light brown ants which, after a month, were displaced by much larger, sturdier black ones. It is the latter that remain today. I think we have Vaeos in our house.

Sometimes I take my tea and sit on the porch and think about my horror at the bug and rodent population. I don't ordinarily consider myself squeamish, but you couldn't prove it here. Noah had a Sri Lankan classmate over the other day as I was in the process of launching a rearguard attack on a procession of ants. I embarked on my daily litany about the ant population. The boy smiled and said, "So?" I carry this word around with me and let it settle in for months. Get your fingers dirty, Adele. The ants were here first. We are the squatters.

With the geckos I made my peace early on, perhaps because for the most part we each respected the other's living quarters. Mainly they live behind the pictures on the wall or behind the stove. I disrupted their habitat only once in the course of a year when I decided to rehang some old pictures. One indecorously invaded my personal living space only once—the morning when I woke up to find it nestled in my hair. When I told the story at work, a colleague was interested in knowing on what part of my body the gecko had fallen. After initially being somewhat taken aback, I was subsequently introduced to the fundamentals of gecko lore. Known as *Houm Sastraya* in Sinhalese, it is a compendium of belief according to which a gecko can bring either good or ill fortune depending on factors as variable as what part of your body it falls on, the direction that its cry comes from, and the day of the week on which the two preceding events took place. If, for example, a gecko falls on your head or body on a Wednesday, Thursday, or Saturday, it is fatal. If on a Tuesday, it is fatal to your wife (the *Houm Sastraya* is silent on the subject of when or if a gecko's fall is ever fatal for the husband), and if on a Friday, one is obliged to leave one's native country. Sunday is more auspicious; on this day the gecko can bring good luck and success, particularly if it chooses to run all over your body that day. My encounter took place on a Thursday, not an auspicious day for a rendezvous with a gecko.

Something about this house nags at me. It has essentially three people taking care of it; two people and a fine specimen, our new German shepherd pup, Samba, actually inhabiting it; a porch with a loveseat that I have refurbished; planters with flowers—and yet it struggles to come to life. Sometimes it seems that if we relax our efforts to breathe home into the place it will revert immediately back to its pre-lived-in condition. Is it just the insect war that is being waged or is it something else?

By the beginning of December, our shared domestic life suffers a precipitous reversal. We are invited down to Colombo for an embassy function for the weekend and upon our return find that our house has been reclaimed. Two and a half days was all it took. Over the weekend the already precarious lines of demarcation drawn between house and jungle have collapsed. Our first hint that something has gone awry is that the puppy greets us sporting a new toy between her teeth. I look carefully and then gently remove a monkey's skull from her mouth. A quick survey of the kitchen reveals that we are not alone. A family of rats has moved in, if it had not been there already. I walk into the kitchen only to find one of the weekend infiltrators looking down at me from the shelf above the stove. The top has been flipped off the rice cooker. Something has moved in, gorged itself, defecated in the cooker, and moved on. There have been other realignments as well in the kitchen. Something has broken loose from behind the cabinets, depositing an entire colony of ants and two queens on the kitchen counter, all of which are engaged in a frantic search for their lost home. Between the living room and the hallway, an impressive-looking sand mound has appeared, evidently constructed as the future dwelling place of our Vaeos. For days, their efforts to rebuild are as fruitless as ours to sweep them away. We are at face-off.

My bedroom fares no better from the nighttime jungle raid. Having sated themselves in the kitchen, the rat family had moved on into the bedroom closet and helped themselves to the box of Crabtree and Evelyn soap I had brought over as a gift. Half the box is gone, and more than half the soap is no doubt in the process of being digested in some being's stomach here in the house. Medicine containers and cardboard boxes have suspicious little teeth holes in them. Noah disappears into his room but comes out again holding an enormous, brightly colored orange and green gecko—beautiful, really—that had taken up residence on his curtain along with several different species of spider. He gently wraps it up in a towel and releases it into the darkness, but not before we take a picture of it. He does it all quietly and deliberately. For my part, I shudder as I feel my way around a house that has come undone.

The next three nights I lay in my bed, waiting for the sound of the rattraps Velu had set in the kitchen to snap shut.

The well-heeled homes that grace our street, the fancy girls' schools that line the hill, and the general level of city chaos belie the fact that our neighborhood occupies the outer edges of a jungle.

"We live on a monkey path," Kush told me one morning after we were unceremoniously awakened by the scratching of tin and tile on the roof, Velu yelling, and something pinging on the roof, the product of Velu's well-aimed slingshot.

"Pardon?" I asked her as we emerged in our housedresses to watch Velu at work.

"Well, it's a path that the monkeys make along the line of trees, wires and roofs in order to find their way to their favorite fruit source. This is why we don't have decent TV service up here. We tried putting in an antenna so that we can get reception, but the monkeys took it. They come down, twenty or thirty at a time, sit on the roof, and twist the antenna until it breaks. They then carry it back up into the hills into the jungle. Perhaps they think it's some sort of human trophy. Anyway, don't leave things lying about in the open on the porch. They'll take them."

At other times they knock a large jackfruit off a tree, which then slides down the hill and comes to rest in the gutter outside the dining room, precipitating a fight over ownership rights.

Our house is one of many that climb the hill leading to a forest reserve. As I walk up the street, I can see how the neighborhood has been hewn and chopped away from jungle growth. Noah and Nandana have taken to walking up there sometimes in the evening in search of panthers. While I have yet to see one, I need go no farther than our dining room to remind myself that we are all guests in nature here. The room backs up onto a hill from which dense growth hangs precariously, artificially halted by the walls of our house. The previous tenants had installed some screens over the window grating to keep whatever comes down the hill out. Something has made short shrift of part of the screen. I keep meaning to fix it and then don't, partially, I guess, out of the realization that it will just get eaten away again. Sometimes at night I hear rustling in the underbrush or something moving along between the hill and the house. At other times, when the ground is saturated with water, something pulls loose from the hill, tumbles down, and bumps against the house. I learn to recognize certain sounds as things move in and out of the jungle above us. I know that the monkeys are on the move from the particular way the dogs bark.

Like anyplace in the tropics, gardening here consists of cutting back, pruning, chopping, and trimming. Nurseries exist here, but to me they become exercises in redundancy, the purchasing on a smaller and less interesting scale of what is already growing in profusion on our property, up the street, and in the forest. Velu spends at least one day a week cutting back the growth between the hill and the dining-room wall. On some Sundays his entire family is out in back in a communal effort to keep the lines of demarcation drawn. His brother arrives, along with Velu's son and granddaughter, the men in their off-white *sarongs,* the little girl all dressed up in a blue cotton dress, her ears pierced, her hair in tight curls. Velu tells me she is four. I come out sometimes to see her, bringing a candy bar or crayons and drawing paper I've brought from the States. She looks and looks at me. I've learned a Tamil word or two. "*Wannakum*" (Good morning), I say. Sometimes I watch Velu and his family from the kitchen window in back as they repair and prune. Velu will look up; I smile and wave and turn away. At other times I pass by the open storage room on the way to the main house and see him and his family sitting, quietly talking among themselves, just the four of them.

We spend a lot of time here trying to keep the boundaries clear. I am reminded by Kush and Nandana to be sure the gate to the property is closed. Of course, I forget to do it properly one day and return from work to find someone's cows grazing in the yard. These are the same cows I pass on the street every day near the lake, tying up traffic. Now they seem to have taken up residence here. Sometimes I see them standing outside the milk bar at the bottom of the hill.

At night they seem mysteriously to disappear, only to reemerge in the morning to take up their previous day's activities. I try to chase them out, but they are persistent. I go to find an old rope in Velu's storage area and start swinging it in the air. All in vain. Velu makes an appearance, says something to the cows, and they are gone. I am a guest here with ten words of Sinhalese, a fact that turns the everyday into a series of evolving mysteries.

People and things do not occupy the same spaces they do at home. The cows in Kandy are an excellent case in point. Shouldn't they be penned up somewhere instead of occupying traffic lanes? I think to myself, as I dodge one in order to get onto a bus. A wealthy woman in town took it upon herself several years ago to rescue cows that were headed for the slaughterhouses. She wanted to give them to some of the poorer families so that they might have milk. The problem was that the needy families couldn't take care of the cows, so the lady was left with a surfeit of bovines with no place to keep them. And that is how, at least according to one urban legend, the cows ended up on the street.

Over the months I notice that wherever I go I share the road with cattle even though the area of the island where we live is Buddhist, and thus the cow plays no particular spiritual role. Kandy, in fact, is the center for Buddhist culture on the island because it is here that the Temple of the Tooth is located. Thousands of pilgrims journey up the mountain yearly to worship at this holy spot. At 6:00 every evening I hear the chanting of a different sermon by the temple monks in ancient Pali over the loudspeaker system. I walk home from the bus station to the accompaniment of the *dharma,* as the *tuk-tuks,* buses, and cars compete with each other around the lake. But up north in the Tamil part of the country, the cow plays a very different role. There the population is predominately Hindu, and thus the cow is sacred, as in India. And yet, as the months go by, I begin to sense that on this small island one cannot simply draw a line that separates the so-called Hindu and Tamil north from the Buddhist and Sinhalese south. I feel Hinduism's presence here in the central highlands of the island. In downtown Kandy, nestled in between hardware shops, fancy shops, and some Muslim jewelry shops, is a Hindu *kovil,* or temple. Several months into our stay Kush, in the process of applying for a job as lecturer in French at the university, took an offering down to the Hindu *kovil* to set before the gods.

"But you're Buddhist," I said. "Why the Hindu *kovil?*"

"Buddha isn't a God. He did not want us to worship him. It's a philosophy, a way of life. It is inclusive. He did not prohibit us from worshipping the gods we choose to worship. Buddha was human. Do you want to come with us?"

We all went down to the *kovil,* placed offerings of flowers and fruit, and Kush got the job. And the cows, sacred or not, continued to tie up traffic in the land of the Buddha.

It is Velu who sets my rattraps. In the morning he pulls the night's catch out of them because I am too squeamish. He is also the one who trains the dogs, Nandana's dog, Kiki, a Weimaraner, and our puppy, Samba. His room is off the storage area on the side of our house. I sometimes wonder what it looks like, but it is a place I do not go. I hear him in the morning talking to the animals, particularly the caged monkey, Kiriya, who was rescued by Kush's uncle years ago and is consigned to a cage with rare forays out onto the grounds.

When he senses we are up, Velu calls in from the storage shed so that I can hear: "Madam, *pan?*" I go to the door and utter a few imperfectly pronounced words, always after the perfunctory bow. Our domestic spaces bump up against each other but remain separate, demarcations of caste and class that are not as pronounced here as in India, but are nevertheless real. I don't know if I am supposed to cross these lines or not. Velu stands at the threshold of the side door and won't come in unless I ask him to set the traps.

Loku Menike cooks me lunch and then stands next to me while I eat it. Before I know it, we have something like a culinary routine going in the kitchen. Our kitchen life also consists of us watching each other's eating habits while pretending not to. I ask her to sit down, but she refuses. But there is something I need from her —specifically, the knowledge of how to eat curries with my right hand, the only hand Sinhalese and Tamils, like the Arabs, use for eating. They do not use utensils and mix the curries with their right hands. The problem is that I am left-handed and need immediately to become right-handed, or at least sufficiently so in order to eat. I can't express what I need, so I show her what it is I am trying to do. I can't do this at the table because she won't sit with me, so the two of us stand in the kitchen with our plates of curry, and I watch what she does. It's all in the mixing, Sri Lankans say. Add utensils to it and the flavor is spoiled. And so I watch her dexterously blend all the flavors together, using all of her fingers. Sometimes it seems like she is knitting on the plate. Rice, *dhal, sambol,* mango, eggplant curry all manage to congeal together long enough for the journey from plate to mouth. She stops, looks at me and gives me a nudge with her eyes. I start in. Rice, *dhal,* and mango curry seep slowly between the fingers of my right hand, forming a gooey mass on my palm. Loku Menike doesn't even try to suppress a laugh. End of lesson for the day.

Finally, after a month, we manage tea and cookies in the kitchen together, observing each other intently as we do so. Our eating and drinking habits are different. It feels sometimes as if we are doing an ethnography of each other's world and bodies. I notice her staring at my hands. I look down. They have what my mother used to call age spots on them. Loku Menike had never seen this and looked at me semi-horrified. I tried to explain, but I couldn't.

"*Maduruvo?*" she asked, and I stared at her. She paused for a moment and then said, "Mosquitoes?"

I didn't know a word for them, so yes, today my age spots were mosquito bites. "*Maduruvo,*" I answered her, in agreement.

Fevers, rashes, welts, all of these begin to appear and disappear as our bodies try to settle into the jungle. Loku Menike does a quick inspection and announces that we are having body problems because we are mixing hot, or what they call "heaty," and cold (*sitila*) foods. "What do you mean by heaty?" I asked her. "Do you mean spicy, *sarai*? Or hot from cooking?"

"Neither," she told me, with Nandana's help. "It's what happens to the food once it enters your digestive system. Breadfruit has a heaty effect on the system. So does pineapple. Cucumber is *sitila.*"

She asked me how much breadfruit I ate. I told her and learn that it is way too much; it is why I get rashes. "You should only have a little each week. It is too heaty on the system."

Sometimes, if I arrive home early enough, Loku Menike is still there. Together we make our tea. After a month or so, I invite her to sit on the porch with me. At first she hesitates, then after a while if I am working at home that day she will suddenly appear on the porch at 3:00 with tea and conversation. Should Kush and Nandana arrive home in their car during our teatime on the porch, she will rise and bow to them. I think about her a lot. People who have no business working as domestics are doing so, all because of one set of tests that they didn't happen to pass. Sometimes in the afternoon I come home from work to find her, Velu, and Latha all assembled in Velu's work area chatting in the midafternoon calm. I wonder if they are talking about my abject failure to master the art of curry eating. But no matter. I come in and say hello, but I do not stay. This is their space. My shared space with Velu is the plot of lawn in front of our house where the dogs "dance" (*buranava*), in Velu's words, with each other at night. Here on this plot of earth, I learn the words for "moon"(*handa*), "stars" (*taru*), and "bad dog" (*balla narakai*). It is the leveler of all else that separates us.

Some of my students at Peradeniya: (from left) Vihara, Tanya, Nirosha, and Sumudu.

CHAPTER 4

Insurrections in the Hills

"Calling you is like calling Gauguin," someone told me who dialed my cell phone from the States and reached me while I was walking on a bridge over the Mahaweli River. It's my place for birdsong, the place that drowns out all other conversation. I watch from the bridge and banks and listen as the deep, lazy waters of the Mahaweli make their slow journey to the northeast through this bird-dense land. I leave one flock behind and acquire another as I head into a classroom that seems to function as a bird corridor. We throw the windows open, erasing all the boundaries between outside and inside. Magpies, bee-eaters, and kingfishers fly in, then out again. Some pause to listen to my lecture briefly and then are gone. On rare occasions a monkey drops in and settles itself on the window ledge, a phenomenon that I initially find exotic and my students find merely irritating. Soon I start to find them irritating as well. Sometimes I suggest to the girls that we all just move outside and have class under the *mara* tree, a venerable two-hundred-year old giant that comes alive with a profusion of yellow blossoms for three days a year in March. Couples come and have their picture taken backlit by *mara* blossoms.

"Yes, madam, as long as we don't have to sit in the sun," they tell me. I comply, and we make our way over to the stone benches under the tree and proceed to focus on the unlikely topic of American Puritanism in the Eden Ivor Jennings built. We weave in and out of the texts as the campus monkey population unobtrusively begins to descend on us from the top of the hill near the Senate building, fanning out as they approach, moving in on us from several different directions until we look up to find ourselves surrounded. They are here for rice and curry. That we don't have any seems not to have any noticeable effect on their insistence. Sometimes entire groups of students will vacate the benches under the tree as the monkeys assume squatters' rights.

Outside we often break a little early and just talk. It is here under the tree that I slowly become privy to the lives of my students. Tanya reveals that she is a concert pianist, and won't I please come to her concert in Colombo? I find out here that Vihara is getting married soon, that Rozmin lost her father several years ago, that Kanchuka is an artist and that her father is a professor of philosophy here. Sumudu and Nirosha seem less forthcoming initially. I will wait to find out more about them.

One day the six of them asked me if I knew that we were sitting on Polonnaruwa.

"On what?" I asked, moving over, thinking I had inadvertently sat down on a bug.

"Madam, we call it Polonnaruwa. It was one of our ancient, medieval capitals. It's not so far from here, up north in the dry zone near Anuradhapura. The benches are like the stone pillars used in the medieval Sinhalese capital by that name. That's why we call this place under the tree Polonnaruwa."

"We also call this place the strike tree," Kanchuka added. "We say *strike gaha*. Rallies and strikes are called here. There was a famous one here. It was the food strike."

"Is the food that bad here?" I asked them. "In the States all college students complain about the food, but as far as I know no one has ever gone on strike over it."

"Well, madam, we weren't here, but the students marched to the vice-chancellor's office, carrying plates of string hoppers. Have you had string hoppers yet, madam?" (For the record, they are one of the staples of the Sri Lankan diet: rice flour and coconut milk are pushed through a sieve so that they emerge in the shape of noodles. They are then cooked and eaten with *dhal* or in a coconut and a chili dish called *sambol*). "Everyone thought the hoppers were too sticky, so they marched to the vice-chancellor's office and threw them at the wall."

"Have the string hoppers gotten better?" I asked.

"A little," they told me, a couple of them screwing up their noses.

"Have there been any other strikes here?"

"Yes, madam, lots."

I was curious about them, but we were off to the next class. Different class, same benches.

One day I walked into class with the announcement that Lord Byron had a crush on the wife of Governor Horton, one of the governors of Kandy under the British. Smiles. Giggles. I had a feeling I'd just reinvented the wheel. I wasn't sure anyone was interested in this, but I told the story anyway.

"You all know the Udawattekele Sanctuary just behind the Temple of the Tooth and Trinity College?"

"Madam, we know. This is the place where couples go."

I too had noticed them, sitting covered by their umbrellas on the thick stone benches that line the paths that disappear into the forest.

"When I go there," I told them, "it feels like I am turning back the pages of history. Those benches that the couples occupy today were built for the use of the young English girls of Kandy. They used to walk these paths and take their morning rides here during the British Raj."

"Yes, madam, we know."

Okay, I *had* reinvented the wheel. Walking in the forest I had found myself in the thick of the nineteenth-century British presence on the island. Along the deep jungle paths, from time to time, one comes upon small signs, pointing to Lady Gordon's or Lady Horton's Road, the mark of order and aristocracy in this otherwise completely wild forest zone. I have started to construct a life for these women. I imagine them more than a century and a half ago in crinolines, corsets, and high-necked collars, using their umbrellas as walking sticks. Victorian women, British women. I had stumbled upon a story in the Kandy Municipal Library that I was eager to share with the girls. It seems that Governor Horton, who served as governor of Kandy between 1831 and 1837, named the entire area Lady Horton's Forest after his wife, who was known for her beauty. As she went for her morning walks along the paths, she was escorted by three soldiers, one fully armed, in case an elephant, leopard, elk, or wild boar made a sudden appearance. Governor Horton also happened to be Lord Byron's second cousin. Byron was evidently not indifferent to his cousin's wife's charms, either. It was to her that he penned the lines:

> She walks in beauty, like the night
> Of cloudless climes and starry skies;
> And all that's best of dark and bright
> Meet in her aspect and her eyes.

"It's one of Byron's most famous poems," I told my students, "and it seems to have originated right here."

"Have you read Leonard Woolf's novel *The Village in the Jungle?*" my colleague Nihal asked me one day. "All the English students here are made to read it. You should have a go at it. He talks about this jungle of yours."

This comes as a complete shock to me. For me Woolf has always been the shadow behind Virginia. Founder with his wife of the Hogarth Press, he was a member of the Bloomsbury Group and was English literary aristocracy par excellence. But here on this island he is known for something very different. He spent time here, seven years to be exact, between 1904 and 1911, as a member of the Ceylon Civil Service. He learned Sinhalese and Tamil, as all officials were required to, and kept the daily diaries that the British colonial government required of each of its officials. He arrived by steamer in Colombo in 1904 with ninety volumes of Voltaire and a wire-haired fox terrier. After seven years he took a leave of absence to go home to England and subsequently resigned from the civil service, having become increasingly "doubtful whether I liked the prospect of spending my whole life as an imperialist ruling non-Europeans."

As I read his diaries, I come to believe that even after he returned to his own roots—to the intellectual ferment of Bloomsbury, of Lytton Strachey, Virginia, Clive and Vanessa Bell—he left something essential of himself behind on this island. And that fundamental something propelled him back here after Ceylon had freed itself from the imperialism that Woolf came to abhor. I think that his passion for this place was something he never shared with Virginia. Fifty years later, twenty years after his wife committed suicide, he returned to Ceylon, a country free finally of the British. In the long intervening years, I think he never got the island out of his system.

After Woolf came back to England in 1911, he set about writing the novel that Nihal wants me to read. It takes place in a village in the south and is about two young girls and their father, whose lives are turned upside down by the forces of change that threaten them from without. I lie in bed at night under my blue mosquito net with my pocket flashlight, reading it. It is a dark and mysterious book, something completely out of character for the Leonard Woolf I associate with Bloomsbury. I think he loved the mystery of the jungle, though for him there was also something ultimately horrifying about it, a rough mystery that lives according to its own laws and that ultimately reclaims and even swallows up its own.

This jungle at the edge of our town has become a haven of solace for me. I take walks up there when I can, and am often struck by the fact that there is something in us, or perhaps something in the jungle itself, that makes me want to learn some abiding lesson about civilization and its obverse by looking at this mass of intricately tangled vegetation, vines, and dense growth. I recognize this impulse in myself while living on its edge, walking in it, thinking about it, and cutting it back.

What would Jennings think, I often wonder, were he to come back to life and journey up the mountain to the university that he founded? There are the obvious differences. I suspect that the place is a good deal shoddier than it was when it first opened its doors. The grounds are not kept up in quite the same way as I imagined they were in his time. There simply isn't money to hire the full-time gardeners that the campus needs. The place seems slightly frayed at the edges—a product, no doubt, of both the war and the economy. I notice, however, in the fall that there is a sudden burst of activity on campus, as gardeners, painters, and general cleanup people are out in force. Students finish their final examinations in March, but graduation, known here as convocation, takes place in the fall, except that it is not really fall because there is no fall. I don't know what to call the changing times of year here. Nevertheless, I note that things are looking up in preparation for the general influx of student family members from all over the island. There have been other changes since Jennings's time as well. A common litany of complaint around campus is that the new buildings have been thrown up in a hurry, destroying the architectural integrity of the earlier ones, all done in the style of medieval Anuradhapura architecture. They have no monopoly on architectural aberration, I tell them. Such things are common on campuses in the United States as well.

Sometimes I walk around the university just to enjoy nature, being careful not to disturb the couples sitting discreetly under umbrellas by trees overlooking the river. I settle myself under a tree behind the Senate building at lunch and frequently take a nap if I can succeed in fending off the local monkey population. Often I eat lunch or take a walk with my colleague Udaya Meddegama, who is head of the Department of Sinhalese. Udaya appeared in my life my first day at the university in response to an e-mail I had sent to the department inquiring whether there was someone available to tutor me in Sinhalese. Short, mild-mannered, and to all appearances massively overworked, Udaya has been here forever and has seen a great deal. I was sitting at my desk trying to organize my thoughts when he walked in, smiled at me, and proceeded to utter something incomprehensible in Sinhalese. He then switched into beautifully rhythmic English, the product of several years spent in the States and in England, and announced that he was here to initiate me into the mysteries of this language. From then on, twice or three times a week we have met in whatever classroom happens to be available at the moment. Before long I am piecing together the days of the week, the weather, fruits. But mainly what Udaya is teaching me is the culture.

"What is the word for 'elephant'?" I asked him one day, having encountered one coming in the opposite direction earlier that morning in Kandy.

"What kind of elephant?" he asked me.

"I don't know. Your plain generic elephant. You know, the big kind." I looked at him with a half smile.

He took it all in stride. "We have three words for elephants. *Aliya* is our general name for male and female elephants. Then *eta* are the tuskers; they're always male. And *etinna* are the females."

I stared at him in linguistic despair.

This is the direction in which our language classes usually proceed. First I learn the words, then I learn the stories that give me the culture. After I get *etinna* into my head, I learn that the mother of the Buddha was impregnated through her womb by a white elephant; that Buddha in his former lives had been born as an elephant; that his rival Mana, the God of Death, rides a monstrous tusker called Girimekhala; and that parents come to the temple in our town specifically to pass their children under the bellies of the temple elephants, an act designed to ensure the child's future protection in life. While Udaya is explaining I am thinking to myself that now I understand why I hear small children screaming at all hours of the day in front of the Temple of the Tooth. All in a day's work in Sinhalese class.

One day Udaya arrived and wrote something new on the board, two words: *chanda kolebala*. "Learn it," he said. "It means 'election violence.'"

"Why are you teaching me this?" I asked him. "I am supposed to be learning how to shop and cook. I'm going to starve with all these abstractions."

"You are learning it because we are coming up to an election, and this will be part of your life. It is almost as normal as shopping and cooking."

The civil war between the Sinhalese majority and the Tamil Tiger rebels on this island had already been raging since 1983, although the roots of the conflict can be traced back to the 1950s. It had claimed forty thousand lives by the time we arrived. But there was another war, one referred to by Sri Lankans as the insurrections, that went virtually unreported in the Western press. It has two histories: one in 1971, when the student violence began, and the other in the mid-1980s, as the economy continued to worsen and as many of the activists arrested in the early 1970s had now been released. By the 1980s the country also found itself engaged in a civil war. The insurrections were a product of a political party called the JVP (Janatha Vimukthi Peramuna), which infiltrated the campus and garnered both student and faculty support for its efforts to topple both the government and the hierarchy of privilege in this country. I have yet to meet a family on campus that has not been in some way affected by these uprisings. I sit in the senior commons room in the Fine Arts Building drinking my milk tea (*kiri te*) and surrounded by faculty members, some of them elderly, who sip their tea with their news. Some are quiet old men with paunches who, I learn only after a year, were either deeply implicated in or victimized by the violence. Either way, for them it is now a thing of the past. What happened on this campus in 1971 and then again in the late 1980s in some fundamental sense informs much of our life here for the next year. It explains things that otherwise have no explanation. Some people who were around in the early 1970s when the violence first broke out have died; others choose not to talk about what happened or even to remember it; still others took meticulous notes so as never to forget it. For everyone these are two decades of difficult memories.

Ashley Halpé and his wife, Brigit, live in the hills of Aniwatta (literally Annie's Garden) up over the town of Kandy. Recently retired from Peradeniya, Ashley is a scholar of Renaissance literature. He is also a poet and, I have heard from colleagues, was asked to take over discipline at the university during the insurrections. I called him to see if he would talk to me, as I wanted to start putting the pieces of what happened together. I drove up with Champika one day into the hills where the Halpés live. Usually lively and often full of song, Champika seemed preoccupied that day. The problem for him is always the same: money. He is in his late twenties and supports his mother, father, grandmother, aunt, and sister on the salary of a *tuk-tuk* driver. On a good day driving his *tuk-tuk* he brings in maybe 1,000 rupees ($10.00). That's on a good day. These things fluctuate wildly, though. He could just as well bring in 300 rupees ($3.00) a day, depending on business. I prodded him to talk a little bit as we sat at the top of the hill overlooking the town. Today the story centered on his younger sister, who is still in high school and getting ready to take her British A levels, the examinations that are key to gaining admission to a university. Champika was having to pay for a special course she was taking to prepare for it, and it was expensive. "First person in family for university," he told me proudly, referring to his sister's prospects. Even then it was not completely clear that she would get in.

These O and A levels have done nothing for this society. The O levels are standardized tests given to all pupils in the equivalent of the tenth grade. Much money and sleep are lost over these tests. The kids need to be able to pass six O-level subjects, including math and one of the languages (Sinhalese, Tamil, or English). Students may take the O levels over officially only three times. After that, even if they pass, they can't proceed on to the A levels. A colleague of mine at Peradeniya was railing against the Kandy police the other day over some matter. "Even these people," he said, "who in general don't use their brains, if they have any at all, had to pass their O levels." He went on to try and explain the system to me. "These kids who do not get through the O levels get stuck in life. They can go to vocational training centers, I guess. Most of them end up as car mechanics, farmers, carpenters, or as politicians. You don't have to have any brains to end up as a politician in this country. But there's another thing. Say you have no brains, but your family has money. You can't get through your O levels. I know of families who send their kids to Russia and to the U.S. for the rest of their education. Here money will buy you what you need. Brains, not always."

Noah is currently studying for his O levels, the only problem being that he will no longer be in the country when the tests are given next year. "Why am I studying the municipal planning of a British town?" is a question he voices repeatedly around the house. I shrug my shoulders, registering the lament. But the real problems for students begin when they have to take their A levels, the significantly more difficult exams given after the senior year in high school. On these all depends: entrance into university, whether here or abroad.

If one passes them, all is well and good. If not, one can retake them after a year, but if the student fails to pass the second time, that is it. No more A levels and no possibility of entering the university. In general, one is consigned to whatever lower- or middle-level job one can get. It is a system I rail against from the beginning of our life here until I leave the island for the second time in 2007. Too much depends on this one set of examinations. Further, it keeps the social structure in place since, for the most part, students who pass the A levels come from more privileged backgrounds, have attended the international or private schools, which give better preparation, and have had private tutoring in order to help them with the exams. There are, of course, exceptions, but not enough to justify the system.

"Going and coming?" Champika asked me, depositing me at Ashley's gate.

"No, just going," I told him. I wanted to walk back, but I gave him some money for the return trip.

I walked up to Ashley's house, thinking about how poverty gets recycled in this country and how slim the prospects are of breaking out of it. I was greeted by a group of happy, well-cared-for dogs, a rarity here, who escorted me inside the house—most of which was, in fact, outside. It was a place open to breezes, which drifted in, mingling with the sounds of Brigit's piano students and the soft pattering of dog feet on the floor. The living room of the house, graced with stunning paintings by Sri Lankan artists, opened out onto a deck that was not quite finished yet. Ashley came to greet me and cautioned me to be careful where I step lest I fall off the edge into the garden ten feet below. Surrounded by his dogs, we drank tea, as Ashley settled into his memories of the insurrections.

"You know, in order to understand what happened at Peradeniya in the early 1970s, you have to understand what this place was and what it represented to the first batch of students who attended it in the 1950s," he told me. "The first students to study here moved into campus in the 1950s when Sri Lanka was still Ceylon but newly independent from the British Raj. By and large they came from the Sinhalese elite. Most were from wealthy and privileged families in Colombo, families with last names that even today have instant recognition on the island. These were halcyon times. The students studied the classics, read with professors who had studied at Oxford and Cambridge, took part in university games, got drunk at the local Kandy bars and, when the Arts Faculty shifted up the road from Colombo, began reading the works of Marx and Engels."

Ashley went on to tell me that in the early years the student protests didn't amount to much. He remembered one that had something to do with substandard laundry facilities. Then there was another one on campus connected with a stench due to the breakdown of the university water system. I reminded him of the string hopper strike as well. But aside from that, Ashley continued, even as the students read their Marx, they were less impressed by what he had to say than they were by the fact that recent grads had found lucrative employment in the capital and had money jingling in their pockets.

I have thought about that so often. At home when I teach Marx, my students and I talk about whether it is possible to really understand Marx if your belly is full and you are bringing in $80,000 a year. Does Marxism die, I wonder, when our pockets are full?

"By the late 1960s, "Ashley continued, "things were beginning to change. Namely, what was changing was the student body. Formerly from privileged circles, the entering students now were coming increasingly from rural areas and from a more impoverished background. This is important; you need to understand this. Not all who entered knew English anymore. You see, the language reform after Ceylon's independence now allowed for secondary school instruction to be conducted in Sinhalese and Tamil as well as in English. The university ranks began to swell. Now we had a very different kind of student—less worldly. Some people felt that the university was losing its hold on providing an elite education for the crème de la crème of Sinhalese society and had nothing to gain from admitting students from the rural areas. Two things coalesced at this moment—the influx of new and a very different breed of student and an economy that was taking a downturn. The students from the poorer, rural families graduated after four years at university, looked around them and saw that, for all their education, they were unable to get jobs. But the sons of the elite who had attended private school either at St. Thomas or Royal College in Colombo or Trinity in Kandy, because of their connections, were virtually guaranteed a job in the private sector if they could make it through grade eight. This is the moment when the Marxists and Trotskyites found an audience on campus.

"So, that's basically the background. Then there was the reality of what happened on campus. One night a bomb went off in one of the dormitories, Maars Hall. Some people think that the bomb was planted there by the army or the government as a way of giving themselves carte blanche to come in and search the campus. No one knows, but the army moved in swiftly and defanged the entire campus. The student radicals moved up into the hills of the Hantana, and the Peradeniya police superintendent declared that he would give safe conduct to anyone who wanted to leave the campus for Colombo."

Hours later, both of us sated by the stories, Ashley and I sat there and drank our tea. The dogs had settled in and were asleep at our feet.

"You're a writer. Did you write about this?" I asked him.

"Yes, I did. I wrote poems. Sometimes it was all I could do."

Days later I found some of Ashley's poems in the university library.

APRIL 1971

I do not know
The thin reek of blood, the stench
of seared flesh, the
cracked irreducible bone; I know
only the thinner reek of pity,
the harsh edge of self-contempt,
the ashy guilt of being too old,
salaried, safe, and comfortable.
I would know their reasons,
The rigour of their hot hate, their
Terrifying faith. But
They have said everything
In dying, a communication
Beyond all our speech.

What happened in Sri Lanka in the early 1970s and again in the mid-1980s is inseparable from the personality of one man, Patabandi Don Nandasiri Wijeweera, alias Rohana Wijeweera, the force behind the JVP. Wijeweera was born in 1943 in a small seacoast town in southern Sri Lanka. His father had been attracted to Marxist and Leninist ideology and passed on his radical leanings to his young son. As important as his father's influence was on him, Wijeweera's most defining moment was the time he spent at Patrice Lumumba People's Friendship University in Moscow. I remember this university from my own student days at Moscow State University in the 1970s. Patrice Lumumba University had been established for international students from developing countries in Asia, Africa, and Latin America that were being courted by the Soviets. I used to see students, particularly from Mali, all over Moscow, suffering from the cold and from deep racism in the land of the socialist brotherhood. The students received their education for free but paid dearly for it in other ways. And they were homesick.

This was also a time of the ongoing Sino-Soviet ideological conflict, one in which Wijeweera took the Chinese side in the debate, not a popular stance those days in Moscow. He came back to Sri Lanka for health reasons in 1963, hoping to go back to Moscow the next year to complete his studies. But when he applied for a visa, the Soviet Consulate turned him down. His years in Moscow and the social and economic conditions in his own country had already left their mark on him. With the help of like-minded Marxists, Wijeweera became one of the founding members of the JVP in the late 1960s.

Not initially a political party, the JVP operated both in the open and underground. As a legitimate enterprise, it organized educational camps focusing on Marxist philosophy and economics. By 1971 there were over one hundred thousand members affiliated with the group, mainly workers, monks from the villages, students, and university staff. Their goal was nothing less than the freeing of Sri Lankan workers from centuries of exploitation, first by foreign powers under colonial rule and now by the elite of Sri Lanka itself. Wijeweera quickly assumed leadership of the organization and ran it literally like a boot camp. He ordered his followers not to smoke, drink, or fall in love, reasoning that if people couldn't obey these simple injunctions, they would never be able to sacrifice themselves for the sake of the revolution. Oddly, his tactics sounded very like those employed later by Prabhakaran and the LTTE.

Wijeweera went straight to the heart of popular discontent on the island. He promised the people that under a government formed by the JVP, all Sri Lankans would have equal access to education. He promised to nationalize the gem industry and announced that the JVP had no intention of ever paying back the money loaned to Sri Lanka by the World Bank. The blue beret that was his trademark gave him more than a passing resemblance to Che Guevara. At a Colombo press conference, a journalist once asked him why he wore the beret. Wijeweera answered by asking the man if he had ever asked Mrs. Bandaranaike (then president and mother of former president Chandrika Kumaratunga) why she carried a purse.

Part of Wijeweera's popularity stemmed from his own class roots. He was also a gifted orator. He knew how to speak to Sri Lanka's rural youth because they were his people. He was the first Sri Lankan politician to come from a poor family with little education, and was the first to stand up to the wealthy elite ruling the country. His popularity was not hard to fathom. He walked the length and breadth of the island, preaching his gospel, often without food or shoes. The persona he created for himself clearly echoed Buddhist and Christian philosophy. But here any similarity between the three ends; the *dharma* Wijeweera was preaching was violence. He felt that the only way to resolve social and economic disparity in this country was through revolution. And revolution meant violence.

By the end of the 1960s, the JVP had begun arming itself. Camps were set up to train cadres in the use of bayonets and rifles. The initial organizers gave lectures on martial arts and on terrorist successes in other countries in South and Southeast Asia. And they were able to recruit several military figures who taught them how to make bombs and firearms.

By April 1970, Wijeweera was a wanted man. In March of 1971, he was arrested yet, Mafia-like, continued to direct the JVP from his prison cell in Jaffna. On April 5, over one hundred police stations throughout the country were attacked or threatened by the JVP, which had put together an abortive rescue mission of five hundred men whose purpose it was to storm the Jaffna prison and free Wijeweera. By week's end, a total of 16,500 JVP suspects had either been arrested or had surrendered to the authorities. Several thousand more had died in the violence.

The spate of violence on campus was bad during the first insurrection in 1971, but gut-wrenching during the second wave in the late 1980s. This time it was more drawn out, most likely because the intervening years had brought no perceptible change in people's social and economic conditions. Tempers in the late 1980s, already at their breaking point, were pushed over the edge by the fact that the country was now in the midst of a civil war that had dealt a blow to the economy. The poor again found themselves in desperate conditions, and the student population at Peradeniya was again infiltrated by the ranks of the JVP.

In 1987 my colleague Nihal Fernando was teaching in the English department at Peradeniya. He gathered his things together as he always did in the morning and set off for work on his bike. His route took him across the Mahaweli River at what I call the birdsong bridge. It was a morning like most. "I always used to come to work across that bridge, and I would see piles of corpses stacked near one end of it. By the next morning that pile had been taken away, and a new pile had appeared in its place. I would look down, and on the waters below there were bodies floating, heading downstream along with random branches or lost pieces of laundry. It seemed like something was always burning at that time—tires, bodies, jeeps. One of the ways bodies were disposed of during the late 1980s was something that was known as tire-pyre. People would get old tires, put bodies inside them and burn them. There were incidents all over campus."

Udaya was here then, too. One day the two of us had taken a walk during lunch before our daily tutoring session, and he had shown me a roundabout on campus called the Alwis Circle erected in memory of the original architect of the campus, Shirley Alwis. In its center sits a classical vase painted pink and white, a tribute to another era and to the intention and design of those who brought this place into being.

"See this circle." He pointed. On a sunny morning in 1987 he had put his two smallest children—Indu and Achala—on the bus for school. They were living in one of the university bungalows at the time, not far from the main campus. "Indu told me that as the bus approached the circle, she looked out of the window and saw little flowerpots hanging on it. She kept looking at them. Probably she wasn't used to seeing flowerpots there. Gradually she realized they were the decapitated heads of students, thirteen of them, hanging from the fountain. The teacher on board pushed all the children to the floor so that they wouldn't have to see. But they saw."

"Even the monks had been the target of violence," Udaya had told me. "A monk in a village not far from here was misidentified. The authorities mistook him for another monk. So they dragged him from a procession and shoved him into a jeep. They took him to a cemetery at the far end of the village and hanged him from a tree. Then the police found the victim's family and set fire to the house where they were living. There was the story of another monk who was forced to jump into an abandoned lavatory pit where he was ordered to look for bombs. He didn't find anything there that could be a weapon and so the police took him out of the pit and tied him to a tree in the temple yard and left. The monk's students untied him and washed him, but the monk could not face society after the humiliating ordeal. After a few days he committed suicide."

Nihal remembers going to his family's land about fifty kilometers north of here. "I passed a body burning and a woman and child crying by the side of the road. There were bodies on the road in completely unrecognizable conditions. One morning, in fact, I was taking my daughter to school on my bike. We passed piles of bodies with their stomachs ripped out. My daughter didn't even recognize the bodies as human, and so in a sense she wasn't really bothered.

"These were impossible times. I remember that the students found two people whom they suspected of being army spies. They tied them to trees in broad daylight and stoned them to death. Some people say it was just the JVP, some say the military, but it wasn't. There was violence on both sides."

———

It was nearly dark when I arrived home from Ashley's. Velu met me at the gate and repeated slowly so that I could understand, "*Chanda kolebala.*" I nodded. Together we listened. In the distance I could hear something that sounded like soft popping, almost like firecrackers from a mile or two away. Kush came down. "Firecrackers?" I asked. "No, grenades," she said. But the election was still days away. "It starts early," she told me. Noah and Nandana would be back soon from their evening walk in the panther forest, and we would all be in for the duration behind our hedge. I changed into my housedress, and Kush and I puttered about while the last light of dusk held. Later that night Noah and I ate the curry that Loku Menike had made for us. I went to bed early, taking care to tuck the ends of the mosquito netting in tightly at the corners of my bed. I wrote in my journal and wrapped myself in the comfort of evening ritual as the preelection grenades drowned out the sound of the last of the buses circling around Kandy for the night.

Aruni, Udaya, Indu, and Achala Meddegama with puppy.

CHAPTER 5

Hot Curry

"Do you have a garlic press to do this with?" I asked Udaya as he, his wife, Aruni, and I set about chopping and preparing the curry in their kitchen for the evening meal. The greens and ginger lay on one counter, onions, chilies, and garlic on another, while the *dhal* began to bubble on the stove next to me. It was a rainy night and Udaya had invited Noah and me to dinner. Noah was cutting the chicken on the other counter. Although Udaya was born in a small village on the island, he had taught in the States for several years and knew about our high-end cooking stores and our tendency to overindulge in completely useless cooking apparatus.

"Just take the back of the wooden spoon, the part that is flat, and press it down on the garlic. There, like that." He showed me. And he swept the garlic up and threw it into the curry.

Aruni stood silently on the other side of the kitchen chopping *karapincha* (curry leaves) and ginger. She pins up her long hair when she cooks, but often I see her walking in the house with it trailing all the way to her knees. I went over to watch how she chops the vegetables. She looked up, smiling, and then turned back to her chilies and onions. It was good to see her cooking. Udaya is somewhat circumspect about these matters, but he has given me to understand that Aruni rarely comes out of her bedroom these days except to get tea and eat dinner. For the most part, she sleeps. I know she suffers from depression, perhaps from something else, but I don't know the details. I don't know how much to ask Udaya about this, but I do know that the lives of the two of them have followed this path since the children were little, and that Aruni's difficulties are part of their every day. In Udaya's study sits a photo taken at their wedding: two young people enveloped in their smiles and in each other, looking into the lens of the unknown. Indu poked her head into the kitchen, declared everything to be in hand, and disappeared back into the living room to be with her fiancé, Sanjeewa. I listened to the thick bubbling of *dhal* and stood staring at a piece of ginger that had been sent my way. "Wooden spoon again," instructed Udaya. Soon I had something close to pulverized ginger.

The seven of us gathered round the dinner table and spooned South Asia's aromas onto our dinner plates. "Utensils?" offered Udaya. "No, we're fine," I told him, and mostly I think we were. What dribbled, dribbled. I looked around as everyone was savoring Udaya's cooking. We had been enfolded into this family. I looked over at Noah, whose plate was piled high with much that we couldn't identify but were learning to cook, latitudes away.

After dinner, the house turned quiet. Indu and Sanjeewa had headed back to the university to practice for an Indian dance recital coming up, and Achala and Noah had taken up their stations at the computer in Achala's room. With the dishes done, Aruni disappeared back into her bedroom as Udaya and I got our tea and took it out onto the front stoop. We listened to the evening train making its way along the Mahaweli as the mosquitoes began to rise. But for the train in the distance I was enveloped in stillness. "I never hear silence anymore," I remarked while tending to my tea.

He laughed. "Yes, we are a very noisy country, especially for a Buddhist one."

The two of us just sat there for several minutes, breathing in the evening air and watching the mist rise from the river below.

"Did you see Ashley?" he asked.

"Yes, we met," I told him, taking in a deep breath. I thought to myself that it often happens that the longest conversations I have about violence on this island take place against the backdrop of something whose beauty is heart-stopping. It is another one of the paradoxes of this place.

"So you know more now about what went on on campus?

Things got so bad around here during the violence that we were thinking of moving back to my village. We lived in one of the campus bungalows then. People would show up at our door. We didn't know what they wanted. One day a guy appeared at my house and wanted me to show him the university library. At that time the JVP was stealing identity cards and jewelry. There were lots of them doing this. The police had just recovered half a ton of jewelry when this character knocked at my front door. I told him I had no authorization to show him campus buildings and that I had to leave to go pick up my daughter. It turned out later that this guy was a JVP agent. I had lied to get rid of him. The children were actually arriving home by bus that day. As soon as they got home, I gathered everyone up and went to spend the night at a friend's house. The next day I found out that this same man had been making the rounds of other professors' bungalows, asking for this and that. I was well known in the country. The JVP seemed to be targeting people with name recognition. Actors had been killed. They killed the vice-chancellor of Colombo University.

"Did Ashley tell you about the Kola-Koti, or Green Tigers? No? Well, these were the unofficial, mobile death squads that roamed the country, putting to death anyone who seemed suspect. Most people believed that they were run, or at least supported, by the government. As if the student unrest wasn't bad enough, we then had to deal with the violence coming from the government.

"This was the beginning of the insurrection," continued Udaya. "It was a very sad time. The university just closed down. A lot of the students left. Those who stayed clashed with police in front of the Science Faculty. The demonstration was massive. There were thousands of students there. They marched out of the university towards Kandy, and the police blocked their way near Galaha Junction. A police inspector gave the students five minutes to disperse and return to their dorms, but they refused. They raged forward and were teargassed. Some broke through the police barriers. The police went after them and beat them with their rifle butts. I remember that all the way up from the science faculty the road was strewn with shoes, slippers, bags, umbrellas, and injured students. That's how it all began."

I asked Udaya about the monks' role in all of this. Robed in saffron, they are part of the visual relief of my everyday life. There are literally hundreds of them studying at the university, where they receive bed and board free of charge while they earn their degrees. I knew that many renounce their vows after graduating and return to lay life. But what puzzled me initially is that every time there is a political demonstration on campus the monks are at the forefront of it. They seem so caught up in the violence that plagues this country—sometimes as instigators of it, sometimes as victims. It seems so counter to the Buddhism I think I know from the peace movements in the United States in the 1960s and 1970s.

"Well, I think their presence really helps the students in their negotiations with the administration," Udaya added. "But for us there is also a long history of political and social activism on the part of these monks. Their involvement is part of the larger philosophy of safeguarding the island as a place where Buddhism can flourish. You need to read *The Mahavamsa*. It's our chronicle. It tells you how Buddhism arrived on the island and how it has been protected and nourished here. I don't know if it justifies violence, but it tells us what we must do as recipients of this philosophy."

Several years later I heard something similar from a Tamil in the northern part of the island when I asked him how the Tigers, most of whom were practicing Hindus, justified the use of force, which runs completely counter to their religious precepts.

"If your entire way of life and your people were being killed," he asked me, "wouldn't you take up arms?"

"The problem," Nihal told me one day as we shared a beer in a tavern next to the Queen's Hotel, "was that the whole country started folding up. No one showed up for work. At night people would find notes attached to their doors saying, 'If you go to work, you will be killed.' Sometimes boys would present themselves at the workplace, hand notes to people, and then disappear. People were so scared when they read the notes that they would close up work and leave. Schools were shut down; the buses weren't running; stores were shut tight. There were power cuts because the pumping stations weren't working since there was no one there to operate the machinery.

The police force had disappeared. The entire country was paralyzed. There was a complete breakdown of just about everything. Curfews were imposed daily. The problem was that we never knew who was imposing them, the army or the JVP. People got used to them. Some people partied. They felt there was nothing else to do."

Several weeks later I asked a colleague how he got through it all.

"My wife and I played *Sergeant Pepper's Lonely Hearts Club Band* and drank. And that's how we did it."

Champika and his venerable tuk-tuk.

CHAPTER 6

Rain

Monsoon is late, bus is late, I am late. I am two days late, actually. Always this is so. For my wedding I did not show up at all.

—Alexander Frater, *Chasing the Monsoon*

"What's that noise?" asked Jon Pearce, the American computer modeling expert we had met the first few days we were on the island. He lived down in Colombo and called up from time to time to see how the people in the hills were doing. His family was still back home in California, though his wife was due here in several weeks for a visit. We seemed to have increasingly interesting conversations about how the other was living—that is, when we could hear each other over the phone.

"It's the rain," I told him. "Why? Isn't it raining down there?"

"No, hot as . . ." His voice faded into water.

"What?" I asked him, yelling into the receiver.

Noah emerged to announce that it was raining in his room and went to look for the plastic tub with the Chinese baby in it.

This is our monsoon. I remember wanting to know in those first weeks here whether the drops that were landing on me from the sky were monsoon. "It's rain," was the usual answer. A colleague of mine has a good, healthy philosophical take on it. He tells me he doesn't think in terms of monsoons at all because there are intermonsoons between the regular monsoons. "So you see," he says, "there is always a rainy season."

Theoretically he is right. Our home is in the hill country in the central part of the island so rain comes at us from various directions. Just as the southwest monsoon gradually tapers off in what we know as the end of summer, the northeast monsoon delivers its first showers, overlapping with the southwest ones.

People here take their rain no less seriously than I do as a southern Arizona dweller, where rain is almost a mystical phenomenon. People who don't live in the parched lands of the southwestern United States find it implausible that we wait for the midsummer monsoons with close to the same anticipation as do people half a world away in Mumbai. In Arizona I watch the July sky expectantly, my temper on edge, my thighs sticking to the seat of our pickup truck—which, improbably, is still without air conditioning. When the local weatherman announces that we have hit five consecutive days with a dew point at 54 or higher, thus marking the official beginning of the Arizona "monsoon" season, we continue to suffocate, our skin burning in a land ready to ignite until the first downpour bursts from the clouds. Living with this phenomenon for twenty-five years prepared me for monsoon living of a different sort as I go out, tea in hand, in the morning to consult with Velu about whether it is going to rain today. "*Vaessa vahinewa?*" I ask him, and he shakes his head, which in American culture would mean no. Here it is the sign of assent.

If a buffalo bellows with his muzzle turned to the sky or a dog wakes with its ears wagging, if ants travel in a straight line, if bats fly close to the ground, if dogs eat grass, or bugs march, it is said in Sri Lanka that the rains are not far behind. On the human plane there is an old belief that if a bride has eaten or drunk coconut water in secret sitting on a stone, it will pour on the day of her wedding! The annual elephant procession in Kandy, called the *perahera,* is designed to help coax the rain out of the clouds. Boiling milk helps, as do offerings to various village gods. If you hear a hornbill (*kadatta*), or a flower crow (*mal kavuda*), a crow pheasant (*ati kukula*) or wing kite (*piya ukussa*) crying in the sky, it signals the coming rain. One of the supreme rainmakers on the island is the Bo tree (*ficus religiosa*), the tree under which the Buddha attained enlightenment in 588 BC. Buddhists believe it possesses the miraculous power to produce rain during drought. Each year just before the full moon, or *poya* day of Vesak in May, pots of water are poured onto the sacred tree by the chief monk of the Uda Maluve Viharaya at the ancient capital of Anuradhapura. Since Vesak occurs just before the start of the southwest monsoon season, villagers all over the country replicate this practice to ensure the coming rains.

The summer before we arrived in Sri Lanka something was off. No amount of water poured on a Bo tree or crying of hornbills or flower crows or elephant processions accomplished what they were supposed to do. In short, the southwest monsoon failed to materialize. The southern coastal areas of the island, already parched, were particularly hard hit. Crops failed and along with them household income for over half a year. The government declared a national emergency to cope with the drought, and relief organizations sent food and water to the stricken areas. Electricity on the island is hydro generated and thus became strictly rationed. The situation deteriorated to the point that the Buddha's tooth was called out to do service. Some explanation is in order here. Across the lake in the Temple of the Tooth, built in the late seventeenth to early eighteenth centuries under the Kandyan king Wimaladharma Suriya II, lies the Buddha's tooth, miraculously rescued from the flames of his pyre in 543 BC by one of his disciples. The tooth was later smuggled into Ceylon from Dantapura in Kalinga in southern India by the daughter of the king of Ceylon who, disguised as a Brahmin, hid it in her hair. Over the centuries battles have been fought over it; it has disappeared from the island only to be brought back again.

Such strong feelings about a tooth initially seem confounding unless, as a Sri Lankan acquaintance reminded me, one remembers that Christianity venerates saints' relics or the Shroud of Turin with the same obsessive devotion. The daily rites and rituals associated with the tooth begin at 6:00 a.m. with *poojas,* or religious services consisting of the famed Kandyan drummers performing outside the chamber where the tooth is enclosed. The *pooja* is repeated again in the evening. At 10:00 in the morning, an almsgiving, or *dana,* takes place. Usually an important family from the island prepares a rice and curry dish for the Buddha that is then eaten by the temple monks, for whom the noonday meal serves as the only meal of the day. Bearing plates of food, the select are escorted into the inner chamber, where the dishes are laid and where they are able to view the reliquary containing the tooth.

According to ancient Buddhist scriptures, the tooth possesses miraculous powers, among them the power to bring rain. Sinhalese historical annals recount how periods of drought have been broken only when the tooth reliquary has been brought out of the temple for public viewing and veneration. In 1828 Kandy received a long-awaited torrential downpour after the tooth was paraded around town, an event remembered in history books as the "Tooth Relic Flood." Care must be taken not to take the tooth out of the temple for too long lest the rains flood the island. In the summer of 2001, government officials, the head monks, and the secular head of the temple decided that enough was enough and that it was time once again to bring the tooth out of its chamber. It was put on display for members of the public who came to pray, bringing flowers while the temple monks chanted *pirit,* or blessings. And on the second day the rains came. For many here, Buddhists or not, it was holy rain. It came and stayed through autumn.

Even as the rains soaked the island, the tanks and reservoirs remained below level, and the country was plunged into rotating power outages. We move about the house at night to a battery-powered fluorescent light made in Thailand. Everyone else in Kandy moves about similarly, and I sit on the porch, watching dim fluorescent lights walking from room to room in invisible houses. Noah does his homework to our one light. My colleagues at the university complain that work at night is completely out of the question. We have perhaps five to six hours of power outages a day, sometimes more, sometimes less. I buy the paper each morning to find out what time I should be cooking that night since the outage times for each area of the island are printed in the paper each day. When Loku Menike comes down the mountain to us, small pots with metal covers sit waiting for us on the stove. On other days dinner hours shift dramatically depending upon what I can see. The rat that has taken up residence in the kitchen finds the forced change in schedule mildly disorienting but still manages to emerge to watch me at my labors. I announce to Noah the time when the lights are going to go out. We calibrate it down to the second, and yet . . . that precise moment when it happens paralyzes us for a few seconds as we bolt from a world familiar into one of primordial darkness. Velu lights small lamps of coconut oil so that we can move between houses. Sometimes he lights extra lights and hangs them in the trees so that the Hindu gods can find their way to our house in the dark. Kandy closes down. We move more silently when it is dark than we do when it is light.

One evening I came home and found the power on when I was expecting it to be off. Must be a misprint in the paper, I thought. More remarkably, it stayed on into the next day and the day after that. The preelection campaigns were in full swing, and the government, in response to what was likely to be a close election, decided to turn the power on in an effort to deflect voter attention away from the ongoing power crisis. The government lost its majority in Parliament, a new prime minister, Ranil Wickremesinghe, was elected, and the lights went off again, at first for one hour, then for four. It all reminds me of stories I had heard coming out of India where elections have regularly been made or broken on the timing of the monsoon. During the 1987 monsoon in India, no less a figure than Rajiv Gandhi was on the phone to the meteorological station down in Trivandrum, checking to see if the monsoon's time schedule was still holding. The promise of rain is one political promise you don't want to break.

South Asia has two major monsoon cycles: the southwest monsoon, which hits at the end of May and lasts until September, and the northeast monsoon period, lasting roughly from October to December. The winds that bring the southwest monsoon to our island originate deep down in the horse latitudes, between thirty and thirty-five degrees, halfway to Antarctica. Oddly, they begin as a whisper, so much so that they used to lock ships laden with cargo in the deathlike calm of the southern doldrums for weeks. And so, to lighten their loads and catch a light wind, the ship captains ordered the horses thrown overboard. Thus was born the term "horse latitudes."

These reluctant southern winds move slowly north in summer-
time in the direction of China and the Gobi Desert. They travel
west until they cross the equator, where they then shift and head in
a northeasterly direction, bringing them directly over Sri Lanka on
their way up into the interior of Asia. When they hit the mountain-
ous interior where we live, they lift, cool, and deposit moisture on
the island.

The northeast monsoons are altogether different. These are the
rains that the dry areas in the Tamil north of the island are fiercely
dependent on. They are much less predictable, however, and not
as wet. The air flow, traveling from the northeast over the Bay of
Bengal, moves over a smaller body of water and thus picks up significantly less moisture than do the southern winds that lie between
the horse latitudes and Sri Lanka.

On my way to the university each day, I pass a spectacular Bodhi
or Bo tree at the Getambe Buddhist Temple. It is situated in an unlikely spot on the busy Peradeniya Road, surrounded by a chaotic
array of *tuk-tuks* and buses, students and patients from the Peradeniya
Teaching Hospital, dogs and their owners from the veterinary clinic,
various municipal buildings, and randomly arranged drink and fruit
stalls. A raised platform on which stands a small *stupa* has been constructed around the tree, adorned by colorful flags sewn by local
women. The site overlooks the Mahaweli Ganga, whose silt swollen
streams below suggest the possibility for solace that can still be found
in unexpected places. At night in particular, people come here to
light oil lamps and to watch them burn as the cool of the river rises.
It is a place to linger. As I pass on the bus, I often see women sitting
on the platform playing with their children, braiding their hair, or
sometimes just talking. Compared to most *stupas,* this one boasts an
unusual level of activity. People pause here on journeys. *Tuk-tuk*
drivers stop to put coins in the charity boxes on either side of the
road to help support the monks as well as the government, since it is
the latter that pays for a lot of the religious festivals, and in the hectic
confusion of traffic and diesel fumes, people manage a moment of
prayer before forging on. My daily bus ride to the university always
transports about fifteen more people than can comfortably fit on

the bus. And yet, as we pass the *stupa,* people who have been lucky enough to find seats improbably pull themselves up with both hands and bow low as we lurch by.

The activity here is not accidental. In 1947 a devastating monsoon hit Peradeniya and Kandy during the month of December. Records show 30.38 inches of rain that month, falling at one point for thirty-six hours straight—perhaps nothing by the standards of Bangladesh, but enough to cause significant damage. The university was flooded, the railway bridge crumbled under the weight of the water, and the river rose ten feet over its highest flood level ever. There were deaths; houses were washed out and roofs caved in. K. M. de Silva, who was a student at the University of Peradeniya at the time, wrote this about it:

> I had never seen—and have never seen—anything like the floods of that year. The railway bridge collapsed, the road bridge was on the verge of suffering a similar fate. The waters rose dramatically and unexpectedly in the night. When we got up that morning we could see just one sheet of water, part of it moving remorselessly ahead, taking everything in its path along with it. This included a large mara tree, dozens of coconut palms, and the wondrous sight of an elephant being rolled along in the waters along with the tree to which it had been tethered in the campus by one of the contractors.

Local residents began to panic. Having nowhere to go, they crowded onto the raised platform where the *stupa* stands at the Getambe Temple and took shelter under the Bo tree. When the rains finally subsided, people found the tree standing safe with a small statue of the Buddha beside it. For Buddhists on the island, but particularly for those who live along the banks of the Mahaweli, Getambe is blessed with miraculous properties. One comes here to give, and to rest in a place sanctified by miracle.

I was going up to Ampitiya today to see a Jesuit priest named Fr. Quéré, whom I had nicknamed "the rain man." He has been teaching theology at the National Seminary since he was fresh out of his own seminary training in Brittany in 1952. With the exception of small trips back to France to visit family, he has remained here ever since, charting the rainfall in this area every day for the past fifty years.

As I walked from the bus stop up the hill, I thought about how it is only here in this part of the world that one's job description includes measuring rainfall! I was reading Leonard Woolf's memoirs of his years spent in the Ceylon Civil Service. One of his duties as office assistant in Jaffna was to keep statistics on daily rainfall. In his diaries of the years 1904 to 1911, he wrote that in order to distract himself and others from the boredom of a lack of social life:

> Every day we had a sweepstake on guessing what the rainfall had been in the previous 24 hours. As Office Assistant, I was administrative maid of all works, and among my infinite duties I was responsible for the elementary meteorological records, including the daily rainfall statistics. So every morning when I went out to lunch, I had in my pocket a paper recording the rainfall during the 24 hours ending at noon on the previous day. Mrs. Price had in her possession pieces of paper on which each of us had at the previous day's lunch written what we thought the rainfall of the previous 24 hours had been.

I climbed the hill toward the seminary and entered another world. Leaving the honking of horns and the diesel fumes behind, I wended my way into cloistered space essentially untouched since colonial days. Some seminary students took a break from cricket and waved to me. I rounded a bend and found myself in a world of manicured lawns, spreading coconut palms, well-tended gardens, and a Romanesque church. The place breathed at once with the sparse lines of seminary life and the abundance of nature that had been carefully trimmed and pruned to complement it.

Fr. Quéré came out to greet me in his white cassock. His hair, once sandy, I guessed, had gone light gray with the years. He was still an imposing figure in his robes. He asked me if I would like a quick tour of the seminary before we got down to the business of rain. I nodded, and he showed me into the church.

"Are you Catholic?" he asked.

I told him I used to be. A long, long time ago.

"Then maybe you know that today is the first day of Lent."

Actually, no. I had forgotten. I knew that on the 27th of this month there would be another *poya* day and that in honor of it there was a major elephant procession down in Colombo. We walked past the altar draped in purple, and I thought about the ebb and flow of one's deeply rooted beliefs and practices when they are deposited into another culture; how over time they slowly begin to merge with the belief system of the world in which one happens to be living. The rhythm of the days and weeks had begun to look different to me now. Someone had given us a calendar from a local pharmaceutical company. It hangs on our wall over the telephone in the dining room and charts our lives according to the necessary *poya* days, Hindu and Muslim festivals. They are, by and large, what determine Noah's school year and my own. And they have begun to determine our own internal calendars as well. But sometimes when I want a refuge—a little less of the new, the exotic, and the incomprehensible—I go to St. Paul's Church in Kandy and just walk around or sit and take in the familiar. Here I know the order of the service, when to stand and when to sit, and how to pull out the prayer stools. The place is a slightly diminished relic of a bygone era. On its walls are marble tablets, memorializing the nineteenth-century British parishioners for whom Kandy was home. They came here as planters, as engineers, as surgeons, and as missionaries. And they brought their prayer books with them.

Fr. Quéré and I walked through the seminary library, a venerable old place, smelling of England. "So, you want to know about monsoons." He looked quizzically at me. "Well, here they refer to me as the meteo [weather] man since I am French."

We headed up the stairs to the second floor of the seminary, where the priests had their personal quarters. Along the wide hallway hung pictures of the Last Supper, the Virgin Mary, Christ, and the rainfall chart since 1905. Here in the finely penned handwriting of three Jesuits was the record of rain deposited on these seminary grounds from 1905 to 1999. The later notebooks Fr. Quéré kept in his own quarters.

"Why do you do this?" I asked him.

"I am a Jesuit. We are the meteorologists of the Catholic Church. I inherited this job from my predecessor when I first came. We are also of all the orders the best educated. From the very beginning, we were directed to found colleges and universities in Europe. Collecting knowledge and disseminating it have always been part of who we are."

He took the chart down, and we stood looking at fifty years of rain.

"Entry for 1933: We had 123.03 inches that year. That's the heaviest since we started recording. In 1976 we had the least rain, only 47.33 inches. The most for any one month was in December 1957. I had gone back to France. Cardinal Spellman was visiting here. He practically got rained out. We had 30.38 inches in one month. Here, look at this. In 1965 we had 163 consecutive days of rain, and on the 13th of February that year we had 3.42 inches in one day."

We went to his quarters, sparsely furnished and stuffed with books. "Please excuse the mess. I am writing a book on the history of the missionary movement in Sri Lanka. It creates vast disorder."

He pulled out a book and read. "Feb. 20th 1627: A terrible cyclone struck Jaffna in the north, producing a tidal wave of unparalleled proportions. Houses, buildings, and churches collapsed. People died of cold in the trees where they had sought refuge. At that time the Portuguese captain of Jaffna, Filippe de Olivier, died from exhaustion after attempting to lead his people to safety.

"There were fierce storms at the time of the Dutch, as well. But my brain does not work as well as it used to, and I cannot find the reference for you just now," he said, looking through his files. "You know I am going to be seventy-eight in two days. Some things are not so easy for me anymore. Come, let me show you the grounds."

We headed out onto the back lawn, where Fr. Quéré fed the ducks, the rabbits, and a bird or two, and then onto the forest path cleared over the years by the priests and seminary students. We talked about the forests, about the clear-cutting, about the displacement of animals, about regrowth. I told him that everywhere I looked, as fast as I saw decay, I saw nature regenerating itself.

"Well, it is not so simple," he said. "Some things don't come back. Look here."

We passed not one but five or six trees eaten away by termites. He pulled the remaining bark away to reveal a colony of red ants that had moved in. "They are doing cleanup. This tree is gone and nothing will come after it, not on this spot."

"Vaeos," I thought to myself.

"You know, sometimes the jungle kills itself. See this Tarzan vine? It's strangling the tree it's wrapped around. Development kills the jungle, but the jungle also turns on itself."

"What lives here?" I asked him.

"Oh, my dear, what doesn't live here? The worst are the boar, who trample everything. What do you want to know about?"

"Cobras? Polangas?"

"Oh yes, we have all of these, but only the viper, the polanga, causes problems. Here, I will tell you a story about cobras. The most important thing to remember about them is that they are gentle. They will not attack unless we attack them. They are not naturally aggressive. Some like to live in people's houses. There is a belief that they will protect the inhabitants from harm. I guess that cobras love milk because there is a story from one of the villages nearby that a certain cobra kept coming to a hut when a mother was nursing her baby. He must have smelled the milk. The mother knew what the cobra was after, so she took some milk from her breast and put it into a small dish and lay it on the floor. Soon the cobra came inside, crawled over to the milk dish, and drank the milk. And that continued until the mother finished nursing the baby. After that the cobra left and didn't come back."

I had read stories not unlike this before. Several weeks ago one of the local papers reported a young mother from one of the villages feeding two baby cobras whose mother had died with milk from her own breasts. Buddhists believe that cobras, particularly those that come into people's homes, are the spirits of one's ancestors and that, if treated properly, they will protect the dwellers from harm. Some of this belief goes back to the time when the Buddha found himself caught in a torrential downpour. While he sat contemplating the seven-day deluge, a cobra covered him with its coils and hood.

From this story originated an almost endless number of tales that have become part of Sri Lankan cobra lore. My students at the university reported that one day while they were sitting under the *mara* tree, eating their lunch, an enormous cobra dropped onto the bench alongside them from someplace up in the tree. The cobra watched them for a few seconds and then slid along on its way.

Fr. Quéré and I continued our stroll through the seminary woods. "Your name," he said, "the *prénom* is French, but the surname is English."

"My grandmother was French. I am named after her and after my mother."

"And where did she come from, your grandmother?"

"From Normandy, but she left and came to the United States. She took a boat from Le Havre with her older sister when she was sixteen years old. They landed in Canada and came to the United States through Montana. She married an Irish lawyer out there who brought her to New York. I never knew her. She died before I was born."

The path threaded its way through leaves, vines, roots. We stopped at an overhang and surveyed the Mahaweli River in the Dumbara Valley below.

"Have you seen a lot of changes on the island? You've been here almost fifty years?"

"I have, but when you live on an island there are always changes. People think that living on an island is to be isolated. It is actually just the opposite. When you live in a place like this, you are at the crossroads of many larger forces from without. Not just the winds and the rain but other things as well. We are at the intersection of many currents here."

"Have you ever wanted to move, to be anyplace else?" I asked him.

"No, why would I want to do that? I came here after seminary, and I guess I will always be here. Until I die, really. But I do go back to France from time to time."

The forest path eventually circled round and opened up onto the seminary gardens, where we stood and talked for a while. It was nearly 5:00, and I had told Noah I would be home soon. I looked up at the sky and asked Fr. Quéré if he thought it was going to rain today.

"No, not today," he said, testing the air on the palm of his hand.

Evening service was approaching, and the two of us said our good-byes. I was headed down the drive when he hailed me. "Your grandmother was brave," he called out in French. I nodded and smiled and waved good-bye.

Fr. Quéré was right; it didn't rain that day, nor the next either. But it was November, and the brown patch of lawn in our compound that Velu lamented over as the dogs did their dance upon it in the evenings would soon turn green again as the northeast monsoon began to move in. Soon the only sound heavier than that of rain falling on our roof would be that of the gutter attempting to handle the runoff. Soon I'd be using the red plastic laundry pan with the picture of the Chinese baby on the bottom to catch the leaks as they fell from the ceiling of my bedroom. The wires of our phones would soon crackle from the moisture, competing in volume with the cacophony of crickets and the pelting of the rain on tin and tile.

That night I sat on our porch with a cup of tea, sipping it along with improbable visions of water buffalos with their muzzles pointed straight at the sky, water being poured onto the sacred Bo tree, and elephants being swept along in flood waters. I thought as I headed in for the night that only by mixing a complex curry of South Asian lore with straight science and rain charts laboriously crafted in a Jesuit's hand over fifty years can one begin to reckon with rain in this part of the world.

"Mom, the roof's leaking," Noah called from down the hall.

Kush, Nandana, and Samba.

CHAPTER 7

The War Next Door

One day Kush and I were washing clothes in our plastic tubs by the outside spigot. Tucked discreetly off to the side on the back porch at the foot of the hill, the washing area is rimmed in rock, providing just enough room for one or two pails. I had chosen carefully what to wash since the clouds portended rain for the next several days. Wearing freshly dried clothes wasn't looking like a realistic possibility for awhile. As we shared a box of soap flakes, I asked Kush how long Velu had been with them.

"December 14, 1998," came the answer, as she wrung out a T-shirt. "We are all still celebrating that date. But he moved from the estate on which he was born much earlier. He came originally from a place called Rajavella near Digane. He was brought up on a big coconut estate there. He is estate Tamil. His ancestors came here sometime in the mid-nineteenth century to work on the coconut, tea, and rubber estates. His father was a storekeeper on the estate. I think it was owned by a British company called the Pallekelle Group, but since the British left, the whole area has been converted into an army camp. Once I asked Velu how much his father made in a day, and he told me it was three rupees."

"That comes to three cents a day," I told her.

"I know. Even by our standards it's horrendous."

"What brought him here?"

"Well, after he finished his schooling he left the estate for two or three years and worked as a tailor in Mahiyagama. Then he came back and got married. It was an arranged marriage. That is very common among the Tamils. The girl's parents were from the estate. So, they married; the children came; and in 1960 they all went to Colombo where the work and the pay were better. They ended up on a farm owned by the Maliban Biscuit people—you know, the crackers that you buy. He worked there for twenty years and took care of the cows. I think he looked after the milking machines. After the riots he went back to Colombo. I guess he felt he was more protected there."

"You mean the 1983 anti-Tamil riots?" I asked her.

She nodded as she handed me some more Sunlight soap flakes.

"It's strange that he felt safer there," I remarked. "Colombo was the epicenter of the problem."

"I know, but I think there was a general feeling among the Tamils at this point that safety was to be found in numbers."

"And then?"

"And then he remained in Colombo until 1993. A lot of people who had worked on estates got land from the government. It was called Mahavelli Land. He built a house on it. That's what he was doing in Kandy when we met him. He got land up here."

"I don't understand why he came here if he already had a place to live."

"Well, that's another story. Essentially what happened is that he gave the house and the land to his son, who is still living on it with his wife and children. He stays with them when he goes over to Digane for the religious festivals."

"You mean the son who comes over here on Sundays sometimes with his little girl?"

"That's the one." I detected a note of disapproval in her voice.

"He gives everything to him. He keeps nothing for himself."

"Is the son working?"

"Who knows?" she said with a shrug of the shoulders as she emptied the washing tub.

The 1983 anti-Tamil riots in Colombo are the barometer against which all else in this war is measured. Though they spread to other parts of the island—Kandy, Gampaha, Kalutara, Matale, and elsewhere—Colombo saw the worst of them. When people talk about the riots, these are the riots to which they are referring. They were the final catalyst that precipitated the civil war between the Sinhalese central government and the Liberation Tigers of Tamil Eelam (the LTTE), a group that, led by Vellupillai Prabhakaran, has been fighting for an independent homeland for Sri Lanka's Tamils since 1976. The events of 1983 have entered into the collective lore and memory of everyone living in Colombo at that time. What prompted them were decades of mounting tensions between the Tamils and the central government over issues of language, job discrimination, and access to education.

Much of the tension between the two sides was initially created by the Official Language Act of 1956, making Sinhalese, also known as Sinhala, the official language of the country. In 1948 the British had pulled out, giving Ceylon, as it was then called, its independence. The country was left with three languages: Sinhalese, Tamil, and English as the bridge language. The Tamil language is Dravidian, close to but not exactly the Tamil spoken in the state of Tamil Nadu in southern India. Sinhalese is an Indo-European language, and many Sinhalese for their part see themselves as part of an Aryan family of peoples. But the language issue seems to reflect something larger than itself and has become a flashpoint for issues of culture, tradition, and identity.

By 1956 a Sinhalese-only bill was introduced in the House of Representatives, infuriating many Tamils who felt that not only their language but their rights, their culture, and their status as equal citizens of Sri Lanka would be jeopardized by the passage of this bill. They staged a *satyagraha* (peaceful protest) in Colombo, and on June 5, a mob of Sinhalese protestors went after the two hundred Tamils who had assembled on Galle Face Green just next to the Galle Face Hotel in protest against the bill. The Tamils were stoned. According to reports, one was thrown into a nearby lake, another had his ear bitten off. That same night rioters embarked on massive anti-Tamil looting throughout Colombo.

There were sporadic incidents between the large-scale riots. Two years later there was another major wave, this on the heels of the passage of the Sinhalese-Only Official Language Act of 1956. The immediate cause of the riots was a train derailment on the way from

Colombo to Vavuniya in the north. The Tamils on the train were beaten. Simultaneously, anti-Tamil riots flared up again in Colombo, with thousands of Tamils rendered homeless. After this, Sinhalese who were living in the north were attacked. There was massive uprooting of populations on both sides; Tamils who had lived in Colombo fled north; Sinhalese living up north fled south. A Tamil friend told me that for him this was the moment when he felt that he was no longer part of the country and that the government could no longer protect him. "It felt like apartheid in South Africa," he said. As the Tamils were losing faith in the system to protect them, many Sinhalese were jumping on the nationalist bandwagon, fanned by the passage of the Official Language Act and the belief among many that the island was destined as a refuge and homeland for Buddhism. It was this belief that galvanized many Buddhist monks to become rabid nationalists and leaders in the anti-Tamil demonstrations and the ensuing violence.

For the Tamils, most of whom are Hindu, the atmosphere was becoming increasingly intolerable. Initially, the violence in the 1950s was directed at the Ceylon Tamils, as distinct from the estate Tamils. There is a difference between the two. The former have deep roots here, some say as far back as the third century BC. They are members of a professional class both up north and in Colombo—doctors, lawyers, engineers—and they tend to be successful businesspeople. They live not just in the north but all over the island. Their command of English is, on the whole, excellent, as many have been educated in missionary schools up north. The estate Tamils, on the other hand, arrived on the island much later, in the mid-nineteenth century. They were brought over from South India by the British to work the tea, rubber, and coconut estates. To this day many continue living on the estates, earning subsistence incomes, and with a lower level of education than the Ceylon Tamils, some of whom are members of the central Sinhalese government. There are Sinhalese who view the Ceylon Tamils as upstarts and usurpers, since many were thriving economically in the post-British era in a way that the Sinhalese were not. But by 1958, rioters were no longer discriminating between the two and began going after both groups of Tamils. According to one pamphlet distributed at the time: "A Tamil is a Tamil." This time the

Tamils in the north did not stand idly by but initiated their own anti-Sinhalese riots in Jaffna, burning Sinhalese property and destroying a Buddhist temple in the town of Nainativu.

In the late 1950s, in response to the increased tensions over the passage of the Official Language Act, President S.W.R.D. Bandaranaike orchestrated the passage of a Special Provisions Tamil Language Act, allowing Tamil to be used for administrative affairs in the north and eastern provinces as well as in schools and universities. Bandaranaike wisely thought that this Special Provisions Act might help ameliorate the situation. He was wrong. When the act was passed, many Tamils felt that it had not gone far enough, while the Sinhalese, for their part, saw Bandaranaike as a traitor to their cause. It was a no-win situation. Bandaranaike was assassinated in September 1959, an event he himself had presaged, by one of the extreme nationalists, a *bhikkhu,* or monk, by the name of Talduwe Somarama, in protest over Bandaranaike's efforts to find a compromise solution with the Tamils. Upon his death, his widow, Sirimavo Bandaranaike, took over his post, despite the fact that she had no qualifications for the job other than that she happened to be the president's widow. With no political experience, Sirimavo adopted a no-compromise position with the Tamil cause. In the opinion of many, this may well have been the single greatest force behind the militancy and terror that began to engulf the country beginning in the 1970s. Some of it was economic in origin. After a period of growth in the 1960s, the Sri Lankan economy began to take a downturn in the 1970s. Much of the frustration in the country was directed at the Tamils, who were perceived as being financially better off and more privileged. The Tamils, for their part, particularly the Tamil youth on the Jaffna Peninsula, had become radicalized by what they felt was a deliberate move on the part of the central government to eliminate their language and their culture, to say nothing of their representation in the government. They began robbing and killing Sinhalese as well as Tamils whom they saw as siding with the central government. What was new about all of this was not just the radicalizing momentum but the fact that it started taking organized form. In 1970 the Tamil Students' Federation came into being, renamed the Liberation Tigers of Tamil Eelam (LTTE) in 1976.

Something else had changed, too. The assassinations, bombings, and killings on an unprecedented scale, which were to become the hallmark of this civil war, began in earnest in the northeast in July 1975. The mayor of Jaffna was gunned down for his presumed loyalty to President Sirimavo Bandaranaike. The assassin was a twenty-year-old by the name of Vellupillai Prabhakaran who came from a fishing village on the northern coast of the Jaffna Peninsula near Point Pedro. A year later he took charge of the newly formed LTTE, an organization that was no longer content with reform but wanted secession. And it wanted it at any price. Local Tamil organizations in the north under the leadership of Prabhakaran were employing increasingly violent tactics in their demands for a separate state. The police and Sri Lankan military stationed up on the Jaffna Peninsula were using tactics no less violent against the Tamils. One riot gave birth to another, one act of violence to another. In May of 1978, the government passed an act proscribing the LTTE. Violence on both sides continued to escalate. There were regular reports of beatings and rapes of Tamils on the Jaffna Peninsula, and the LTTE, for its part, stepped up terrorist activities. And then came the burning of the library, part of a larger rampage that took place between May 31 and June 2, 1981, during which the market, the offices of the Tamil newspaper, the home of an MP, and the Jaffna Public Library were all destroyed. It was the burning of the public library, however, that struck the hearts of the people in Jaffna. For them this event became irrefutable evidence of Sinhalese desire to obliterate their entire culture. On the Sinhalese side, the act was viewed as direct retaliation for the growing violence directed at them, violence that was all too soon to relocate south directly into Colombo.

The 1983 riots are still in the air here. They pushed a lot of people over the edge. In July of that year, eighteen Sinhalese soldiers, traveling in an army convoy up north in Tinneveli in an LTTE area where they were stationed, were killed and mutilated by members of the LTTE. The corpses were brought back to Colombo and displayed in the central cemetery in Borella. The fury over the condition of the bodies signaled the beginning of the anti-Tamil riots, which began initially in Colombo but spread throughout the central and southern portions of the island. Many have described these riots as a virtual pogrom against the local Tamils. Initially, rioters in Colombo looted and burned property and Tamil-owned businesses. Then things got completely out of hand. A rumor had started that the LTTE had infiltrated Colombo to avenge the anti-Tamil violence. This precipitated another round of violence by both sides. Cars were stopped, and if there were Tamils inside, the mob poured gasoline over the passengers and set them aflame. Houses with people inside were burned. People were hacked to death in broad daylight. Tamils were put into the Welikade Maximum Security Jail and then murdered by Sinhalese prisoners and Sinhalese guards. Nearly seventy thousand Tamils were made homeless during the riots. Some fled north, if they could; others took shelter in schools in Colombo and elsewhere throughout the country. Some ended up in refugee camps because there was nowhere else to go. Others were taken in by their Sinhalese friends and neighbors with whom they had enjoyed normal relations for years.

It's not easy finding people to talk to about the 1983 riots. Many Tamils left for Australia, New Zealand, Canada, and elsewhere in the wake of what happened. Others, who wanted to stay in the country, moved out of Colombo up north to Jaffna. I'm not able to get up to Jaffna to talk to anyone because the A9 road linking north and south is closed. Since 1996 this road has gone back and forth between government and LTTE hands. Government troops presently control the Jaffna Peninsula, but portions of the road from Thandikulam to Kilinochchi are still in LTTE hands, thus making it impossible for the government to ship provisions up north. Jon knows some people in Colombo who might be willing to speak to me. I call them only to find out that they had been out of the country at the time of the riots. I need to have an entrée for this kind of conversation. Over the next year and then again in 2005 and 2006, I try to find someone who witnessed them and who will talk with me. These are not times that people want to remember. People who were here and remember them are reluctant to speak about them because of fear of reprisals—not only from the Tigers but from the central government as well. I am starting to get a sense here that one pays heavily for one's honesty in this country.

My search came to an end one day in Colombo. Nalini arranged for me to meet a Tamil family at the home of a friend with whom they were staying. They live in New Zealand now, having left after the riots, but were back visiting. I was given their address and went over there late one afternoon to drink tea and listen to their stories. As the *tuk-tuk* threaded its way down graceful, tree-lined lanes just blocks from the ocean, we passed houses rimmed by white walls, the mark of prosperity and caution in one of the upper-end Sinhalese neighborhoods of the city.

Dressed in an elegant yellow *sari,* the woman opened the door before I had a chance to ring the bell. They had been waiting for me. She introduced herself as Kalmathi. Children of various ages stood behind her, and a man whom I took to be her husband ushered me into the living room and invited me to sit down. I looked around, trying to put the pieces of this family together.

"No, we don't have quite this many children," Kalmathi smiled, anticipating my questions. "We are just the four of us, my husband and I and our son and daughter."

A young woman brought in tea and sweets for us.

"You see," Kalmathi told us, "we still keep to the traditions even though we don't live here anymore. I suppose Nalini told you that we live in New Zealand now. We can live normally there. But here, drink your tea and have some of our Tamil sweets. Nalini said that you wanted to hear our story. It is hard to get the local Tamils to talk. There is so much fear in the air. But our lives are different now, so I can tell you some things."

Adjusting the folds of her sari, she settled back and began her story. "My husband and two children and I were living in a sort of flat with several other families right here in Welawatte. A few days before the 1983 riots my husband's mother arrived to stay with us. There was talk around Colombo that something might happen because the soldiers' bodies had been brought back, and emotion was running high. The people at the cemetery were enraged, but then separate mobs began to form the day after the burials. I was really anxious, but my husband went off to work anyway and told me not to worry. After he left, some neighbors came round and told us that bands of people were going from house to house in our section of the city—it is Tamil, you know—and attacking anyone they saw.

"Mother said to all of us, 'Let's pray,' but I couldn't pray. I was trying to find somewhere safe for all of us to go. Mother wouldn't let us go anyplace because my husband wasn't home. We actually went over to our neighbors'. They had a bit bigger place. There was a Burgher boy who either lived with them or was a friend. I've forgotten. [The Burghers are Sri Lankans of Dutch or Portuguese heritage, born originally to Sinhalese mothers and Dutch or Portuguese fathers who came to the island between the sixteenth and twentieth centuries.] The boy told us all to get into the bathroom. You know, in our culture we have the toilet room and then the bathroom. But still it was crowded; there were ten of us in there. We heard glass shattering. People had gotten into the flat and into the other flats in the building. I looked out the bathroom window and saw cars aflame all up and down the street. People were lighting them. The worst was that my three-year-old son started crying. I was afraid they'd hear him and come after us. I managed to quiet him down. After about twenty minutes it seemed that the rioters had moved on. I have no idea why they didn't check the bathroom. I could hear them in every other room. It was a miracle we were saved.

"I went out onto the street after things seemed to have settled down, and a bunch of us ran to the other side of the road where some Tamil missionary people were living," Kalmathi went on. "In the midst of all this, my husband came home. He had walked all the way from Slave Island where he worked. You know, he had a Sinhalese coworker who accompanied him all the way and then stayed the night with us. I don't know who the rioters were. In our section of the city, there was a kind of shantytown along the canal. I think some of the mob came from there. But I don't know because I was hiding."

I myself have heard it said from many different quarters that the violence after the burial of the soldiers felt increasingly organized. Some say they saw government buses bringing people in. But when the smoke cleared, it became apparent that it wasn't just Tamil homes that were being targeted but Tamil businesses in both middle-class and the more well-heeled neighborhoods as well. The mob that took over was a mix of the employed and the unemployed, factory workers, and students. And the anger was both specific and general. Some Sinhalese felt that the Tamils had enjoyed disproportionate economic success in business compared to the Sinhalese. But there was also a more generalized anger at a system that had educated the populace and then either underemployed them or failed to provide jobs altogether. This is what spilled out onto the streets during those last days of what became known as Black July.

"How exactly did the mob know where Tamils lived?" I asked.

"Well, it was pretty straightforward. The area where we were living was mostly Tamil, so I guess they just took their chances. But somebody told me they had voter registration lists. On these lists it says what our ethnicity is. Also you can tell by people's last names. So I am wondering who gave them all these voter registration lists."

"It feels odd," another one of the family members joined in, "to talk about these riots as turning points in the war. Now it may seem so, but at the time we were getting up in the morning and going to work just like we always did. Even after the riots, I was going to work; my husband was going to work. We went out to get bread. We were going and coming just like we always did.

"There is something else, too. Everyone talks about the disintegrating relations between Sinhalese and Tamils since the 1950s. We were middle-class people living in Colombo. We never felt anything. When the police came the morning after the riots, we were all herded into vans and put into prison. We got food and help from our Sinhalese neighbors. The government turned these schools and public buildings in the neighborhood into prisons. They put us in individual classrooms where we stayed for two or so weeks. I remember at first I was eating from little tubs of yogurt and drinking water from the tap. Usually I wouldn't do that. I'd boil the water at home. But my son was so thirsty. But the main thing is that it was the Sinhalese who brought us food from the outside. No Tamil dared to come near the jails for fear of being arrested. We received food from Sinhalese people we had never met. That was 100 percent sure."

We had talked enough about the violence this one day and sat sipping our tea and taking refuge in small pastries.

"Come back tomorrow," the lovely Tamil woman said. "I have a friend who wants to meet you."

I thought that night about what my students had told me several weeks back as we sat under the *mara* tree talking about the war.

"Madam," said Kanchuka, "did you know that the last kings of the Kandyan Kingdom were Tamil? We were all one back then."

And this from a friend: "I don't know how all of this got started, this ethnic superiority mess, but I'll tell you this: there was a time in history when we were all speaking each other's languages. Sinhalese kings and other high-ranking officials were using Tamil for their record keeping. That was in the fourteenth century. The Buddhist *pirivenas,* it is our name for religious schools, were teaching Tamil. A lot of these Buddhist monks were preaching in both Sinhalese and Tamil. It worked the other way, too. There were Tamil authors composing in Sinhalese as well."

Indeed, the reality of life here is that Tamils and Sinhalese have been working and living side by side for centuries. And it is not just Tamils and Sinhalese. It is Tamils, Sinhalese, and everybody else. I have never lived in such a small place with such a hybrid mix. I keep remembering what Fr. Quéré told me about how living on an island is not to be isolated but to be at the cross stream of many different cultures. There is intermarriage on the island between Tamil and Sinhalese, perhaps not as much now as prior to the conflict, yet still in all, it exists. Udaya's eldest daughter, Atulya, who lives down in Colombo, is getting ready to marry her boyfriend, Gopi. Atulya is Sinhalese and Buddhist; Gopi, Tamil and Hindu. The issues the two families are trying to sort out have nothing to do with intermarriage or religion. Religion has never been a factor in this war. The big questions these days in Udaya's family are how the service and the reception are going to be arranged. They are to have a Hindu wedding in a Hindu *kovil.* In Buddhist tradition there is usually a large reception at a hotel afterward. Atulya is trying to keep the fuss to a minimum. Udaya is leaning toward the hotel reception. He confided in me one day that some people at the university whom he knew thanked him personally for allowing the marriage. As each side in this war is grabbing the headlines from the other, marriages between Tamils and Sinhalese are quietly taking place.

Intermarriage here is not only between Tamils and Sinhalese. There are close to a hundred thousand Burghers on this island. Our neighbors up the street, the Fernandos, are Portuguese Burghers; the writer Michael Ondaatje, author of *The English Patient* and *Anil's*

Ghost, who now lives in Toronto, is Dutch Burgher. I meet people with the last names of Smith, Wellington, or Murdoch who turn out to be Sinhalese, a product of intermarriage with the English and Scots. Other forms of hybridization exist here as well. To be a Sri Lankan Moor is to have Arab blood mingled with Indian blood from Malabar, India, and the Coromandel Coast. Arab traders began arriving in Ceylon as early as the tenth century. Their descendants still live here, primarily on the eastern and southern part of the island as well as in Kandy. The Malays in Sri Lanka—at last count between fifty thousand and sixty thousand of them—are descended from the Javanese who accompanied the Dutch to Ceylon as early as the mid-seventeenth century. It is all part of the mix of this place.

I went back the next day for more conversation, stopping on the way at the Bombay Sweet Shop so that I wouldn't arrive empty-handed. The couple's children, grown up now, and wearing jeans and T-shirts, sat visiting with their own friends before heading out to a café. We waved good-bye to the kids and settled in for more talk with tea and scented sweets from India.

"What happened when the riots quieted down?" I asked Kalmathi, helping myself to something with pistachios in it.

She tucked her legs up onto the sofa, noticeably more relaxed today. "We didn't know exactly where to go." She looked at her husband for confirmation. "Some of us returned to houses to find them razed to the ground. It is what happened to us. My husband went back after a few days and saw that only his passport and his briefcase had survived. We have no pictures of our children from their first years because they were all burnt by the mob. Some of our friends decided that they were better off going to the north. The government was shipping Tamils back to Jaffna and Batticaloa, and for many of us this was a good opportunity. We stayed, though, but we began to think seriously of getting out. I mean getting out altogether, going to another country to live. I thought of Canada, Australia, Pakistan, New Zealand. Before this I had never experienced any anti-Tamil feeling, but I started picking up on a little of it after 1983. My husband worked for a really good company. He was supposed to go to Singapore for two years as the company's rep. At the last minute he was turned down, and they gave the posting to someone else. This happened yet again, maybe even two times after that. I can't say it was direct, but yes, we felt something. I wanted a home that I wasn't going to lose again. And so after a while we left for New Zealand."

Theoretically, it is possible to visit this island as a tourist, head south to the beaches, and have little or no inkling that the country is at war. The success of beach tourism here has been based on making this war invisible. The local hotel owners receive much help from the U.S. media, which have continually underreported the civil strife in Sri Lanka. The U.S. government has shown little interest in the war, partially because the island poses no security threat to us and exports no products we rely on. Interest in Sri Lanka has been growing in Washington, as in Beijing, because of Trincomalee's harbor, the fifth-largest natural harbor in the world, and large enough to accommodate a U.S. naval carrier. The BBC has been more conscientious about reporting the war, presumably because of Britain's past colonial presence on the island. But in all fairness to the media, even those journalists who have tried to write about the war objectively have been denied access to the very areas they need to cover. Most tourists thus arrive at the newly refurbished Bandaranaike Airport in Colombo, whose face-lift began after the attack on it by Tamil Tigers in the summer of 2001, and are whisked away in a van down to the southern beaches.

Given a slight adjustment in one's vision, however, the war can become more visible. When violence escalates, beach tourism is down. Moreover, in an economy already devastated by the war, many of the villages that lie next to the big tourist hotels are not profiting in the way one might expect. Only a few of the resorts actually employ people who live in the neighboring villages, and those they do employ work in menial jobs, barely eking out a living wage. Most of the resorts bring in employees from the outside, often from abroad, who already have hotel experience. And so, the village that sits alongside the hotel shows no visible signs of the prosperity that might otherwise come its way. The village of Unawatuna is an exception to this general rule only because the beach has yet to be taken over by the huge hotel conglomerates. Here the villagers have been able to operate their own small concessions, renting out rooms, taking tourists scuba diving, and running *kades* and eateries just feet from the ocean. But for the most part, the people who live in the villages adjacent to the big beach resorts sell souvenirs on the beach—if they are allowed on the beach at all—and the bulk of their proceeds goes to a middleman who has provided the goods they sell. The local economy remains stuck, decimated on the one hand by the war and untouched on the other by a tourist industry that with few exceptions operates as if the villages didn't exist.

When we first arrived on the island in 2001, the war was no more visible to us than to the beach tourists down south. Some of this was due to the absence of overt conflict in the city of Kandy where we were living. Were the garbage, the dilapidated storefronts, and the young men standing idle along the streets simply signs of garden-variety developing-country poverty and mismanagement, or were they a function of something else? What I know is that this island was touted as the next Singapore twenty years ago as it stood on the cusp of an economic boom. Something had gone terribly wrong.

Our life in Kandy continued in those first months to keep us immune to the war. We lived in a Sinhalese bubble. I have Tamil colleagues, Tamil students; we have several Hindu *kovils* in town, and a sizeable Muslim population, but fundamentally this is a Sinhalese and Buddhist company town. Pilgrims, both Sri Lankan and foreign, come here primarily because of the Buddhist presence—the monasteries and the Temple of the Tooth. The talk on the street, at home, and at work does not articulate the Tamil perspective on this war.

And yet, 150 kilometers to the north, one enters the war zone. Sometimes pieces of the conflict break off and reveal themselves in odd ways. After our first week in Kandy, Noah and I made an impromptu trip 20 kilometers south to the Pinnawala Elephant Orphanage, where we watched some sixty elephants of varying sizes being herded down to the river for their afternoon bath. Sri Lankan families with their children stood at the water's edge, children squealing amid much picture taking as the elephants cavorted and splashed around in the river. A *mahout* approached me and asked me if I would like to bathe an elephant. I took my first tentative steps into the river as the *mahout*'s charge lay half submerged on his side, waiting for my ministrations. I was handed a brush, and I worked my way through wiry hair on tough leathery hide as one big eye on the side of one large elephant kept me in close range.

"Madam, see elephant. Only three legs, madam."

Somehow we had missed her. She stood at the water's edge on her three legs, her spine horribly out of kilter, while the baby elephants ran in and out of as many elephant legs as they could find in the herd.

"What happened?" we asked the *mahout*.

"Land mine, madam," he said, smiling. "Two year old when it happened. Claymore mine." I watched her as she stood on the banks of the river, not venturing in any farther. On the way out, I asked one of the administrators there about her, wondering if she was accepted by the rest of the herd. "They tolerate her," he told me, "but they don't go out of their way to include her. The strong always favor the strong and ignore the weak."

Even the elephant population of the island can claim no immunity from the war. They step on mines and become war casualties. Those who survive end up at the orphanage. In addition to the three-legged elephant that resides there, some of the babies have been orphaned by the death of the mother, often an unwitting victim of the war. Sick or wounded elephants are brought here as well. Here in this place along the Kelani River, they have a home safe at present from land mines.

The war comes at me from an obtuse angle as I am stuck in a traffic jam in downtown Kandy. Traffic here presents the sort of problem for which there is no obvious solution outside of Buddhist contemplation, as buses, cars, *tuk-tuks,* and pedestrians all vie for the same square foot of space on streets with no clear traffic lines on them. No one from New York or the Beltway around D.C. or the L.A. freeways has any right to say a word about traffic woes until they have spent time on the Kandy roadways. Kush and Nandana tell me that the traffic has gotten worse since 1998.

"What happened?" I asked them one night when we were all sitting in their kitchen drinking tea.

"Two Tiger suicide bombers drove a truck right through the gate of the temple. It was in January 1998. Eleven people were killed as well as the two suicide bombers. Actually, we were lucky. The car and the bomb didn't get any further in than the outside wall so everything was safe. They were going for the reliquary, for the Buddha's tooth. They closed everything down immediately. Now you can't even get close to the temple in a car, but it has made the traffic—well, you see how it is."

This was the first time the war really took hold in Kandy, and it became apparent to everyone that this was a war no longer confined to the northern tip of the island. As it happened, the bomb went off just a week before the fiftieth anniversary of Sri Lanka's independence from Great Britain, which was to be celebrated in Kandy. Kush told me that the festivities were shifted down to Colombo partially to protect Prince Charles, who was due to attend. Charles arrived, the celebrations by all accounts were low-key, and the bombs went off again just hours after his plane had taken off for the UK. A month later a school bus was detonated, and thirty-three children were dead in Colombo. And the traffic patterns up in the hills in Kandy got rerouted for the next five years.

I do my everyday shopping in the center of town. I go to the open-air markets now and am learning to shop the South Asian way. The sellers are patiently teaching me what it is I want to buy. They cut off slices of papaya and mango for me, peel tiny succulent bananas as I pass by with my sack. I take aim down the sidewalks, threading in and out of shoppers and rows of young men hawking their wares— bright cottons, bed linen, Columbia sportswear, made in Sri Lanka and then sold for ten times the price in the States. Other men sit alongside, or just stand watching, all young, none with permanent jobs, all waiting for promises from the next politician, victims of an economy that has gone south during a war in which the only clear winners thus far have been the arms dealers.

"Good quality, madam," a hawker shouts as I am borne along by the wave of people down the street toward the vegetable market.

—————

"Do you want to go to the American Studies Conference?" Udaya asked me one day. "It's down at one of the beach resorts. We can all go swimming."

The lure of the beach is one invitation I never turn down. But it was also a good time to get away. Noah had been having his own problems at his school, problems that I wasn't even fully aware of until they had exploded one evening the week before. I had been sitting in bed under my mosquito netting. We were in the midst of our daily power outage, and I was reading, flashlight in hand. Noah had gone with some friends from school to a musical at one of the other local schools up near Katugastota. It was one of the few nights he went anyplace, and I wanted to stay up to get the full report. Around 10:00 I heard the front door close. Samba scrambled and slid on the red wax floor in her efforts to greet him, and Noah in his khakis came in, looking somehow much older than he had when he had left a few hours earlier. He unfastened the mosquito net, slipped in under it, and told me the story of the evening. He had gone out for a Coke at intermission and was lured into the parking lot by a boy from one of the other schools, who proceeded to threaten him. Soon the group expanded, and one of the boys alluded to the fact that he had guns in his car that he would use against Noah. A group from Noah's school appeared, and one of the teachers finally defused the situation. Noah hadn't even known the boy but suspected that he was put up to it by some boys from his own school. We talked for a long time. He was frightened, but he was also angry. This sounded bigger than a schoolyard brawl. We talked a little about what his next step would be when he went back to school. I told him not to fight violence with violence, that we had enough of that here already.

"I'm not going to take the first swing, Mom, but if one of these guys hits me, I'll hit back. I swear I'll do it."

"Suppose you don't hit at all. Suppose you just walk away. Then he doesn't have a target."

"I don't buy it. Then he'll think I'm a coward."

"But if you stay and engage, then you give him what he wants, which is a good fight."

"But if I walk away, he won't have a target, and he'll feel frustrated and want one."

We were trying to piece it all together. To both of us it felt like this had been planned but by whom? Was there some sort of city-wide interschool gang activity? Had Noah somehow precipitated this in ways he didn't understand? There were questions as we sat in the bedroom that night that we simply had no answer to. There is a large Muslim population in Kandy, many of whom send their sons and daughters to private international schools. Was this Muslim anger at America getting diffused into fourteen- and fifteen-year-old minds and then playing out in dark parking lots? What had happened in lower Manhattan just months prior to this led us all too comfortably into seeking an explanation for what had happened in anti-Americanism on the part of Muslim communities. That was the simple explanation. But we had no way of knowing if these students were even Muslim and if they were whether these larger events had motivated them. We had to be careful.

We spent the next morning at the Katugastota Police Station, filing a report and being told that there is a pattern of interschool gang activity up here. Noah was the new kid on the block this past year. No doubt it complicated things for the Muslim students that he was American. He came in later than the other students and was evidently targeted before he ever set foot in the school. The harassment started during the first week and continued on and off for seven months. Noah's response initially was to laugh it off. After that he began to internalize it until it reached this new plateau.

So as we headed for the beach, I was aware that we all needed sea breezes. Noah and I needed some time to absorb what had happened, and Udaya and his family needed to get away from the daily grind. And so we piled into the van that would take us to Wadduwa just south of Colombo for two days. Udaya and I left Noah and Achala doing battle with the waves and headed indoors to hear what my Sri Lankan colleagues had to say about America. The United States had just gotten itself embroiled in Iraq against the better judgment of everyone I knew, including myself, and I was curious to discover how Sri Lankan academics viewed this. I took a last look at the waves slamming the shore and our sons with them, and remarked on this to Udaya.

"It's a pre-monsoon ocean," he replied.

Inside no one wanted to talk about America. Instead, American studies specialists from all over the island were discussing what was eating away at their own country. I sat and listened to a conversation about a war with no end in sight. A man stood up and gave an impromptu talk about memorializing the dead. "I don't know if you respect the dead," he began. "We Sinhalese have no Day of Remembrance for those who have perished in this war. The Tamils have it, but do we?"

A man who was clearly Muslim spoke out. "The Muslims in the east of this country are very bitter. Their land has been taken by the Tigers. There have been 144 Muslim slaughtered in that part of the island; they have been chased off two thousand acres. They have been expelled from Jaffna; they were given twenty-four hours to leave. The whole north and east of this island is a powder keg. And what are the Tigers doing in the eastern provinces anyway? This is not traditionally the land of the Tamil people. There are Muslim shrines there, Sufi shrines. And there are Buddhist statues there."

A young scholar from the University of Colombo then got up and went to the front of the room. "The LTTE is the kind of party it is impossible to have a durable agreement with," he began. "The Tigers are not a religious movement, but they are made up of the same fanaticism that we find in religiously based organizations. Prabhakaran is tapping into the idea of the chosen people. But he is neglecting the moral aspect of living. They talk about liberation, but it is terrorism. The Tigers are being accused of draining Sinhalese soldiers of their blood and then killing them. Is this terrorism or liberation? The U.S. is calling the bombing of Afghanistan liberation. The people in Afghanistan are calling it terrorism. As a Buddhist, I believe in the moral precept that violence begets violence."

Udaya had sat quietly the entire time, and I was taking notes. The discussion felt like a political impasse mixed with a casualty list of atrocities perpetrated by the Tigers. People were simply at a pitch where it became impossible to talk about this war rationally.

Udaya got up. Our eyes met as he headed to the front of the room. Quiet and self-effacing, he is generally not one to speak at larger meetings such as this. But he also frequently has a different take on things that provides an unusual perspective. The room was silent as he began to talk. "The question as I see it is this: where does the violence come from, where does the terrorism come from? Is it just bred by the war or do we see it in our daily lives? I see it on our own campus at Peradeniya. I see it in the ragging. I see it in the way the Sinhalese boys treat the Sinhalese girls. The girls are regularly threatened by the boys on campus who tell them they can't use the campus pool. 'If you get into a bathing suit,' they say, 'just wait and see what will happen to you.' And so the question is, what form does this kind of attitude take as these people get older?

"And there is another thing," he went on. "We need to talk about the atrocities committed by both sides. The burning of books and libraries is a part of Sinhalese culture. It's been a recurrent feature of our national history. The burning of the Jaffna Library was nothing new. It happened at Polonnaruwa in the thirteenth century under Kalingha Magha. There is a passage in *The Mahavamsa*. It says, 'They set fire to the manuscripts, piled them up as high as Sri Pada [Adam's Peak, a mountain sacred to Buddhists, Christians, and Muslims in Sri Lanka] and burned them.' This is an accepted way of taking revenge here."

Later the two of us went down to the beach. Noah and Achala were still taking up arms against a sea of pre-monsoon or inter-monsoon trouble. We fetched beers, sat on some chaises, and watched our sons emerge from the ocean, looking like seaweed. I was thinking about what Udaya had said about the possible origins of violence in this country and Noah's own situation at school. And about each side going after the other's cultural monuments, one of the most disturbing aspects of this war to me, as is the recruitment of children by the Tamil Tigers. It has echoes of the Taliban going after the ancient Buddhist monuments in Afghanistan.

"Listen," said Udaya, "the suicide bomber who tried to destroy the Temple of the Tooth in 1998 was a Tiger, but the general feeling is that it was in response to another horrible event. The Sri Lankan Army had leveled the cemetery up in Jaffna in 1995 where the war dead are buried. One act of violence set off another. It has been a series of reprisals. It goes back even further than that. In the early 1980s Anuradhapura was attacked by the Tigers. Over one hundred pilgrims and monks were killed. We've gone back and forth like this for decades, maybe for centuries, attacking the symbols of each other's cultures."

I reminded him that the Sinhalese didn't have a monopoly on book burning. There was Hitler's Germany. Goebbels used his own perverted notion that history was being rewritten as the excuse to confiscate and burn thousands of books. The Serbs managed to destroy half a million books in three days during the war with Bosnia in 1992. There's a line by the Russian writer Mikhail Bulgakov in his novel *The Master and Margarita* in which one of his characters says, "Manuscripts don't burn." But Bulgakov was talking about how finally it is impossible to stamp out creativity and intellectual life even during an era of terror. He was convinced that creative life would outlive Stalinism. I'm not as thoroughly convinced that the culture here is going to survive this war. I don't know at what point the line is crossed where more has been destroyed economically, intellectually, and above all spiritually than can be restored and brought back to life. Sometimes I think to myself that this culture is quickly approaching that line.

"Something else is bothering me," I thought out loud. "I still can't buy the notion that Buddhist monks are involved in political violence. I know what people say and that presumably they are doing what they have to do to protect the island as a home and a haven for Buddhism. But look, 72 percent of the people living on this island call themselves Buddhists, and Buddhism subscribes to an ethos of nonviolence. This Buddhist involvement in the student insurrections, in the war, runs counter to everything I think I understand about Buddhism."

"You understand only some of it," Udaya replied. "There are theories that the violence comes out of Buddhist culture itself, that it is not counter to but rather endemic in it. Some say that it is a philosophy that fosters repression and denial."

Sufficiently Freudian in my thinking, I buy the fact that what we repress and deny must find outlets for expression in other ways. But

I don't know that this explains the level of violence that has become the hallmark of this particular war. Some people tell me that what we are seeing here is a conflict of sorts between the philosophy the Buddhist monks espouse versus the background and culture they originally come from. Many of the monks come from poor, rural areas and took the robes in order to get an education, a roof over their heads, and food in their stomachs. Many were initially attracted to movements such as the JVP because they fought for rights for the disenfranchised. The JVP was populist, anti-Western, deeply nationalistic, and anti-Tamil, and much of their platform found common ground with Buddhist belief that the country needed to be safeguarded as a refuge and home for Buddhism.

Everybody has an opinion about this war. Most people just want it to stop. I have met very few, though I have met some, who are fierce nationalists on one side or another. Most understand that ultimately there can be no winner in this debacle because of the deplorable state of the country that the winning side will inherit. A friend one day, discussing this impasse with me, said: "We Sinhalese are a majority in this country. We make up 74 percent of the population. But we are a majority with a minority complex. Possibly the Tamils are a minority with a majority complex. I don't know about that. But somehow we Sinhalese think we are going to be obliterated as a culture, as a people, if we grant the Tamils linguistic parity with us or if we grant them the same access to education. It's nonsense.

"We're not Sri Lankans anymore," he continued. "We're Tamil or Sinhalese or Moor. We have no national identity left. I don't know how we got into this mess. We complained about life under the British, but then when the British left, look at the mess we made of things. We should be ashamed. All of us."

CHAPTER 8

Colombo

The train from Kandy to Colombo is a latter-day holdover from the British Raj. It's a three-hour trip down the mountain (or three and a half or four or four and a half), depending on the state of the train or the tracks. We travel from the cool of Kandy to the heat of the city down precipitous inclines as the train brakes through slopes of banana, papaya, and mango, skirting small, barely visible villages nestled within jungle growth. After an hour and a half the ground gradually levels off, giving way to fields of rice paddy. I watch men bending over as they move through the paddies, harvesting, weeding, or sometimes transplanting the paddy saplings. I look at what they wear in wonderment. Villagers don't have shorts as we do in the West but instead tuck up their *sarongs* and make a kind of pant out of it called an *amudaya*. I see Velu sometimes in one, working the gardens. Later in the day this same piece of cloth mysteriously reverts back to a *sarong*. Only feet from the slender green blades that feed the island, egrets survey the world from their perch on the backs of cattle as the terrain continues to flatten. I watch men on bicycles and women with their umbrellas shielding them from the sun moving along the red clay paths. Passengers begin to gather their belongings as we pass over the Kelaniya River, a big swath of water that, when the rains come, lumbers onto the land, into the tin slab huts, through the lean-tos, over the modest kitchen gardens of settlements only barely recovered from the floods of the year before.

As we creep into Colombo Fort Station, the towers of the Hilton Hotel come into view, as do other kinds of residences consisting of straw mats and a few bundles, on which the elderly, small children, and those in between eke out something like a life two hundred yards from the $250.00 a night rooms. And when I walk across the bridge over the train tracks, moving with the throng past the ticket collector who takes our train receipts, I can choose my lifestyle for the next several days. Or at least I think I can.

There are people who commute weekly between Colombo and Kandy for work. Two of my colleagues have their primary residences in Colombo but dutifully take the train up and down the mountain to their jobs at Peradeniya. Our trips to Colombo are more erratic, propelled less by necessity than by friendship.

"Take a cab, will you?" Jon has implored us if he is not at the station to meet us himself. On one occasion he even managed to show up with a diplomatic car from the embassy. It is unclear to me how he finesses these transportation miracles. But there he stands, waiting for us, six feet two or three, white hair tucked under a floppy hat, towering over smaller heads of thick, black hair.

Me: "Let's take a *tuk-tuk*. They're cheaper."

Jon: "No they're not. A cab is the same price. Besides, it's safer. You might actually arrive at my place alive," referring to the fate of an embassy employee who was killed not long before riding to work in a *tuk-tuk*.

Jon wins. We take the cab.

A mathematician and computer scientist from San Jose State University, he was over here on 9/11 teaching on a Fulbright at the University of Colombo. Funny, brilliant, strangely incompetent at certain things, and always with a band of people in tow, all committed to his welfare, he has opened his home to us when we come down. I think he is glad for the company, though it is company he hardly needs.

"Do you always have this many people around you?" I asked him once.

"I had nobody around me, nothing until 9/11. On the day it happened suddenly people from the university came to my office. I haven't been alone since."

Jon lives in Colombo 7, the tonier section of the city where one is likely to find most of the embassies, diplomatic residences, and upscale homes. His is a well-appointed apartment complete with air-conditioning, a TV set and VCR—and no monkeys. He is also our access to the beach; Noah's to pizza, potato chips, and American movies. And he is sometimes, though not always, our access to a life without ants.

He calls up with his usual comment about the phone lines or the rain on the roof. "Come on down. I've got Peet's coffee here."

Our experience of this island is different, our knowledge base different. There is a certain level of information one acquires living in the capital that we are not privy to. He knows things about the political life and the history of the war that I don't yet know. We sit on his balcony in Colombo 7 early in the morning before the heat rises, he with his coffee, me with my tea, and talk in our *sarongs,* pretending that we are much more Sri Lankan than we really are. We are curious about how the other lives. I tell Jon we love coming down the mountain to Colombo to see him, but sometimes I feel that I'm not in the culture when I come here. I feel like it's sanitized, too Western, too something. I feel like I have to go up the mountain to be in the culture, to really be here.

"Half of the civil war has taken place down here," he responds. "Suicide bombers have blown themselves up here. Two presidents have been assassinated here. Isn't that culture enough for you?"

"You're right. Maybe I'm talking about indigenous culture and the culture of daily life. I just feel that I'm closer to something up there—well, village life, for one thing."

"For you being in the culture means doing everything the hard way. There can be a million easier ways to do something, and you always take the hardest one. Why do you take *tuk-tuks* in Colombo? You could take a cab."

"We've been over this. I don't want to take a cab."

"Is your life more real because you take a *tuk-tuk*? Is it better because you live with ants?"

"In a way, yes."

For my part, I tell him I think he travels too much with an entourage. "There are too many people wanting to take care of you;
you need to get out and see things by yourself."

I remind him of the famous Friday evening when he called from
somewhere over beyond the university at Peradeniya, probably
from one of the bungalows. He was up for the weekend, giving
some lectures through the Post Graduate Institute of Science. We
were going to meet the next day.

"I'm in the middle of nowhere, at the top of a hill," he told me
over the crackling of the phone line. "There's nothing here, including people. Can I stay at your place?"

"Sure," I said. "Come on over, but just so that you know, we
don't live your style. It's pretty basic here. There's a problem with
the shower in the bathroom you'll be using. Also the rats have built
a nest in the plumbing line running from the toilet."

"See you in an hour," he said.

That night in Kandy we sat on the porch and talked, two pairs of
eyes fastened on the same culture, until Velu had taken the dogs in
and the last bus had roared around the lake for the night. We envy
each other, but we stop short of wanting to live each other's lives.

"You know," he said, looking around, "I don't think Ronna
could stay here when we come up to Kandy to see you. I think I'll
book a room at the hotel down the street."

"It may save our friendship," I said, smiling.

I kept thinking that Jon worried too much about whether his
wife, Ronna, would like something or not. Once in Colombo he
and I did a dry run at a restaurant in preparation for her arrival from
the States the next week. Noah had opted out to watch a video in
Jon's living room. So Jon and I did a dress rehearsal. We sat outside
under small Italian white lights and ate something wrapped and sim-
mered in banana leaves.

"She'll love it," I told him. "She'll be here with you in South
Asia. That will be enough."

"You're a bad test case, though. Everyplace I take you to you
love. I could take you to the garbage dump and you'd find something wonderful in it. Oh, by the way, add that to your list when
you come out to Santa Cruz to see us."

We laughed over it, weaving a friendship together.

"Here, I'll show you something," I said, that next morning in Kandy as I took him down for a tour of the lake and a visit to the Temple of the Tooth. I pointed at a large, black, slimy creature that looked like an oversized eel surfacing just feet from where we were standing.

"Good God, what is that?" Jon yelled.

"It's a monitor lizard," I told him. "We have several of them residing here."

Jon's eyes bulged as he ripped out his camera to take pictures of what became known in certain circles down in Colombo as the Kandyan version of the Loch Ness monster.

He stared at the lake with the residue of the last downpour floating in it. "See that leaf floating over here?" he said, pointing to where a couple of large leaves lay waterlogged on the lake. "If this was Africa and you saw something floating that looked like a leaf, you could be pretty sure it wasn't. Here it is probably a leaf."

Jon had spent time in Africa and still carried a lot of it with him in the way he saw things. I looked first at the leaf and then at Jon. Today, at least, a leaf was just a leaf and the lizard was still a lizard, at least until Jon got back down to Colombo.

A few weeks later, Noah and I walked into Jon's apartment in the late afternoon. The American ambassador was having a Christmas celebration at his residence for Fulbright students and scholars, and reconnecting with Christmas felt like the right thing to do. Ronna had arrived from Santa Cruz, and we came down the mountain for two days to spend time with the two of them. We managed to get ourselves as far as the door of the apartment before we were greeted by a noxious odor of uncertain origin. All hopes that it was coming from somewhere else quickly vanished as the same putrid local air seemed to have taken up residence in every room of the apartment. Jon dutifully pawed through the garbage; I looked under the beds and in the closets; Ronna checked the living room and curry prep kitchen; Noah examined the balcony.

Then, in a small plastic tub—meant, perhaps, for garbage—in the bathroom we found it. Had it somehow flown in, crawled in, and then gotten trapped in, trying to extricate itself? What was it? Bird? Rat? Something else? We all stood looking at a small, black, gelatin-like mass, indecipherable in its decomposition. Jon and I stared at it with our two pairs of eyes, and he uttered two words: "Organic matter." As the weeks wore on, "organic matter" became our personal term for anything on the island unrecognizable but alive, or perhaps once alive, or at the very least a relative of something living, that we couldn't recognize or had no other term for.

"What is this?" I would say, pointing.

"Organic matter" was always his answer. Or mine.

"Now do you feel like you're back in the culture?" he said, with just a hint of smugness.

If I stand outside the Fort Station, I can easily hail a three-wheeler and head past Colombo 7 down Buddhaloku Mawatha and into the whirlwind of the neighborhood known as Colombo 6. I leave the foreign enclave behind and enter what seems to be the heart and life of the city. I feel as if I move closer to the culture here. There are no more embassies in this section of the city, none of the higher-class shops catering to the privileged. This is Wellawatte, the Tamil section of the city, known by many as Little Jaffna. Here Buddhist temples cede their places to Hindu *kovils,* whose gods look down from dancing poses onto the traffic moving alongside them. Its street life, like much of street life on the rest of the island, erases the distinction between shop and street, as merchandise, ranging from plastic buckets to fruits to textiles, competes with pedestrians for the remaining two feet of space before the curb ends precariously, sending one spinning down onto the street. Sandwiched between the larger stores are smaller communication hubs—phone, fax, international direct dialing, and e-mail centers where the local Tamil population communicates with the Tamil diaspora abroad in Canada, Australia, and England. Toronto has the largest Tamil population in the world outside South Asia, reported to be over two hundred thousand, with twenty-one Tamil newspapers, several radio stations, and a TV station, and is thought to be the fund-raising hub for the Tigers. The exile community there has swelled since 1983 with people fleeing the hardships and the violence in both north and south.

The *tuk-tuk* driver lets me off at Nalini's, where I have rented a room at the back of the house for when I am in Colombo. Nalini and her family are Sinhalese and live on an island of Sinhalese culture in Colombo 6. She was born in this house, grew up in the house, and, once married, continued to live here with her husband, Nimal, her daughter and brother, and with Mutto, who is Tamil. I ring the bell and can hear the doors and bolts unlocking, and soon Mutto lets me in to a haven of unlikely calm. A small, nicely tended garden, some potted plants, and a fishpond sit sedately behind the walls that keep the street out and us in.

Nalini came to me via Jon, who had inherited her and her family from other friends in Colombo. To bring in a little extra on the side, Nalini, like many in Colombo, rents out rooms in her house. Jon will be leaving soon, and we will need a place to stay when we come down. Thus the relationship with Nalini and her family was born. Nalini greets me from upstairs. During the day Nimal is usually at the tea board. His work took them first to England and then to Pakistan to live. They came back to Sri Lanka in 1995, and now are not sure they did the right thing. It seemed impossible that the violence would last this long. And then there is the problem of their daughter Chitra, a young woman, almost thirty now, always beautifully dressed, her hair done to perfection, an eternal smile gracing her face, who was born deaf. In the UK. Nalini and Nimal had her enrolled in a special school for the deaf, where she was doing well. And then they returned to Sri Lanka, where this kind of specialized education is unavailable. Now Chitra does hair and nails out of a small salon set up for her at home. Customers come, but only in a trickle. People cancel and forget to call. And yet I watch her moving about the house, working in the kitchen, cleaning, tending to the everyday practice of keeping a house in order, and seeming to take infinite pleasure in the life of the home. Nimal takes her swimming once a week. Nalini takes the two of us shopping; we go to teashops. I take her with me when I'm going someplace I think will interest her.

It is always Mutto who meets me at the door. It is Mutto who, when I arrive at odd hours, always has tea waiting for me. He has turned on the overhead fan in my room and shut the windows to keep the mosquitoes out. Short and wiry like Velu, he has infinite stores of energy. I turn over in bed and look at my watch; 5:00 a.m., and I hear him already at work in the kitchen. Soon he knocks gently at my door with the words, "Madam, *te ohne, da?*" (Would you like tea?) "*Te ohne,* Mutto" (Yes, tea, please). I answer lazily and adjust my *sarong* as he brings tea in on a tray and sets it down. I watch him survey the window to be sure I have followed his order not to open it. I slowly drink my first cup, then another. I am so surrounded by people's servants. I explained to Mutto one morning that it wasn't necessary to bring me tea and that I was doing fine. He wouldn't hear of it. I talk to Nalini and Nimal about how endlessly busy he is. They have tried to curtail it, but Mutto will have none of it. Sometimes I think that it is more than a case of a servant doing his assigned chores. Mutto's relationship to this place occupies a range that I have yet fully to comprehend. He is both master and servant. I rail against Jon's life of privilege in Colombo 7 and fall back into it in Colombo 6. It feels like colonialism redux.

"He is freeing you from laundry; he is freeing you from cooking and all of the other things that get in the way of your writing. Tend to your writing," says Nalini, "and to moving about. Mutto will tend to everything else."

Mutto came to this family in June of 1970 when Nalini and Nimal had first gotten married. When they went to England, he stayed on with Nalini's parents, who found him employment in an office until they returned. As Nalini and I sat upstairs with our tea one day, she told me of the problems they have had off and on with anti-Tamil sentiment in the city.

"Mutto has been with us throughout. This is why it is so sad that we have to register him at the police station just because he is a Tamil. This compulsory registration of Tamils all started in the late 1980s. Mutto is registered here at our house, and I think that probably saved him over the years. At least twice during the late 1980s, police came round to 'register' all the Tamils living in Colombo. Then a year later it all took place again. So now whenever there is some sort of flare-up, the police come round.

"You see," continued Nalini, "a lot of the Tamils here have

no address at which they're registered. They fled here to Colombo when things got bad up north. They were staying with friends, relatives, wherever they could. So the police were coming round, actually even before the riots, to check everyone's registration papers. If you were Tamil and weren't registered at your address, you were put in prison. If people were arrested on a Friday, they had to sit it out in jail until Monday since police intelligence services didn't work on weekends. If you were putting up Tamils for the night, you had to go down to the local police station and register them. A lot of the Tamils were staying at hotels in Pettah and Kotahena since there were cheaper rooms to be had there. The hotel owners had to go down to the police station every day and register their guests. After that everything got out of control, and full-scale war started. And it continues today," she added, stirring her tea thoughtfully.

In the mornings in Colombo 6, Mutto's breakfast preparations bring us all out from our bedrooms. Nimal is up now. In his *sarong* he prays at the statue of the Buddha on the balcony to the accompaniment of life honking its way down the street outside. Sometimes I watch him silently from the door of my room as he worships, unmoved by the frenzy below. I remember something the Indian philosopher Krishnamurti said about meditation being something one is able to accomplish on a bus. The only thing I am able to accomplish on a bus is the act of getting in and out of it. I turn around, feeling the cool of the floor on the balls of my feet and surrender myself to my own morning ritual of tea and reading.

Early on at Nalini's I acquire a shadow. A pair of eyes watches me from around corners, from the kitchen when I eat in the dining room, upstairs when I am downstairs. The eyes belong to Mutto's niece, who comes in from the village on weekends or sometimes for a longer stay. Perhaps she is about twenty, perhaps younger. She moves through the house silently.

"We want her to see something outside the village," Nalini tells me. "We're trying to teach her some English. She's smart but very, very shy."

I tell Nalini that I seem to be the object of enormous curiosity. I try to talk to the young woman, but to no avail.

"It's possible that you are the first foreigner she has ever seen.

I think that's why. We have had people here from India, but I think for her you are the first white person."

I relax and let myself be on display. White skin, white hands, blue eyes, freckles, what I eat for breakfast, how I talk and dress. I come back to an ongoing conversation Jon and I have about how hard it is to be alone in this culture. But there is something else, too. I am always just on the edge of this culture, sipping stories with my tea of lives I will never live, lives I will never thoroughly understand.

CHAPTER 9

Colonialist Torpor

It's early Saturday morning, and I am feeling lazy. I don't need to get up and unlock the front gate to let Champika and his *tuk-tuk* in to take Noah to school. I am vaguely aware of some small stirrings outside. The bats are returning from their nightly feed on jackfruit and mosquitoes. A random bus makes its way around Kandy Lake, and I hear the buzz of a mosquito on the other side of my netting. I am mulling over the day in my head, moving in and out of sleep. I have to do my weekly shop for vegetables at the outdoor market. Sometime late morning Kush and I will take the bus down to the central market in Kandy. The Getambe Temple over near Peradeniya is having its annual *pooja* for students preparing for their O and A levels, so the traffic is likely to be worse than normal. I will buy my vegetables and come home. Then Kush has promised me she will show me how to oil my hair. Probably this afternoon I will walk down the street to the Hotel Suisse and do my laps in the pool. If I swim on my back, I can watch the bats hanging from the trees. Floating in the pool, I observe their sleeping habits and learn that they are not silent sleepers. They toss and turn, preen, and chatter even during the daylight hours to protect themselves from mongoose or snakes stalking the unaware. In the pool I am safe from flying bat guano. The sidewalk down the hill is another matter altogether.

I lie lazily in bed until Samba can stand it no more. She has developed an irritating habit of squeaking when she wants attention, and so I extract myself from the complex meshes of my thoughts and my mosquito netting and let her out into the enclosed area between our house and Velu's quarters. She heads straight for his room, and I hear him talking to her in Tamil. There is some leftover chicken curry courtesy of Loku Menike that I will give her later. Prepared dog food is starting slowly to make its way into the economy here but at such a price that for most people it is actually cheaper to cook for one's canine.

I shuffle into the kitchen, check for the rat, and make the tea. I now own a porcelain teapot. Loku Menike watched for the first week or so as I boiled the water. She then took the kettle, poured two cups of the boiling water into the pot, swished it around, and threw it out. One teaspoon of tea leaves for the pot and then one per person, she instructed me, then more boiling water; stir and put the lid on the pot. Let it brew for two to three minutes, stir again, and put the lid on once more. Let it stand for a few more minutes. I do it, and learn to make perfect tea.

I go down sometimes to the Royal Tea Store on the corner of Colombo and King streets, owned by the father of one of Noah's school friends. Abdul Jabbar, a Sri Lankan Moor, sits with his own father, age ninety-six, and a gaggle of male relatives in an open-air store on a raised platform smaller than some people's walk-in closets in the States. Here barrels of tea are sold daily, both retail and whole-sale. The grandfather still sits at his abacus at the front of the store. I asked Abdul one day why so many people appear to be working in such a small place. Two could easily handle the work. He told me that they are all relatives, and that since he is the manager, it is his responsibility to support them all. He also told me that he is planning on quitting because he'd rather take a straight salary and let someone else take care of all the other relatives.

Now, with my tea brewed to perfection, I make my way out onto the front porch in my bathrobe, cup in hand, and settle myself into the old rattan love seat that I have recently recovered. Kush used to sit on it when she was little and came up from Colombo to visit her uncle. I drink and mull over my tea. Muted horns in the distance are punctuated by the sound of tennis balls on the court below at the

Kandy Garden Club. I am reading Leonard Woolf's memoirs *Kandy,* published in 1907, about the place and about the more exclusive Kandy Club up the street from it, still a bastion of privilege:

> Night after night we all went up to the head of the Lake to the tennis courts, a grander and more social ritual than that of Jaffna with a continual flutter of females including a fluctuating stream of visitors, planters, army officers, and their wives and daughters.
>
> After tennis I usually went down to the Kandy Club. In those days in an Asiatic station where there was a Club, it was a symbol and center of British imperialism although perhaps we might not be fully conscious of it. It had normally a curious air of slight depression, but at the same time exclusiveness, superiority, isolation. Only the best people and of course only white men were members. At the same time there was none of the physical luxuriousness, spaciousness or at least comfort of a London club; it was, indeed, a poky, gloomy, and even rather sordid building. . . . the atmosphere was terribly masculine and public school. Even if we were not all gentlemen, we all had to behave, sober or drunk, as if we were, although when some of us were drunk—and drunkenness was not infrequent— it often seemed to me a very curious form of gentle manliness.

The residue of British imperial life in Kandy repeats its rhythms on the courts below. On weekdays I sometimes watch a schoolgirl returning her instructor's serve at 6:30 a.m., taking her daily tennis lesson before classes start. I don't need a watch here. From the sound of the bats returning from their nightly feed, I know it is time to get up. And when the soft thumping of tennis balls ceases, I know it's time for Noah to leave for school. On weekends their reverberations become a metronome to the rhythm of my thinking, as I sit pondering and listening on the porch.

By 7:30 I am on my second cup of tea. I watch a flock of small, soft, yellow lorikeets returning to the lake from the north. Toward evening, about half an hour before the bats depart from their diurnal perches around the Hotel Suisse, the lorikeets will fly north over the lake again. I keep a pair of binoculars out on the love seat so that I can better spot the white-breasted kingfisher, the gray-headed flycatcher, the white-throated babbler, the white-bellied drongo. Two baya weavers have built intricate nests in the shape of a dome in the aurelia tree between Kush and Nandana's house and ours. Last week we saw the mother bringing food back to the nest in her beak and knew the babies had hatched.

I have brought with me to this island a small volume by the French writer Pierre Sansot entitled *Du bon usage de la lenteur* (On the Good Use of Languor). On the cover sit two French ladies, facing each other in a rowboat, from the 1879 painting by Auguste Renoir. The one who is paddling has momentarily rested her arms in her lap while both young ladies are engaged in the act of watching the paddle. Theirs is the kind of languor that Sansot preaches in his slim volume. "Slow beings," he begins his book, "do not enjoy a good reputation. They are seen as awkward, maladroit, even if they execute difficult movements." Sansot's book is a defense of the art of choosing to live one's life without haste, to choose, by modern standards, to do nothing. He speaks about the condition of happiness this way:

> For happiness I guess that you have to drag your boredom into an ordinary village. From your loft you inspect the route of an event, the roar of a motor, a gypsy cart. At the end of the afternoon, you will be satisfied with the hours passed at the window of your loft.
>
> One should understand that the phenomenon of going slow is not a trait of character but a life choice.

He talks about the relationship of place to our ability to sense and reflect: "My friends and I have chosen certain parks such as the Luxembourg and Parc Montsouris at less frequented hours. We stroll along the paths and side-paths. I enjoy singling out the paths. They are more civilized, better protected from the wind, the noise and from other people's eyes by the trees. Their intimacy permits us to better weigh our words, to listen to what is said to us, and to reflect here."

The hedge just beyond my porch is my wall of intimacy. Kept carefully trimmed, yet not too much so, by Velu, it allows me, standing in my pajamas and my bathrobe, to observe long and deliberately yet not be seen by the people who pass below. It is my Luxembourg, my Montsouris. But I also know that what Sansot calls my "waking sleep" is not simply a function of this island on which I am living. Even with a substantial workload here, I am able to look and linger, mull over a word, watch bird flight or wait motionlessly on a forest path for the appearance of a Himalayan bird of paradise. I give myself over to Sansot's world in a way I do not allow myself to do at home.

We receive letters infrequently. When they come, we linger over them. I don't have to perform triage every evening at the front door from the surfeit of whatever it was that was shoved into my mailbox that day. Velu brings me our letter, bows respectfully, and with both hands places it in my hands, as is proper in this part of the world. Velu and Loku Menike marvel at the stamps, and we open the envelopes, knowing that what is inside is of a personal nature, something for us—letters from friends, pictures from home. I show Loku Menike the blond, blue-eyed boys, children of our friends Robby and Susan in Tucson. The phone rings with the same frequency as the mail comes. When it rings it is Kush or Udaya, Jon from Colombo, or sometimes Al and Eileen from the States. Welcome calls. I tell my colleagues about the phenomenon of phone solicitations in America and how I am free from them here.

I do not respond to stimuli in these hills in the same way I do at home. And yet daily life is anything but problem free. I worry about the rats; I worry about whether the plastic tub I have positioned in my bedroom will hold the rain dripping from the ceiling. And there is the not insignificant matter of a stubborn civil war always providing the unspoken backdrop to all other permutations of life on the island. And yet, with all of this, I am also free from the detritus of living in the so-called first world. Would it be different were I more than a visitor on this island? I cannot answer that, but I do know that there is a deliberateness and slowness about the life I have chosen for myself here that eludes me at home.

I've brought my notebook out here and start on my Sinhalese. *Ade vahinewada?* Is it going to rain today? I ask Velu who, even before there is a cloud in the sky, seems to be able to calibrate the possibilities. I am memorizing new words. *Awa,* sunny, *muhuda,* sea, *ire,* sun. This week I am supposed to learn the days of the week, soul-destroying multisyllabic words that, despite being part of an Indo-European language, resemble nothing, just nothing, that I know. After several months I stop doing anything on Tuesday because I can't remember the word. *Angaharuvada,* a word that is pronounce-able only if it is implanted on a piece of paper in front of my face. Meetings take place on a Monday or are put off until Wednesday. Preferably everything should be done on a Thursday, because *Brahaspatinda* flows like liquid off my tongue. In English there's something very German and heavy about Thursday which is, after all, Thor's Day, but in Sinhalese the soft consonants turn Thursday into something close to a linguistically erotic experience. Velu sees my lips moving silently and smiles. I recite the days of the week to him in Sinhalese, as nearly as I can. He repeats them in Tamil. I get an appreciative shake of the head from him and a *hari hondai* (very good) as he heads off with Samba at his heels to trim the hedge.

Noah will probably sleep until 11:00 today unless there is swim practice up the hill. But when there is no practice, he sleeps in, his mosquito net pulled tight, creating a hollow tent-like structure over his bed, the window curtain pulled even tighter, the only sound in his room the slow click of the metal fan that always needs oiling and never gets oiled. I am starting to worry about him. I have pulled him away from his world. Sometimes I don't know if I have done the right thing. In the long run, maybe; but in the short run I have uprooted him from everything that grounded him. The swim meets have become a godsend. I sit there with other parents and watch Noah swim his way into acceptance at his school. But they do not take place with the same regularity as high school sports events do at home, and so on the weekends and afternoons when there is no swim meet he lies behind his door, listening to his music or sleeping. People here reach out to him with abandon. Nandana takes him for walks to search out panthers; his schoolmaster makes sure to check in with him; Jon and Noah seem to have bonded, and trips down to Colombo have become high points. Aside from that, his situation tugs at me constantly. It had all seemed so simple initially. Life on the island is beginning to extract its own form of payment.

I start making mental lists for the market. I need leaves for curry.

I need to buy *karapincha* and *gotukola,* greens that season curry to perfection. Kush has bought me a straw *kude,* or basket, to put my purchases in. The big acquisitions for today will be several bunches of small, very sweet bananas. I also have to pick up some mangoes for the curry. The mango man at the market calls them *kohu amba.* They are a kind of fibrous mango and grow all around Kandy. I will get the green ones today. They're not quite ripe yet and thus better for sautéing. On my way into town, I always pass carts with vendors selling these *kohu amba.* They scrape off the skin, slice the fruit, and then sprinkle chili and salt on them. I get them almost every day coming home from work. Sweetness fired with the spice of pepper. Different weeks bring different mangoes. Sometimes while I am fingering the mangoes, gently prodding them for their sweetness, I remember something Udaya taught me in Sinhalese class. *"Amba yaluwa,"* he told me. "If someone is your best friend, they are your *amba yaluwa,* your mango friend." I smiled at the sweetness of that image.

I am still waiting on *mee amba,* or honey mango. They grow in the wild on tall trees in bunches of about fifty to a hundred fruits. My friends tell me that the fruit is much smaller than the regular mango and that you can just pop them into your mouth and suck the juice out of them. I ask my *amba* man when we will have *mee amba,* and I get a shrug of the shoulders as his eyes seem to roll up to the heavens. Someone else tells me I must search for parrot mango, or *gira amba,* so called because one end of the mango is shaped like a parrot's beak. According to Udaya, there was a time when they were on all the vendors' carts, but now they have practically disappeared. Why? No one knows. Udaya remembers that when he was growing up, the best were the Jaffna mangoes called *karatacolomban.* But that was before the war. "Can I find any in Kandy?" I asked him one day. He told me that the only things being imported from Jaffna these days are bodies of war victims. He looked at me. "When the bodies stop coming and the mangoes reappear, we will know that the war is over."

Noah is up now. I make him and myself a cup of tea, the fourth of the day for me, and together we head out onto the porch. Samba hails him, doing a little round dance accompanied by squeaking and yelping, maneuvering herself in and out of his legs. When this performance has ended, Noah announces that there is nothing to do. It is the litany for him of all the free time outside school. In one sense, there really is nothing for him to do. I cannot tempt him with my discourse on mango shopping nor my endless bird watching, or the joys of simply sitting. His bike was supposed to be shipped to him once we settled in. But we both quickly realized that biking here is tantamount to setting oneself up as roadkill. And so the bike stayed in Tucson, and for Noah there is nothing to do but long unceasingly for home. Some friends of his have introduced him to a video store in town that sells spin-offs of American and British films, pirated in Indonesia. He plays some of them on our laptop. His friends come over and they gather round, watching the backs of the heads of the Indonesian audience watching the original in the theater. This is the way he has seen the James Bond film *Golden Eye* maybe eight times. I have watched it a couple of times with him. TV has not been possible since the day the monkeys ripped off the antenna from the roof. In the two days we had something resembling reception, Noah stared blankly at fuzzy faces of people reporting the news in Sinhalese, a Sinhalese entertainment show, and the usual run of Hindi movies.

Sometimes I think to myself that Noah's boredom is a function of being American, of being part of a society in which we overprogram our kids, inculcating in them the notion that you aren't really living unless you are active and out doing something. And we do it to ourselves as well. In his world, sitting on the porch and drinking countless cups of tea does not qualify as doing anything. It is what we do between doing things, between the various activities with which we have clocked and choked our days. It is what Sansot quietly rails against.

As the months go by, I come to realize that something else is at work here, too. It is not just Noah bored to death in a culture where, by American standards, there is little to do. I keep bumping up against other people's encounters with this culture at different moments of history: the British, for example, who arrived here as civil servants, military personnel, and as planters in the nineteenth century. In addition to the memoirs that people were mandated to keep as part of their job requirement, there were other kinds of personal accounts left as well that today sit behind glass bookcases in the Ceylon Room at the university. Over the course of a year, I sit paging through tomes with titles like *Fifty Years in Ceylon* by Major Thomas Skinner, *Description of Ceylon* by the Reverend James Cordiner, A.M., Late Chaplain to the Garrison of Colombo, *The Rifle and Hound in Ceylon* by Sir Samuel W. Baker, *Sixty-four Years in Ceylon: Reminiscences of Life and Adventure* by Frederick Lewis, *An Account of the Island of Ceylon* by Captain Robert Percival. In addition to what he was required to write, Leonard Woolf also kept more personal diaries of his life here; Sir William Gregory wrote at length about the island in his autobiography. Frederick Lewis's mother came out to visit him from England and meticulously recorded each day in her diary. I sit here in the afternoons reading these memoirs, half lulled to sleep by soft whispering in Sinhalese behind me. There is something in all of this I am trying to understand that is both puzzling yet at the same time completely comprehensible. Here were the British, finding themselves suddenly on an island paradise, brimming with life in certain ways and yet to foreign sensibilities quite empty and rather dull, something quite short of paradise. A line I read in George Orwell's "Shooting an Elephant," the best anti-imperialist tract I know, has implanted itself in my head. "I had to think out my problems in the utter silence that is imposed on every Englishman in the East." He wrote this line in Burma, but I think he was also talking about the loneliness that power imposes on one as a white *sahib* in Southeast Asia. Physically he was surrounded by hordes of people, but spiritually and emotionally he was alone. I both sense and don't sense what Orwell experienced. I welcome the silence, the deliberateness with which I move about, the rarity of the phone, the long-awaited letter. But some things have changed since Orwell's time. I move with Sri Lankans, many of whom have had some experience of the West, and so we share a certain unspoken context. But I also know that I am always on view here, in some places more than others. In public I am watched, never maliciously but always deliberately and persistently. My answer after awhile is to retreat inside myself. Such visibility imposes its own rules of isolation upon me.

Perhaps the Englishman who knew this island best was Frederick Lewis, who was born in Ceylon, his parents having come by ship from England around the Cape of Good Hope on a journey that had taken five months and four days. They had come as coffee planters, as had many British and Scots in the early days of British imperialist presence on the island. With typical English reticence Lewis, demurring from anything other than the most cursory reference to his emotional life, produced a volume of memoirs in 1926 entitled *Sixty-four Years in Ceylon*. The book was penned by a man who became completely absorbed by his work and by his life here, so much so that when he went to England in an attempt to recover his roots, he ached to get back to the only real life he knew. In general, he seemed determined to be very British about his sense of place and duty in Ceylon even though, born as he was on the island, he had virtually no knowledge of the country he was meant to be representing there. He planted his coffee bushes and in between had a small harmonium shipped out from England, the country he had yet to visit but felt he ought to be more tied to than he was. Subsequently he took up Euclidian geometry. New planters arrived and brought with them the *Illustrated London News* and *Punch*. One even brought Defoe's novel *Robinson Crusoe* with him—not the best choice, I think to myself. In December 1875 he and other British planters formed a small quartet. A neighbor in a bungalow not far away took up storytelling. Lewis, in due course, took up ornithology and made drawings from life. "I feel no inconvenience from my lonely existence," he wrote in his memoir. But about his mother's emotional life, he was more openly concerned over the threat of loneliness and despair. He recounts the time his father took over ownership of a tea estate in the Ballangoda district near Ratnapura. The entire family loaded their possessions into a bullock cart and moved down south. The nearest white female neighbor was over thirty miles away, which Lewis termed an "impassable gulf" in those days. Thinking back on that time, he recounted: "Had it not been for my mother's devotion to her husband and family, I do not believe she, or any woman, could have lived cheerfully and contentedly in that solitary spot, and yet, for over one year and a quarter she resided there, and was never, as far as I can remember, discontented with her fate."

I feel these people's presence here when I walk over to the Old Garrison Cemetery on the other side of the lake where many of the British are buried. I walk between gravestones and read their lives between the inscriptions that tell of their deaths:

> Neale and Charles Swinburne, infant sons of Capt. Swinburne 83rd Regiment. The former departed this life, aged 6 days. The latter, aged four years, 8 months, 19 days.

> May Ann, daughter of Thomas and Mary Ann Proudfoot, 78th Regiment, aged 1 year and 20 days.

> Erected by a few friends in Kandy in memory of A. McGill, who died suddenly from Sunstroke at Rozell Estate, Ambegamoa, aged 36 years.

> To the memory of Archibald Montgomerie, 45th Regiment, fifth son of Alexander Montgomerie of Annick Lodge, County of Air, North Britain, and of Elizabeth Montgomerie, his wife, who died the 2nd of March, 1821, of jungle fever, in the 20th year of his age.

> This memorial is erected by his sorrowing parents to the memory of John Spottiswode Robertson, Esq. Of Hillside, Dolosbage, born in Edinburgh 13 October, 1823. Killed by wild elephants.

> David Findlay, who was killed by the falling of Mullegodde house, Kandy . . . aged 38 years.

Sometimes I talk to the Sri Lankan curator of the cemetery, Charles, a middle-aged Singhalese man of slight build, who tells me stories about the people who lived here as he tends to the graves. "Not so many people were killed by elephants as you might think," he told me one day, pointing at Robertson's grave. "Robertson was only the seventh European who died this way, at least according to record. He was also the last. More people were killed by trains, some from lightning, lots from cholera."

"Is that what is meant by jungle fever?"

"Yes and no. People get fevers all the time in the jungle but the fever isn't necessarily cholera."

I told him about the fevers that Noah and I contract without any apparent reason and that leave a few days later with no apparent ill effects.

"Yes, the British used to complain about that a lot. Not everyone died from the fevers," he told me reassuringly. "Just some of them."

John Lewis, 1894:

> Some time after I had finished my work in Gillimali, I had the misfortune to get a bad dose of fever, and on the top of that a chill, which brought on a dangerous attack of double pneumonia, that completely prostrated me. I had a house at Ratnapura at the time, and there I was attended by the local doctor, but as I grew worse, it was decided to send me to Colombo for hospital treatment. I was too ill to travel by road, so under the kind and affectionate care of Mr. Aelian A. King, who was the grain commissioner of the district, I was taken by boat to Kalutara, but so ill was I that after we had passed the lower rapids on the river, I could not bear the vibration of the boat, caused by the action of the rowers. Mr King, therefore, made the boatman hand-paddle, and in that way we got to Kalutara at about 2 a.m.
>
> I was then gently lifted out of the boat, placed upon a couch, and carried to the old rest-house, where we arrived about 2:30 a.m. I was first left in the sitting room until a bed was prepared, and there I lay panting. Over my bed was a hole on the roof of the building, through which I could see a star twinkling, and I remember thinking if I did not actually say it aloud "good-bye, star. I shall see you no more." I was next carried to the bed and very gently laid on it by Mr. King, who after doing so went off to find a doctor and somebody to take care of me, before he left me on his own business. There I lay and felt as if I was on an inclined plane, down which I was slipping into a sort of purple-black vortex, that got nearer and darker, as I felt myself sliding towards it.

Charles told me that a lot of the British and the Scots never made it into Kandy to be buried here. Many came out here alone to make their fortune, intending to return home, rich from coffee and tea plantations. That was until the coffee blight. Many died alone out on their estates from cholera, fever, diarrhea, or dysentery. I found out later by reading the records carefully copied in longhand on lined index cards in the gatehouse that some managed to make it by bull cart from their estate into one of the Kandy hotels before succumbing to one of any number of tropical diseases. Others, according to the records, seem to have been finished off by the whiskey bottle, which became a useful tool for combating boredom and loneliness.

I walked back home to *ambambambamba,* listening as the sellers strung the word for mango together in a refrain that seemed to create a million mangoes out of one. But I was lost in thoughts of burying three children in one day or sweating out the last stages of cholera alone in the Queen's Hotel.

After a month here I begin French lessons at the local branch of the Alliance française. In many ways the Alliance is the social hub of Kandy for foreigners and for those preparing to leave for assignments abroad. Under Kush's able hand, the Alliance offers classes, art exhibits, concerts, and whatever else may come its way. On Wednesday evenings the former Indian ambassador to France and his wife, a few Sri Lankans preparing for work assignments in France, a British planter's wife, a teacher at one of the private schools, and my friend Anna, a reporter for the BBC whose husband is working for Oxfam in the Kandy area all sit and play word games in French, while Marie, our instructor from Normandy, presides over the hilarity. Six degrees north of the equator, 5,287 miles from Paris, we conjugate the verb *aller.*

One day after French class our teacher asked me if I'd like to go to the Saturday night function at the Citadel. I asked Anna if I should go, and she rolled her eyes. "You need to go once. You're writing," she said. "It's the whole expat thing, mostly British expat. It's where they socialize with other Brits."

I decided to take Anna up on her suggestion and that Saturday night decked myself out for an evening at the Citadel. This is one of the spectacularly beautiful hotels designed to gracefully interlace nature and edifice; it sits along the banks of the Mahaweli. The open-air bar was framed in moonlight, which dipped down into the pool terraced just over the river. Stunning young Sri Lankan women in *saris* passed us hors d'oeuvres, while elegant waiters in white circled us with silver trays, bearing white wine. All of the guests but one were white. Talk ranged from the local book-lending club to the local cricket matches to trouble with Sri Lankan help. A gentleman asked me what I've taken up here.

"Taken up? Well, nothing really. I'm working here. Well, maybe French."

"Well, we've all got to take something up here, don't we?" the gentleman replied and then disappeared in search of a whiskey sour.

By 9:00 we had all been properly seated and sated with wine and were about to be fed. The pairs sat together; I was installed between two British couples. We had good English roast beef, something unknown with a béarnaise sauce, all spiced and peppered with the scent of colonialism. I stared into another glass of wine and by 10:30 realized I had had it for the night, excused myself, and headed out. The doorman asked if he should call a cab or *tuk-tuk,* but it seemed a good time to take advantage of the light from a nearly full moon. I walked a mile or two along the stillness of the river back toward the main road. Oddly, with all the violence in the country, I move about safely—enveloped, perhaps, in the protective mantle of being foreign. But I am also in a city that has remained immune from the worst of the civil strife. As I walked along the lane bleached by moonlight, once or twice I thought I heard a fish rise to the surface. Velu and Noah would be waiting for me when I got home. And the dogs would be dancing under the stars.

By January I have taken out a membership at a small gym in Kandy to work off the effects of coconut milk. It is a large room next to a dentist's office on one of the residential side streets. On days when I don't have classes, Champika takes me there at 8:00, goes and visits in town with friends, and then picks me up again at 9:00. It's a modest place in a modest neighborhood but serves its purpose. I work out on the Stepmaster and the Exercycle, all the while watching Hindi movies, creating possible plots in my head based on what I see on the screen. Anna gets me involved in the local Kandy women's football (soccer) squad. We are one American, two British, several Sri Lankans, and one German on the squad, ranging in ages from early twenties to mid-fifties, and we're in heaven because we can wear shorts. We bump around crashing into each other, and somewhere along the way become passable football players. Husbands, kids, and random employees from the nearby club watch our progress, and probably our legs in shorts, from the sidelines. Later Anna and I dissect the game over a Carlsberg.

"Sometimes I think that all these things I'm doing—the French, the ladies' football—are terribly colonialist," I tell her. "It's the sort of thing they did to fill up the empty spaces. But I don't feel as if I have any empty spaces—or rather, to put it another way, I am relishing the empty spaces. You know, the memoirs I am reading are written by people who are trying to replicate the lives they lived at home. One man actually had a harmonium shipped out. But for others it seems as if they ordered their lives to keep from going mad. Do you know Charles at the cemetery? He has some stories about the British and Scots planters who let their isolation get the better of them and took to the bottle."

"A lot of these people were planters out near Haputale," she tells me. "And when they weren't out planting, they had nothing to do but sit on the porch of their bungalows and swat at mosquitoes. This was their life. Miles of tea bushes and tea pickers who didn't speak English. And I guess some of them curled up with their bottles."

"I think I have a term for it," I tell her. "'Colonialist torpor.'"

"Monowada karenewada?" (What are you doing?) I asked Velu one day, as I saw him sitting, rocking back and forth on his haunches in the area between our two living quarters. I thought to myself that his position looked incredibly uncomfortable. *"Mame nikan innawa,"* he answered. I was puzzled. I hadn't heard these words before. He said it again, *"Nikan innawa,"* and put his palms to the floor, smiling. I still didn't get it, but he smiled, and I shook my head, smiling back

as I made my way over to the main house. The next day between classes I went in search of the words to Udaya's office, a place that had overnight turned into a firetrap. On the floor sat stacks of exams numbering in the hundreds tied up in bundles from students who were taking their university degree by correspondence. Udaya was staring at them glassy eyed, clearly in despair. "I have come to add to your burden," I told him. "I have a question. What is *nikan innawa?*"

He laughed. "*Mame nikan innawa.* If I say that, I am telling you that I am doing nothing. I am just here, not doing anything special. That's what it means. People say it a lot. 'Why did you come here?' or 'What are you doing here?' and they'll say, '*Nikan innawa.*'"

"But we say it all the time in other languages," I told him. "In English if someone asks us what we are doing, we can say, 'Oh, nothing special.'"

"Yes, that's true, but here there is something about it that is specific to our culture. Have you read Robert Knox's *Historical Relation of Ceylon* yet?"

I told him I'd gotten through the chapters on ants.

"Well, keep reading. He talks about the *nikan innawa* phenomenon. He says our people are content to sit by their huts, chewing the meat of the arcana nut. I think he uses the word 'indolent.'"

Later I ran into Nihal and asked him what his take was on the concept. He told me that if I went into the villages, I would see people just sitting on their haunches, either chewing betel nut or not. "This is *nikan innawa,*" he told me. "It's part of the culture."

Sometimes on the island one will hear comments about a certain group of people being lazier than others. I've heard it said that the Sinhalese are lazy. If one wants something done, one is better off hiring a Tamil. But the phenomenon of *nikan innawa* has nothing to do with laziness or lassitude. It is something else, informed by a kind of deliberate intent. It seems a practice of both Tamils and Sinhalese. For long hours Velu will sit on his haunches. I glance in as I pass by his work area and see him just sitting and rocking. Sometimes he is sharpening a piece of metal, at other times mashing the leaf of the betel in mortar and pestle. Sometimes just rocking. Velu is Hindu, yet this willingness to just do nothing for hours seems decidedly Buddhist.

It is easy to wax eloquent about doing nothing if you have a job and can put a meal on the table. But there are a lot of people on the island for whom this is not a given. And this is where *nikan innawa* gets peppered with the spice of economics. Along the main street of Kandy stand hundreds of young men with nothing to do but stare at whoever passes by and talk among themselves. Almost all are out of work. They hawk whatever they can—watches, bed linens, underwear. They were the first people we met when we arrived in Kandy because they attached themselves to us, perceiving us to be tourists. One offered to take us up the hill to see the statue of the Buddha; another proposed a journey in his *tuk-tuk* down the mountain to the elephant orphanage. But, as I learn, this is a particular kind of *nikan innawa,* one devoid of anything remotely Buddhist and one ready to erupt at a moment's notice. These are the young men who didn't pass their O and A levels and for whom university education and access to good jobs are now closed. The civil war and the resulting collapse of the economy dealt devastating blows to the job market, which was then followed by 9/11 and the bottom falling out of the tourist industry. And so, groups of young men loiter, waiting for the next tourist or for the next political candidate who can promise jobs. Much of the anger these days is focused on the president, Mrs. Kumaratunga who, in the minds of many, has failed to deliver on her promise to end the civil war and restore the economy. And when the elections come, tempers and despair that have been kept at bay along the sides of the street erupt into violence.

By early December we were facing an election for members of Parliament. For weeks cars with public address systems attached to their roofs had been blasting their way around the lake along with the buses. From time to time curfews were imposed because of street violence. I was trying to finish Dostoyevsky's *Crime and Punishment* with my students over on campus before the next *poya* holiday, which would be followed shortly thereafter by Christmas. My students were now used to my protracted laments over the endless number of holidays in this country, twenty-nine public ones at last count plus the monthly closing of everything for the full moon. This is the only place I have ever lived where I do my syllabi according to lunar cycles.

"We need to finish this before *poya,*" I announced to my students.

They looked at each other, and I knew I was in trouble.

"No, not another holiday," I whined in despair.

"No holiday," they told me. "*Chanda.* The election. The university will be shut down. There is always election violence. We are all supposed to go to our homes and stay there."

My colleagues in our communal English department office confirmed the news. It was now two days before the election, and I noticed that Carmen, whose desk sits across from mine, and Nihal were beginning to gather up work to take home. Noah arrived home with the word that his school would be closed on Election Day.

"How long am I supposed to stay at home?" I asked Naomi, the secretary in the English department office. A shrug and a rolling of the eyes, which essentially meant "as long as you need to."

The day before the elections I took Samba over to the campus veterinary clinic for a persistent ear infection. I stopped by the office to check on things. Udaya was shoveling a batch of correspondence exams into the trunk of his car. My colleagues Sumathy and Thiru had already taken the train down to Colombo. Champika and I headed back to town, where he let me off at the Alliance. I picked up Kush to do a last-minute vegetable shop, leaving Champika and Samba to make their way home. Kush was taking this seriously. She closed the Alliance early, and the two of us hailed a passing *tuk-tuk* and made our way over to the vegetable market, which also seemed to be closing early. That done, we stopped by Food City, the up-scale food store in town, only to encounter a mass of upper-crust Sri Lankans and some British, three times the number that the store could comfortably handle, vying for breathing room at the meat and liquor counters and the checkout line. I grabbed a quart of milk, Kush some cereal, and we stood mutely in line for forty minutes, listening to talk of violence. I took a look at the shopping baskets, odd combinations of English biscuits, Dundee marmalade, and Scotch whiskey.

The general consensus was that this was going to be a nasty election, a referendum of sorts on Mrs. Kumaratunga's presidency. The three major political parties in the country were all vying for a majority in Parliament. Mrs. Kumaratunga's party, the People's Alliance, was in hot contention with the UNP, the United National Party, for the majority of seats. If the UNP won, the party would have achieved the right to elect the new prime minister.

Barricades had been set up on the streets. Two days before mounted police appeared. They patrolled the streets and the sidewalks. The lingering of the young men along the sidewalks had now acquired a distinct edge to them. Kush and I loaded our vegetables into a passing *tuk-tuk* and made our way home.

I woke up in the middle of the night to the sound of grenades rattling our windows. I lay awake trying to pinpoint the direction they were coming from. Some seemed to be up on the hill, others from Ampitiya. Worrying over us, Kush moved down to the main part of the big house in case we needed her at night. On Election Day the two of us did our laundry and dried it on the bushes. Kush and Nandana disappeared at one point to go vote and were back within the hour. I had asked if I could come along to observe. Nandana thought it better for me to stay put. "It's not a comfortable time," he told me. Velu had gone the day before to Digane to vote and had come back immediately. There was a sullen stillness in the air. We listened and waited, going about our own chores with scant attention. Toward evening Nandana emerged from his study to report the news that five people had been killed at a polling place in Kandy. Other casualties mounted around the country as we sat silently on our porch.

"This is not the worst," Nandana told us. "The worst will be when the results of the election are announced."

By the next day the results were not yet in. But Noah's headmaster, frustrated by all the closures, had insisted that school reopen. Just as Noah and Champika left for school, the curfew was lifted for several hours so that people could do a minimal amount of shopping. An hour later Noah called to announce that he was returning home since only twelve students out of several hundred showed up for school. Nandana came down grim faced with the news that twelve Muslim men traveling in a van had been killed up near the Katugastota Bridge, not far from Noah's school. Within seconds I was ringing up Champika on his cell phone to tell him to avoid the bridge. As I was attempting to get through, Champika and the headmaster, as I learned later, were going head to head as to who would take Noah home and by what route. Meanwhile, the dead were being removed from the crime scene by the police and local Muslim leaders. Right then so much was rumor that it was impossible to sort it all out. Kush, Nandana, and I stood looking over our hedge and talked quietly among ourselves. Velu emerged from his room, and we waited nervously for Noah and Champika. We asked questions to which, at 10:30 on this particular morning, there were no answers. Why these Muslims, this in a town where Hindus, Buddhists, Muslims, and Christians live in peace? My post-9/11 nerves sprang to the surface, and I wondered about reprisals, so much so that within an hour of Noah arriving home I had packed him off on the train to Colombo to stay with Jon for a few days. Jon would pick him up. He reported that Colombo was calm; Kandy far from it. I returned home from the train station to wait it out.

By the next day we knew that the UNP had won a majority in Parliament. We also learned that the Muslims had evidently been killed on orders of one of the local warlords for crossing party lines. Nandana claimed that the man responsible would never be put behind bars because he was the son of a high-ranking general who also happened to be a member of Mrs. Kumaratunga's Cabinet. By the end of the week, what the Kandy police had done was nothing. What the Muslim community had done was bury its dead and return for Friday evening prayers at the local mosque. I had caught up on some work, watched the lorikeets and the bats at nightfall, and listened to the grenades.

After a week the university reopened. My students returned, primed to read Tolstoy. Udaya had made it through two hundred of the eight hundred correspondence exams, and Noah had arrived back safely from Jon's in Colombo, sated with Coke and American videos. We were all tired of *nikan innawa* and ready to get back to work: all but one colleague who reappeared only at the end of January, claiming that he had heard a rumor that the university would be closed for a month and a half. As for the hundreds of young men with nothing to do, they took up their positions again on the streets of Kandy, another election behind them, hoping that a change in the prime minister's office would create more jobs. From my porch above the lake, ringed and secured by my hedge, I settled once again into my world of blithe abundance, where, tea in hand, I reflected on the joys of a life lived not in haste, but by what Sansot terms "le sentiment de la non-urgence." Below me on the streets were the people for whom *nikan innawa* was not a choice but a daily repetitive act of standing and observing the world go by, a form of doing nothing made harsh by necessity, one that could find its only outlet in *chanda kolebala*. It was a lesson in more than language.

Noah at Minneriya Tank.

CHAPTER 10

Life in a Different Key

In December Jon was packing to leave for the States. Noah and I both realized we were going to miss this man. The protective mantle under which he seemingly moved about the island hadn't shielded him from all the quirky, mysterious information he had managed to pick up about the culture. In the few short months I had known him, our different visions of life here, planted and nurtured on different parts of the island, experientially distinct, wrapped around each other like a double helix, each completing the other. It felt a bit as if part of that strand was unraveling as I watched him pack. He was to leave the following week. I told him that it felt as if he was taking half of Colombo back with him to California.

"Only a quarter of Colombo," he laughed. And indeed two or three months later two of his students followed him to study at San Jose State. A significant number of their family members showed up in the fall to visit the students who had left. One remained in the States. The next fall one of his deans came to teach. One student married an American; then the father arrived several months later and took up what seemed to be permanent residence on their sofa. But it was all in the nature of things. And Jon seemed to handle it with ease.

Back in Kandy the months rolled by, and classes continued. Noah dutifully memorized the layout of the typical British town in sixth form geography, made his way through a combination of algebra, geometry, and trig and lamented the lack of a decent soccer field at his school. I spent most of my time preparing lectures and working with Kanchuka and Tanya, who were both in the midst of applying to graduate schools in the States and the UK. Together we sorted out the application process and dealt with financial aid hurdles. My colleagues in the English department all agreed that there was no need to encourage students to apply for an undergraduate degree at a U.S. college since the quality of their undergraduate education in Sri Lanka was every bit as good, if not better, than what they would get in the States. There was no need to persuade me. It is graduate school, though, where the United States has the edge in terms of financial support available to the students, the state-of-the-art laboratories and technology, and a wider choice of coursework than is available in Sri Lanka.

On the domestic front I continued to deal with the unsolvable mystery of why it had taken close to five months to get someone over to deal with the ongoing plumbing problem in the house. And when the plumber finally did appear, Kush and Nandana gently instructed me in the proper custom and ceremony that one must follow when workmen come. And so I ran down to the Bombay sweet shop to fetch some sweets, and Loku Menike served up tea. The process took up most of the day. Here it is one thing at a time, often with very slow, measured steps. Life simply moves to different rhythms. If I fight it I will lose. More importantly, I will not get the plumbing fixed.

I know I need to adjust my rhythms. A friend of mine in Tucson, Dick, who has spent years in South Asia, is after me about it at home. Noah is on my case as well. I arrived on the island, as did Noah, encased in a cocoon of two feet of personal space, which is what I thought I needed in order to move about in public. South Asia, Sri Lanka, Kandy, the streets, my bank, the milk bar down the street— all are oblivious to the invisible web I have wrapped around myself. I steel myself as I plunge into the throng at the bank, where people conduct their transactions by simply pushing forward en masse to the tellers' windows. Were lines ever here? I think to myself. Surely the habit of queuing must have come with the British in the eighteenth century. "Actually, we had queues way before then," Udaya tells me. "Our Buddhist monks always walked in single file according to seniority. When they go out on their alms begging or go to donors' houses, they always observe this practice. You've seen them do this, no? People started pushing and shoving during times of shortages. When Aruni was expecting Atulya, someone told us that we had to keep garlic in the house, that it would help with the pregnancy. So I went over to the cooperative shop and waited three hours in line for the garlic. When I got to the counter they told me they had no more. This was when people started going crazy and pushing to the head. If they waited there would be nothing left. And so it continues to this day. But not in our religious practices. There it is different."

Sometimes at the bank a young woman, one of the assistant managers, plucks me out of the crowd and politely takes me back to her desk, where she deals with my banking matters. I am rescued no doubt by my color and status, and yet I also spend most of my time wishing I wasn't in many people's minds the white lady (*sudunonna*), or perhaps more appropriately, the "white lady tourist." Noah, who is originally from Paraguay, blends in better than I do. In Tucson he's the dark one to all his Anglo friends. Here he's the white boy at school. Our colors change as we move between cultures. Someone had told me that after a few weeks people would stop seeing me as a tourist. But someone else who knew better told me not to believe a word of it and that no matter how long we stayed we would still be tourists. They were right. "Taxi, madam," drivers call from across the street. "Postcards." "You need map of city." "*Mate epa*" (No thanks), I say, on cue. "*Mame mehe innawa*" (I live here). "*Mame tourist ne*" (I'm not a tourist).

Blending is good. I would love to blend. In November I buy two *chalwas*, two-piece cotton outfits consisting of pants with drawstrings and a long dresslike top. I love them. I feel like I'm wearing pajamas. I still don't blend, but at least the outfits are comfortable. The reality is that I am tall and white; I do not have a long black braid down the middle of my back. I wear a straw hat instead of carrying an umbrella to protect myself from the sun, and I will stand out forever here by my difference. Noah, after two months, gives up going anyplace in town with me. He is fifteen and doesn't like being stared at. And he doesn't like the person he is with being stared at either. In the morning sometimes I take the bus to work from the bottom of our hill, much to the consternation of Champika. I change at the central market, and in forty minutes I'm at the door of the Faculty of Arts. I feel as if I have made my first real inroads into this culture when I figure out where to go in the line at the bus station in order to get on the right bus and get a seat. I learn to read enough Sinhalese to puzzle out words like Mahakhanda, or Gampola, so that I don't confuse the two and end up halfway to Colombo when I am trying to get to work. From time to time, someone will get on board, spot me, and look at me as if I have no clothes on. At such moments I usually take a quick look to be sure that, in fact, everything is on me where it should be and settle back into reading the local news. If I am stared at, I ignore it, stare back a little or, more commonly, just feel big, white, and foreign.

By the beginning of the new year, we have nested and built ourselves a schedule here. I have learned to jostle and hammer my way onto buses along with everyone else, buy fruits and vegetables with aplomb, and wrap my tongue around impossible Sinhalese syllables. Still I rail against the mind-numbing inefficiency in the Kandy Post Office, where I stand at the glue bucket, trying to glue envelopes closed with an oversized glue brush. And yet something else has taken up residence inside me up in these hills. I sit on the porch in the twilight hours and look for repetition and sameness in this exotic world that enfolds my life. The birds of Kandy Lake have their own daily routine. There are 420 species of them on the island, 230 of which live here permanently. The others come for the winter from western Europe, the Himalayas, and Siberia. Many of them congregate around the lake. I spend hours on the porch watching the fruit bats fly over between 6:15 and 6:45 each evening on their way into the hills to gorge on breadfruit and jackfruit. As the months go by and it gets dark ever so slightly later, the bats adjust their schedules accordingly. There is an order to this nightly migration. It commences at about 5:30, with flocks of small, lovely, green and purple lorikeets—the smallest member of the Ceylon parrot family and unique to this island—flying in pairs over the lake. They are also known as hanging parrots, and toward sunset they set off for their evening roosting places. Their flight path takes them directly over our porch. Soon other species of birds follow suit. I watch as the egrets begin to relocate for the night. The black cormorants wait first for the egrets to settle before flying south from the lake, looking for their own nocturnal quarters. The cormorants fly lower, as they are not strong flyers. They leave the higher altitudes to the large fruit bats, whose nightly procession commences when all the other species have settled in with the dark. Finally, at night the very lowest altitude is reserved for the small bats that feed on the local mosquito population. These smaller bats swoop through the portico of our porch, using it as a passageway to the jungle behind the house. Sometimes I duck in order to avoid being dive-bombed. One night a wing grazes my cheek, sending shivers up my spine. For the most part, each species keeps to its own altitude and respects the flight patterns of the others. And after several months I learn to tell time in the evening to within a five- or ten-minute margin based on bird flight.

I am attuned to things differently than I am at home. There is no fall and spring, only wet and dry seasons. And yet I sense the seasonal changes. Trees lose their leaves when it is hottest outside. The Bo tree becomes brown in March. The aurelia tree outside our porch sits barren for most of October to February and acquires enormous green leaves and fresh blossoms in April. Each plant and tree has its own blooming season. When the rains are upon us, I see small red leaves drifting down into puddles on the street. There is something to all of this. We are just far enough north of the equator that we pick up some of the seasonal variations from the Northern Hemisphere. Thus, in what I am accustomed to seeing as fall, little by little, we feel the shortening of days. In addition to the subtle hints bespeaking change, some trees and flowers lie dormant or lose their leaves while others come into bloom. Daily life gravitates between fall and spring.

What is mundane to most becomes part of our exotic. It is the draw one feels to places so far removed from one's known worlds. Elephants lumber down the street and become part of our everyday comings and goings. Kush's parents were up from Colombo a few weeks ago. Tea, sweets, and social chitchat mingled on the porch with elephant tales. Kush's father, as it happened, grew up with six elephants. He told us that the little ones were actually kept in the house as pets.

"Wait a minute," I jumped in. "Small elephants have a habit of turning into large elephants. So what happened when the elephant got bigger?"

"We just expanded the door so that he could go and come."

Noah and I turned and looked at each other.

Buddha's beast has become part of my everyday. Champika and I round a corner, barely avoiding several tons of elephant coming toward us with his *mahout* on his back. The temple elephants move en masse down the street on the way to their afternoon bath, shaking their trunks as they go. Sometimes they carry their lunch of palm and *kitul* in their mouths as they thread their way in and out of the traffic around the lake. A doctor I met treats patients in the morning and then in the afternoon frequently drives over to Minneriya Tank, where he sits in the brush with his sandwich and spends a few hours just watching the herds. Then there is the story of the local *mahout* who asks me one day if I want to buy an elephant. "Pardon?" I ask, thinking I have misheard. "Madam, *aliyek ohne da?*" "No," I tell him, turning away before I get sucked into a completely insane business arrangement. "I've already got a dog at home."

Before catching the bus in the morning, I go to the local news-stand and grab a copy of the *Island,* one of the English-language newspapers that reports local news and always has a full range of human interest stories, often on village life. The relief of not being battered by the ongoing emotional sagas of American teenage pop queens and the latest sex scandals that pass for news in the mainstream American press is enormous. Instead, I devour the weekly surfeit of elephant stories: "Elephant raids ginger beer establishment," "Elephant saves drunken *mahout* on Katugastota Road," "Lanka's first elephant hospital opens today" are just some of the weekly headlines. In February we are all following the ongoing tragedy of the baby elephant that had fallen into a rock quarry and gotten trapped there while its mother stood at its edge helplessly bellowing for a week, watching her baby die.

Sri Lankans love their elephants. At times I am of the opinion that they are one of the few things, perhaps sometimes the only thing, that people on this island can agree on. There is an irrational and emotional tie to this animal that has roots deep in the culture and has become one of the auspicious symbols of the faith. Buddha, I am told, was an elephant in one of his earlier incarnations. The mother of the most recent Buddha dreamed of a White Elephant while carrying the Buddha in her womb. The White Elephant came down from *Tushita,* or the fourth heaven, where those destined to become Buddhas dwell. It is all part of the culture.

These days the elephant situation on the island has reached crisis proportions as elephant and man compete for the same food source. How to keep elephants from destroying paddy fields and other crops is one of the many unsolved problems over here. The farmers lose valuable income through elephant incursions into their fields, and the elephants, for their part, are frequently injured in the process. They are known to fall into irrigation canals and be unable to get out. Others have gotten killed by trains while feeding near the tracks at night. One of the problems is that roughly 50 percent of the elephant population in this country resides outside the reserves and parks and thus becomes a roving menace to farmers, villagers, and drivers alike. This means that in the drier, lower areas of the country, one is likely to meet them along the roads, particularly at night. The press reports that about three a week are dying from traps, poisoning, and other deterrents designed to keep them away from the paddy fields.

The elephant problem in this country was not always so dire. Under the early Sinhalese kings, the elephant was a protected species, so much so that the penalty for killing one was death. The kings took their special elephant trainers from the Kuruwe people, who come from the area around the city of Kegalle north and inland from Colombo. The Kandyan kings also had a special elephant unit that dealt with all elephant matters. The British, however, left a different mark altogether on the fate of the elephant in Ceylon. Their view of the whole population was that they were good sport and that their sheer numbers on the island made many of them dispensable. Reading the accounts the British left of their hunting exploits in Ceylon in the nineteenth century, it is hard not to be cynical about the imperialist venture. It is true, however, that when they first arrived in the late eighteenth century, Ceylon was literally overrun with herds of wild elephants numbering in the thousands. The Dutch and the Portuguese, who had preceded the British here, did not encounter elephants in the same numbers as did the British, mainly because they confined themselves to the coastal areas. For centuries the Kandyan Kingdom in the central hills had remained free from foreign domination because the area was completely inaccessible. Hills rising eight thousand feet above sea level, dense forest jungle, precipitous cliffs, and a land subject to two monsoons a year were major deterrents to anyone who didn't know the region well. There was also the small matter of the roads. In short, there weren't any. Even after the British laid railway lines throughout the island, Leonard Woolf in his diaries describes getting from place to place in a bullock cart.

Once the British imposed their rule over the Kandyan Kingdom in the early nineteenth century, they found that the only way they could control the territory was through an effective chain of communication. And communication meant roads. The British also discovered that the soil and weather conditions in and around Kandy were ideal for planting coffee, a crop that at the time fetched a high price in Europe. And so, to serve both military and commercial purposes, roads were laboriously carved through and around the Kandyan hills. And the hills had to be cleared and the area deforested to make room for the coffee crops. Thus began the massive displacement of thousands of elephants, which found themselves suddenly without a food source and feeding ground. They moved to lower ground where they could find the palm and *kitul* they needed to sustain themselves while the British provided guns to the villagers to help them deal with the marauding elephants. As the island became a British colonial outpost, the British put the local elephants to work on their coffee and tea plantations to clear the jungle and draw the logs used in constructing buildings. And so, in cutting down the forests, the elephants became engaged in destroying their own food source. Having nowhere to go and being naturally hungry, they began making periodic forays into farmers' fields and villages. The British, in essence, created the very problem to which they were attempting to find solutions. Take away their habitat and their food supply, and the elephants will go where they need to go in order to find food. The problem continues today and on a much greater scale than that ever experienced or envisioned by the British. What the British did was simply set it into motion.

Much of the nineteenth-century thinning of the elephant population was pure sport on the part of the British. Major Thomas Skinner, who spent fifty years in Ceylon, some of them as commissioner of roads, is credited with having shot over 1,000 elephants during his time on the island. Even more famous for his shooting prowess was Major Thomas Rogers, who managed during his brief six years in Ceylon to shoot 1,400 elephants, which, if you do the math, works out to one elephant per day. Rogers's exploits with his rifle so impressed the local villagers that they declared that the only thing that would ever kill the man would be lightning. On June 7, 1845, it was reported that Major Thomas Rogers was struck by lightning near the Rest House in Haputale at age forty-one. Local village lore has it that it was God's punishment for having killed too many elephants. The most egregious of all is the account written by Sir Samuel Baker, an Englishman who spent eight years in Ceylon and constructed a model farm and English village in the hills around Nuwara Eliya. He was also an avid hunter, and reported killing 104 elephants in the space of three days.

In February, on one of those interminable Sunday afternoons, Noah and I on the spur of the moment decided to do a little of our own elephant sighting. I had been languishing on the porch watching the world go by and listening to the tennis balls on the court below. Velu's son and brother had come to see him, and the three were quietly engaged in visiting in the area between our living quarters. Periodically Velu came out to cut some *bulat,* which has practically taken over our porch. Samba had devolved into early afternoon lethargy, and Noah was staring at the fan in his bedroom, listening to his music. And so, on a moment's notice we bestirred ourselves, went down in search of a vehicle at the local hotel, and set off for an area near Habarana, where a local jeep driver took us into the Minneriya

Tank, just on the edge of the dry zone. It was 4:30 by the time we got ourselves installed in the jeep, and I asked the driver whether it was not too late in the day to see elephants.

"Good time elephants," he answered. "Day too hot. Now good elephants, no."

The jeep tracks ran amid dense jungle overhang that we dodged until the track opened up onto a clearing. Here we got our first view of the tank. The terrain was mostly flat, punctuated by several small hills in the distance. The color of the land, a translucent blue at this time of day, seemed to merge into the lake like quicksilver. Several egrets stood motionless at the water's edge, while in the distance the only break in the lovely monotony of land and water were brush strokes of dark brown—a herd of cattle—grazing with single-minded attention, oblivious to the other life slowly emerging from the wood behind. Our driver heard them, though. "*Etinna*" (female elephants), he whispered to us as we watched twenty-five or thirty of them, some massive, others newly born, take their place in the blue of the twilight. Nothing stirred; the egrets continued to stare, stark and still across the lake, the cattle lowed in the field, and Noah and I sat motionless with our binoculars. The group seemed to move as one. If they saw us, they gave no hint of it. And if they smelled us, they didn't care. It was a herd of females with their youngsters. They went on feeding and checked the babies which, still waiting to grow into their trunks, wandered in and out of the group. Quietly I let myself down from the jeep and walked toward them, a guest on this plain. I looked back at our driver, and he motioned that it was okay to go ahead. He knew his elephants. As we struggled to communicate, I think he had told me that you could tell whether an elephant was mad or not depending on the position of its trunk. "Good down?" I asked. "Good down," he answered. "Up bad." We sat watching their slow, languid movements until twilight. The group then began to move down to the tank, and we quietly backed off and returned to our jeep.

We took the story of our afternoon back to 2 Mahamaya Mawatha with us. It became part of our family lore, that place where the exotic and the everyday rub shoulders lightly with one another.

CHAPTER 11

Gihin Ennam

In February, as part of the cease-fire agreement, the A9 road to the north opened up. People from the south who hadn't seen relatives in fifteen years choked the roads leading to Jaffna and Trincomalee. Rumors abounded, as they are wont to do in this country, about what life was like up north. Some friends in Colombo had told me that one of the new chic things to do among well-heeled Colombans was to drive up to Jaffna, get one's picture taken exchanging business cards with the Tamil Tigers, and then turn around and get the hell out. But nobody I knew had been there. We made calls. People were hesitant about taking us in. It was some Muslim friends of ours who finally broke through the deadlock and got us as far as Trincomalee, or Trinco, as it is known here.

The entire family mobilized to convey us over to Trinco, and to see to our safety once we arrived. Calls were made to acquaintances of acquaintances, people scarcely known or not known at all, to see if someone could put us up, hotels and guesthouses having become casualties of the war. Somehow a family was found willing to accommodate us. And as we set out—the Muslim women closely escorted by their male cousins—we were steered through six security checkpoints with one of the cousins at the wheel.

As we entered the conflict zone, one area's rubble became indecipherable from that of the next. War here has had a way of depriving everything in its path of personality. Cities, towns fold up into themselves with a kind of protective coating, spectacularly defined by their sameness. There was nothing to distinguish a pile of rocks or a charred tree in Batti from those in Trinco. But Trinco has also been harder hit by this war because it is further to the north. The town seemed to be in the midst of a massive cleanup as we pulled in. The pristine, translucent blue waters of the bay were rimmed by what had been destroyed and discarded. Few businesses and even fewer signs dotted the streets. We stopped to let an elderly man in a blue-checked *sarong* struggle on one crutch with his one leg to cross the street. Something about this city reminded me of how I felt about our house in Kandy, which sometimes asked too much of us as we strained to breathe life into it. Here it felt as if the city had somehow, beside these tropical waters, seemingly untouched by war, just ceased breathing altogether. And yet the people themselves were stirring. Every family was, as far as I could tell, engaged in a sort of freelance hotel and food service business as a way of shoring up an economy that has festered for decades. Windows wounded by shellfire opened to become impromptu carryout restaurants as the smell of chickpeas, lentils, and rice filled the air.

We were given a room on the second floor of a house in the center of what remained of the city, consisting of two mattresses on the floor and a small, wooden table propped up against the window. The family had moved with their mats onto the earthen floor of the kitchen below in order to make way for us and the rupees we proffered. As we came down the steps the next morning, we passed the kitchen, where the family of five sat on the floor in the dark while the mother prepared *roti* over a gas burner. Enveloped by the fumes from the gas cooker, they looked at us silently, their faces almost expressionless. This was not a town that was used to visitors.

Within the hour we were moving with the throng of pilgrims who had come both to see relatives and to pay homage to a local Sufi saint who, according to legend, had been over fifteen feet tall. We circled his tomb along with teenagers sporting newly pressed Osama bin Laden T-shirts. Noah had pointed them out to me. I turned away, feeling suddenly very visible. I also wasn't quite sure I understood it. No one in our group was sure, either. This area of the northeast is part Muslim, part Hindu, part Catholic and Angli-

can, a mix of worlds that had come here and settled as the traders who brought their religion with them moved on. Were these
T-shirts part of Muslim anger at something much larger than the
catastrophic situation in the north? Was this a more generalized anger at America shared by many in the Muslim world? I thought of
the Muslim community in Kandy that had quietly buried its dead
after several of its members were gunned down in the most recent
election. Up here things are different, though. One could well argue that the mix of peoples in the northeast is on a par with that in
Kandy, and yet the fortunes of war have undeniably dealt this place
a hard blow. This is Colonel Karuna territory. He has been Prabhakaran's top commander over here, and from all I have heard was the
chief strategist behind the Tigers' successful resistance against the Sri
Lankan Army in 1997–98. I have heard it said the Prabhakaran had
taken the lion's share of the credit for the victories that were, in fact,
orchestrated by Karuna. There are other things as well about this
place. There are Muslims up here who were forced off their land on
the Jaffna Peninsula by the Tigers and who have had to resettle in
the northeast. I thought as we all stood there looking at a fifteen-foot
tomb that the whole area felt like a powder keg.

Leaving the crowds of pilgrims behind, we headed over to Nila-
vali Beach, regarded by some as the loveliest beach on the island. A
hotel with panes of glass blown out, its off-white curtains dirty with
the grime of war and heavy from disuse, seemed to be shaking itself
awake as gardeners trimmed palms and brushed away sand from a
stone walkway leading to the entrance, which bore all the signs of
having been shelled. We ate on a beach that the police assured us had
been de-mined and crowded around the fishermen's nets as the catch
was pulled in and people bargained for their meal that day.

By the end of the weekend, along with the pilgrims and the
people who had just wanted to reconnect with family, we turned
back toward the central highlands, passing once again through the
security checkpoints, whose young guards seemed noticeably more
relaxed about all of us this time.

I had promised Noah that at the end of May he could go home. I
kept that promise. Friends back in the States were willing to have

him stay with them. School was out in Tucson, and he wanted "a normal summer" with his friends. And he wanted to get on his bike again. He had earned it. This was a very different country seen through fifteen-year-old eyes. And he had seen all he wanted to see. He wanted home, and he was very clear on where that was. And so at the end of May I packed him up, and he came down the mountain for the last time. I would follow in August. I walked with him as far as I could at Bandaranaike Airport, gave him a hug and a kiss, choked back a tear or two, and watched him head off past security, bike helmet in hand.

Ten days later an e-mail from our friends Al and Eileen in Tucson reported a sighting of Noah's head leaning into their refrigerator and a voice asking, "What's to eat?"

Just days after Noah's departure the southwest monsoon hit. In Kandy it brought more rain. In Colombo it brought a return to something approximating normal living conditions. The call came from a friend in Colombo one afternoon. "*Vaesa, vaesa*" (It's raining). Congratulations made the rounds. And then the phone went dead.

It rained all through June and July. I sat on the porch at night and read exams to the portable light Noah had left behind. Students were writing their tutorials, and I was trying to finish a special seminar on Joyce's *Ulysses* with my girls. I gave strict orders to the cosmos that there be no more full moons and even stricter orders that the government hold no more elections of any kind until I had finished the seminar. I received a vote of noncompliance from the cosmos and a reluctant assent from the government. At home Samba and I rattled around the big house, just the two of us. From time to time, she would poke her wet nose into Noah's room, sniffing to determine his whereabouts, pricking up her ears, waiting for me to tell her where the other family member was. "*Gedera, gedera*" (At home), I assured her. She seemed uncertain and lurked about, sometimes resting her head on my lap as I sat with piles of papers and books at my laptop in our cavernous living room with the red waxed floors. It rained hard some nights. The walls and ceilings gave in to nature's force and molded and dripped. I closed the laptop, covered the books and papers with a sheet, and went out to sit on the loveseat, looking at the rainwater glistening on Velu's *bulat*.

Velu, as always, would come in the morning and ask about the bread. I couldn't eat it as fast as he brought it, and what I didn't eat one day would turn blue the next. Sometimes he came into the kitchen and inspected yesterday's loaf for himself. Loku Menike would appear three times a week to clean a house that really didn't need cleaning. I tried to get home earlier during these months so that the two of us could drink tea together on the porch. Some days I'd have to wait for three or four buses to pass by at the university before one came along that I could squeeze onto without losing a body part. Some days, I think, she got tired of waiting or had something else to do and left. But mostly she was there, waiting for me in her house *sarong* on the porch when I came through the gate. I had managed to get some brown sugar, which isn't available in Sri Lanka, from the U.S. Embassy commissary and taught her how to make chocolate chip cookies. And she showed me things, too, because we both knew that our daily routine, her job, and my life on her island would soon end. Sometimes she waited to make certain dishes until long after she was due to catch her bus. Curries emerged from our joint kitchen late in the afternoon as I stood next to her, writing it all down in a small blue notebook. She checked that I was getting it right. "Lady fingers?" (what Sri Lankans called okra), she queried. I screwed up my nose. She took the lady fingers home with her that evening.

"Why are you leaving?" she asked me one day.

I told her I had this other life that I had to get back to: my son, my students in America. She remained unconvinced, even though she knew it all too well. I, too, was dragging my feet.

People began to sense my departure. I worried over things that had been left undone, people I could not help. Champika and I had a long talk. He confided in me that he hadn't been out of Kandy in five years. More and more these days our conversations revolved around the van he wanted to buy. He was trying to get a bank loan for it, hoping that he'd be able to take tourists to places that he couldn't get to on his *tuk-tuk*. Also, the newspapers were running

daily ads for jobs in Dubai—everything from drivers to heavy machine workers to mechanics. He thought that if he could find work
there as a driver, he'd be able to save money and then come back and
buy his own van if the bank loan didn't come through.

"My life is small," he said to me.

We talked about possibilities. In the midst of all this, I remembered the wooden plaque Dad had attached to the wall above the
staircase at home. It read, "Grow where you are planted." I thought
about how that is fine if it can be a conscious choice, done willingly.

Then there was Harshini, the young woman who worked at
the Internet café in Kandy where I sometimes did my e-mail correspondence. She took care of the accounts and tended to some of the
technical problems when the computers didn't do what they were
supposed to. I had known her now for the better part of a year. In
a radical departure from the hairstyles of many young Sri Lankan
girls, who wear their hair braided down their back in one long plait,
Harshini had hers cut into a bob and sported a bright green Toronto
T-shirt and a pair of snug-fitting jeans. I came to know her when
the monkeys were playing havoc with the phone wires at Mahamaya Mawatha, and I started doing e-mail down at her Internet café.
Harshini and her green T-shirt became part of my daily rounds. She
told me proudly that she had been to Canada but never to the States.
Over the months she gradually revealed a bit more of her story. It
was in some ways a unique one on this island in that she had no family. She was twenty-five, she told me. There was no one left but an
uncle in the States. I learned that she had gotten through her O but
not her A levels and thus never went to university. It was the usual
story I had heard at least once a day since first we came here.

"If I can just get to the States, madam, my prospects will be ever
so much better."

One day I arrived and happened to glance over at the computer
screen where Harshini was busily typing away. Usually she stopped
everything and came over for a visit, but not that day. She was obviously deeply engrossed in something. For a moment she turned
away, and I caught a few lines of what was shaping up to be a steamy
love letter. Harshini glanced up to see me looking, and I apologized

profusely. She told me she was writing to her fiancé, a Sri Lankan who lived in Florida. I asked about him. She told me that she had never met him but that he was the manager of a hotel in Key Biscayne. I was feeling motherly and counseled her on the virtues of holding back just slightly, at least until she had met the guy.

"Madam," Harshini asked, with a broad smile on her face. "Do all houses in Florida have balconies?"

I did a double take.

"Well, no, but some certainly do. I can't say."

"I told him my dream was to live in America and have a balcony."

"Don't you think you should meet him first and see whether you like him?"

"Oh, I think I like him. He wants me to come visit him."

"That's an excellent idea," I told her. "You'll be able to see how compatible you are."

She paused. "If it doesn't work out, I will have no one to call. If I come to Florida, to Miami, and he is not there, will you be able to come and pick me up?"

"Well, you know I live in Arizona. It's pretty far."

"How far? Can you drive over from Arizona to Florida? How many hours will it take you?"

"More than you can wait at the airport," I told her. "He'll be there. Don't worry. But just in case I'll give you my phone number. I think I have a leftover phone card from the States. I'll leave it with you, okay?"

She smiled and looked a little relieved.

Visa application time came, and Harshini was worried. "You think I will get a visa, no? I've traveled before. I go and come. I've been to Canada twice. Always I come back."

"That will help," I told her, trying to be supportive. I'd heard that the Consular Section of the U.S. Embassy could be sticky on these matters.

The next week I arrived to find her in tears.

"No visa," she told me. "They just said no."

I told her I thought the best thing would be to ask for an interview.

"I tell them I always go and come."

"A lot of people just go and don't come. Maybe that's the reason."

By the time I was getting ready to leave that summer, Harshini was still trying to get an interview at the embassy.

During my final weeks in Kandy, Loku Menike and I made two trips to her village with the things from our house that she wanted and we didn't. We moved cautiously up the mountain with Champika in his *tuk-tuk,* the red plastic tub with the picture of the Chinese baby in it holding pots and pans, sheets and towels, a chair, a lampshade, and a box of brown sugar. We managed with Champika's help to negotiate our way across the mountain stream, rimmed by rocks where the village girls were doing their laundry. Giggles followed us. We stacked everything on the oilcloth table cover in Loku Menike's small house and lined up the chair along the wall next to the others she had inherited from the American couple for whom she had worked the year before we came to Kandy. Plastic figurines of birds and babies, and a glass one of Buddha, surveyed us from a blue wooden shelf. I heard soft whisperings outside as her sister, several nieces—one fresh from doing her laundry at the stream—and more relatives, whose relationship to Loku Menike transcended my vocabulary, all arrived. They always came when I visited. With or without me present, they looked after each other, quietly dropping in and drinking tea. It was in the natural order of life here. But this time they had come to say good-bye. We drank mango juice in silence and bowed.

I gave Velu the TV, warning him that reception was impossible. But he already knew that, since he was the one who got out there in the mornings with his slingshot to disperse the monkey population. Nandana helped him set things up. Those last several weeks I heard singing and dancing coming from his room. He had found the Hindi movie channel. One day I followed Nandana into Velu's room as he proceeded to see if he could do anything about the TV reception. I stood for the first time in this space with its small cot and an off-white sheet. On the wall hung a picture Velu had torn out of a magazine of the Hindu God, Ganesh. That was all. It was just a place to lay his head. His home was the compound.

On the morning I left, Velu, Champika, Loku Menike, Kush, Nandana, and the dogs all stood outside to see me off. Samba would follow in several weeks. I reached out tentatively to Loku Menike, and she reached back. I was leaving her with our things, with money for a month, with a package of brown sugar, and with no job. The hardest good-bye was the last. I took both of Velu's hands in mine and told him he was my *amba yaluwa* (mango friend). He repeated it back. We bowed deeply to one another before both of us turned away.

I came down the mountain with two carved wooden elephants—gifts from Champika—and a wrapped-up piece of elephant dung presented to me by a *mahout*, who had explained that it was an auspicious sign to have elephant dung in one's possession. It would bring all good things to me, he told me.

"You say *gihin ennam,*" Udaya once taught me, "when you are saying good-bye but know you'll be back. Our people don't like to say good-bye directly because they are afraid there will be no coming back. They know from the *dharma* about the impermanence of life, and so they say *gihin ennam,* which means, 'I'll go and come back.'"

"I will be back," I promised him. I had promised myself this as well. There were things I knew I had to do. I had seen this war too much through southern eyes. I needed northern eyes to find the balance, the eyes I would find in Jaffna. What I didn't know as I left—what I couldn't have known—was that I would be led back here by something much larger than this war, something that would drag everything in its path back into the sea with it.

Our friends Loku Menike and Latha, who taught us to live the Sri Lankan way.

PART II

After the tsunami, near Batticaloa.

CHAPTER 12

When the Sea Came to the Land

On the morning of December 26, 2004, I woke up with the residue of Christmas in my head. The rest of it was residing on the floor of the living room and on the kitchen counters. Samba squeaked and a cold, wet dog nose planted itself somewhere in the middle of my face as I contemplated the bliss of an unplanned day. I spent a few more minutes horizontally, stroking a dog's ear before heading downstairs to face the detritus from last night's feast. I surveyed the damage while making my tea and settled in on the sofa with the morning paper. It was the usual post-Christmas news fare: only one fire horror reported on Christmas Day; the rest, human interest stories—a soldier's surprise return from Iraq just in time for Christmas, record number of adoptions from the humane society, Mexican family reunited after years of separation across the border. I lollygagged my way through another cup of tea and then went upstairs to do a quick pass by my e-mail before getting into my sweatpants and heading out to the dog park.

Another Warden Message from the American Embassy in Colombo, I noted as I scrolled down the night's mail. We'd been back in the States for two years but were still, improbably, on the U.S. Embassy's Listserv. From half a world away we got invited to talks, receptions at the ambassador's residence, Super Bowl games at Marine headquarters, and we received the latest security updates in the wake of the latest bombings in Colombo. This e-mail seemed different, arriving with several exclamation marks and bold lettering. I opened it.

Sun 26 Dec 2004 14:08:49 +0600
Consular Colombo

!!!!

The Embassy of the United States is transmitting the following information through the Embassy Warden System as a public service to American citizens in Sri Lanka. Please disseminate this message to all US citizens you know, who are not registered with the embassy.

At this time the US Embassy has learned of heavy flooding in Wellagama and Trincomalee districts probably caused by a seismic event. At this time we are strongly advising all American residents not to travel towards the coastal areas. If you are located near the coastal area, please try to get to higher ground at this time, staying as far away from the water as possible. If you have an emergency, please call the US Embassy.

It was, in hindsight, a modest communiqué. It sent me to CNN online, though, where there were reports of a seismic event off the west coast of Sumatra that had triggered tsunami-like waves. I saw murky film footage obviously taken with someone's handheld camera of what looked like a tidal surge hitting a beach and taking everything in its path with it. The film footage seemed to be coming in from Thailand and consisted of the one shot being played over and over again. What I saw was less a wave than a surge carrying beach chairs, tables, and people, slamming them against trees, which then toppled and floated over my TV screen like abandoned logs. The rush of water almost silenced the screams . . . but not entirely. For the next ten minutes I sat waiting for more film footage, watching the same wave washing over the same coastal area. At this point no one in the media was clear about the path this wave had taken or what the level of destruction was. There was a complete communications blackout save for the film footage taken by tourists who minutes before had been enjoying breakfast in Phukat. I went downstairs and turned on the TV. Same film footage. Everything else on the news had been preempted. There was only one story: this wall of water.

Jon was due to leave for Sri Lanka in several days with a group of ecology students from San Jose State University. Forgetting the time difference between Arizona and California, I rang him up and jolted him and his wife Ronna awake with the news. Jon told me he would get on the phone and try to call friends in Sri Lanka to determine what was actually going on.

"Look at the times these messages were sent," I told him. "There's a thirteen- to fourteen-hour time difference between us and Sri Lanka. One of these messages was actually sent yesterday our time. So whatever's going on started last night our time."

"Just wait. I'll find out. I'll call you back later. Your people are up in Kandy. Mine are in Colombo, so they'll know. If you can't get through, send e-mails. Just keep trying, okay? I'll talk to you later."

I hung up and watched tidal surges on CNN for the next several hours. New film footage was coming in, this time from Sri Lanka. It looked again to have been taken by tourists. Noah came downstairs in time to watch places we knew down near Galle on the island's southern end disappear into the sea. We watched Hikkaduwa dissolve, then Bentota. Clearly no one had been able to get down south to report on what was happening. Somehow, almost miraculously, this film was making it through to the TV stations, and thus we sat watching another human tragedy play itself out in front of our eyes on TV. Jon gave a quick call. He wasn't able to get through to Sri Lanka. The lines were impossibly tied up.

"How much more can this country take?" I asked him.

"I don't know. I don't know," he murmured. "Look, let me keep trying. Are you okay?"

"Yes. No," I answered. "I've been thinking. Do you know what date this is?"

"I know. It's Christmas."

"And it's *poya,*" I added. "It means the country's closed down. Everyone's moving about. And it's Boxing Day. I guess the expats celebrate it. Jon, everyone's on the roads or they're down at the shore. They're coming and going."

"I know. I know. I'll bet my student Ruckman's parents are up in Kandy feeding the elephants, so they're okay. But, look, it's no use speculating. One of my students, Anton, is trying to ring his mother. I'll call you later."

I picked up the phone and tried dialing Kandy to the accompaniment of people's screams on our TV. I couldn't get through to Udaya. It wasn't even clear if I was getting a line through to Sri Lanka. I tried a few more times and then gave up.

I kept checking for more Warden Messages. I migrated between the TV and the phone, watching the same images of the same surge for the next four or five hours. What no one knew outside the immediate area at that point was that the roads in the east, south, and southwest were all but impassable and the railroad track south of Colombo a mass of contorted metal. It is now known that at about 8:20 a.m. the first wave slammed into the east coast of Sri Lanka near Adalachchena in the Ampara district just north of Arugam Bay on the island's east coast. Between 8:30 and 9:15, most of the eastern coast was submerged. We were eating Christmas dinner in Tucson. I had been playing with the seasoning on the yams, mixing in more cinnamon and nutmeg brought from the market in Kandy. The wave lumbered south, engulfing the southern tip of the island and then the southwestern beaches between 9:15 and 9:40. We were probably finishing the chocolate mousse and passing around yet another bottle of wine. The east coast received at least three, possibly more, hits; the southern coast was hammered with only two. Near Trincomalee in the northeast, seven were recorded, near Ampara further south, five. We were all hugging and kissing at the door at the end of a long celebration. I went over to the Christmas tree and took a last lingering whiff of the French soap a friend had given me before I headed for full collapse in bed.

The casualty figures were not in yet. The media had not even begun to grasp the full extent of what had happened. More images from Banda Aceh on Thailand's southern peninsula were beginning to come in. A sickening feeling took hold in my stomach. It was becoming clear that no one could have survived this. I looked at my watch; it was just after 11:00 p.m. in Sri Lanka. Jon called back. He still hadn't been able to get a line through.

"Adele, this is hideous."

"I know."

We stopped there. We were having trouble talking about it. Jon was starting to get calls from students and from students' parents asking if the trip was still on.

"How is there supposed to be a trip if there isn't an island there?" was the last thing he said before another Warden Message came across my e-mail screen.

> Mon 27 Dec 2004 12:57:14 +0600
> Consular Colombo
> PLEASE READ!!!!
>
> To All American Citizens
>   At this time the US Embassy has received reports of increased water levels in Galle and south of Colombo and the outlying areas. Continuing seismic activity is resulting in aftershocks from the earthquake and will continue to generate high waves and flooding in coastal areas. At this time we are strongly advising all American residents not to travel towards the coastal areas. If you are located near the coastal areas, please exercise extreme caution and vigilance, staying as far away from the water as possible. If you have an emergency, please call the US Embassy.

In his account of the tsunami, Satinder Bindra, New Delhi bureau chief for CNN, described how he was on holiday with his family in Sri Lanka. They had gone to one of his favorite restaurants in Colombo the night before, a perfect place for seafood called Beach Waddiya. It's the kind of place I love—an open-air restaurant directly on the beach with a sea breeze and sand in between one's toes. While they were sitting at their table, less than fifty feet from the water, someone commented that the sea was unusually noisy. The earthquake would not hit in Indonesia until the next morning, and yet as the arrack and holiday mood flowed, someone in Bindra's party sensed something unusual about the ocean. The next morning he and his family headed out from the hotel around 9:30, which was exactly two hours and thirty-one minutes after an earthquake registering 9.2 on the Richter scale jolted the seabed under Sumatra and set in motion the waves that would kill over 230,000 people in South Asia. It took two and a half hours for the first wave to reach Sri Lanka. As it arrived, Bindra got in his car with his family to head over to Paradise Road, an upscale store popular with tourists, to do some shopping. From his car he saw waves coming up as far as the outdoor tables at the restaurant where he had eaten the night before. A number of people were running toward the shore with cameras, waving excitedly. Intrigued, but not particularly worried, he thought it was high tide and kept on driving. Then his phone beeped with a text message from CNN in Atlanta: "Please call; it's urgent."

While Bindra was dialing Atlanta, a train known as the Queen of the Sea was making its way from Colombo south to Matara with eight coaches full of people heading down to the shore for the holiday. The train had left Colombo's Fort Station at 7:10 a.m., and, in an astonishing departure from its usual schedule, arrived in Moratuwa just south of Colombo on time. It was the usual sort of train, the kind we used to take from Kandy down to Colombo: slightly shoddy, seats with the sticky residue of whatever the last passenger to sit on it was eating or drinking. Like most trains in Sri Lanka, it jolted along an old single-lane track first laid during British rule and, like the entire railway system of the country, badly in need of repair and major upgrading. But for any deficiencies on the train one is royally compensated by the view of the shoreline from the window.

About 9:30 the Queen of the Sea made an unscheduled stop, its brakes grinding and screeching in a village called Peralia. The signaling system that enables conductors to communicate between stations was evidently not working that day. It was unclear when it last *was* working. Some people came and crowded around the side of the train nearest the shore and reported, as Bindra wrote in his book *Tsunami: 7 Hours That Shook the World*: "inky, black water hurtling towards them like a 'herd of thundering black elephants.'" Within minutes the entire train was hit by an oncoming wave that caused it to list precariously. People were scattered from the impact; some lay unconscious. Others managed to get out and started running, but at this point the train guard began shouting at everybody, telling them to get back into the train where they would be safe. A few minutes later another twenty-foot wave smashed into the shore, this one sending the train hundreds of meters inland and ripping the track up off the ground. More than one thousand people died in this one place in a matter of ten minutes.

Movement up and down the west coast was impossible. Everything was engulfed, and the dead, like everyone else, simply had to wait their turn. Slowly over the next few days the realization sunk in that if the train had been late, as it normally was, the one thousand or so people whose bodies lay strewn about—that is, if they could be found at all—would still be alive. Likewise if there had been an early warning system. The people in Banda Aceh had no chance, as the tsunami hit them immediately after the seismic event. But the people in Sri Lanka had a two-and-a-half-hour lead time to evacuate and knew nothing. Oddly, the official communiqué I received from the U.S. Embassy, sent though it was after much, though by no means all, of the damage had already occurred, was precisely the sort of communiqué that reached virtually no one in Sri Lanka.

As I waited anxiously for news, the e-mails started arriving.

December 27, 2004: e-mail from Atulya, Udaya's daughter, in Colombo:

> Yes, we are okay, though barely. My whole family (including the newlyweds) did go to Kataragama on the 25th and were returning on the 26th. I was in Colombo. So I was frantic. Finally they called around 1pm and said they managed to escape. They had been in Hambantota on 26th morning, headed towards the beach cos Achala had insisted on going for a swim in the sea. As they were passing a row of houses, they had seen water coming out of a house and swirling across the road. So they had stopped to see what was happening and then suddenly a huge wave knocked the house down. Fortunately my Dad had ordered the van driver to turn around, so they had gone into a narrow path into the land and got stuck on a hill kind of place which was the highest area where all the villagers were gathering. They all stayed there for a couple of hours, and when the water subsided a little, they got away. Yala Safari Lodge completely destroyed including all staff and guests except for one worker. They've found the bodies of the chief accountant and his wife on top of a tree, dead, hugging the tree. They've had to cut down the tree to get the bodies down. So you can imagine the horror. Whole families have been washed off, including huge vehicles like Prada jeeps, buses, trains.

Of course Udaya and family were on the road; it was a three-pronged holiday. Of course he would want to take the newlyweds to Kataragama and have their marriage blessed. It all made perfect sense. No one who could afford time away on this island was home. People from the mountains, if they could, went to the shore. Those who lived near the shore went up into the mountains. Much of the population shifted, passing each other on roads and in train stations. I kept coming back again to the timing of this catastrophe. It was, in a word, heart-stopping: the height of the tourist season, the Christmas holidays, Boxing Day, and *poya* day. From the other side of the globe I thought about Buddha and *poyas,* each of which marks an event in Buddha's incarnation on earth. My first lesson in Buddhism on the island had come from Kush. "What happens in this life is not a function of his will," she had told me. "He is the maker of neither good nor evil."

By the morning of the 27th Jon was immersed in phone calls from Sri Lanka as I was trying to put the pieces together from my end. Improbably, he was hearing from people in Colombo, among them our friend Nalini, who had not even known there was a tsunami. By the time the wave had reached Colombo, the damage it inflicted was minimal since it had lost force moving up the west coast. The worst was some fairly severe flooding. Nalini had learned of it only because someone who came over to have Chitra do her hair reported on the flooding. But that was Colombo. Move ten miles down shore, and it became a very different story altogether. Jon was also getting e-mails from various people on the Sri Lankan side who were involved in organizing his study trip and who told him that he and his students should come ahead, not cancel. People simply didn't know what they were dealing with in those first two or even three days. But by the 28th it was completely clear that there would be no travel.

Late at night on the 27th I called Jon to report on Atulya's e-mail. He seemed oddly muted.

"That's not the worst," he told me.

I steeled myself for the news of one of our mutual friends.

"Ronna left me today. I think she was going to do it when I was in Sri Lanka with the students. Now it looks like I'm not going, so she pushed her departure up a bit."

"This is not possible," I told him, more perhaps out of my inability to absorb another kind of catastrophic loss. I thought to myself how the timing of this stank.

"Had you two talked about this?" I asked him.

"No, nothing. Things were fine. Well, at least I thought things were fine. Well, there were the usual problems, but not this. I had no warning, no warning at all."

He cried softly into the phone as waves carried away other lives on our TV screens. I tried to wipe away tears through the phone receiver, promised to call in the morning, went into my bedroom, curled up, and softly wept.

The next morning more e-mails arrive, the first from Udaya.

> Dear Adele,
>
> Thanks so much. Yes, we are now ok. Perhaps by the blessings of the Buddha or God Kataragama. Although I am not a strong believer, after this ordeal, I am obliged to believe in certain invisible powers. I don't know who or which karma saved me and my family, including the newlyweds. We were right there at Hambantota, the worst affected spot. Sunday morning 9:30. We were just passing through the town when the Waves hit, right in front of my vehicle, just a few yards away. We saw this huge wave breaking through houses into the street, throwing some boys and men into the street and then taking them away. First we didn't know what was going on, but I shouted to the driver to reverse and turn back. But there was no going back, as there were many vehicles trying to run in the opposite direction, telling us that the whole town was under water. The market had collapsed, killing some hundreds and things like that. Then we managed to drive down a narrow lane trying to find a higher place. It was so difficult, everyone trying to squeeze through the same lane. People were crying, shouting, yelling, cursing and children crying for mothers, mothers calling for children and crying for the babies snatched away from their hands by the waves. Fortunately, or by the power of someone, a man, yes a strange man, got into our van uninvited and offered to guide us to a safe place. But he too couldn't do much because all the lanes were packed with

vehicles, trishaws, trucks, busses, cars. However, that strange man helped us to reach a clearing amidst some houses and left us saying that his help was needed by others and assuring us that we were safe there. Then he disappeared. And thanks to him, we were saved. We stayed there receiving some encouraging words from the neighbors and others stranded like us for three hours. Then as soon as the word came that some of the main road was clear and the big waves had receded, I helped the driver to go down to a junction, about 8 km away from where we could turn into a road running inland, away from the ocean. Finally we reached home. Everyone was so shaken up and listening on the way to radio news about the disaster happening all around the island. This is just a little bit of our experience. Probably you never thought that we had this near miss, that we had been so close to death.

The death toll is rising every day. The real numbers are much higher than the official ones. We will keep you informed.

Udaya

I am five feet six. Udaya is much shorter than I, maybe five feet three. An involuntary image of him standing under a wall of water estimated by tsunami experts to have been thirty feet high, even higher in Indonesia, hitting the shore at a speed of thirty to thirty-five miles an hour, settled in on me like lead. The reality of what the island faced was enough. I didn't need my imagination interceding.

I called over to Santa Cruz the next morning. Perhaps Ronna was back. Instead Jon's children were with him. Friends had come. I had noticed in the past year when Noah and I had gone out to see them that Jon's life moved similarly in Santa Cruz as it did two oceans away. Always there was the buzz of phone calls, the friends making plans. He was always up for a party. Eleven people over for dinner was nothing. But he was also a person who found the time to sit alone on the beach or in the woods with his books and journal. He read poetry, thought out solutions to physics and math problems, and read deeply in religion and philosophy. Those were the two nonintersecting sides of his life. Nothing seemed strong enough to sustain him right now. The shock had plunged him into the one place he had not yet visited, for all his travels. Oddly, we had talked about this. He had over the three years that I had known him commented several times that he had never known loss. His parents were still alive; there had been no serious illness in the family; he had not known sickness; his marriage was intact; the kids were fine.

"You are living a charmed life," I told him.

"I know," he answered. "This cannot last forever."

I wondered now if I should drop everything and go out to Santa Cruz to be with him. For the time being I stayed in Tucson partially because I believed that Ronna would return. I was no longer quite sure of what I should do other than be there at the other end of that phone.

I thought to write to Alan, my British friend who had purchased a bungalow on a tea estate some miles from Kandy. Before I sat down to write, though, his e-mail came across my screen.

December 30, from Alan near Teldeniya:

> Dear All,
>
> Thank you for the various messages of concern and sympathy which have arrived since the Boxing Day catastrophe. Don't be concerned about us up on the estate or our immediate circle of family and friends. We are all safe. Sunil had a bad time when an aunt and family of seven went missing down south. However, they have all turned up safe and well. The Kandy British Council gang are all OK though there were some miraculous escapes. Nick and Kathy and friends were literally washed out of their guest house at Mirissa and ran for their lives. All safe and uninjured. Prasad (head boy at school) and his family were at Trinco. He was injured, one member of the family killed; otherwise, somewhat miraculously, they survived.
>
> So, we are ok and life is proceeding more or less normally in Kandy and elsewhere. The stories pouring in from the South are absolutely ghastly, however. The BBC has only reported from Galle so far, where the situation is tragic far beyond description. Also Hikkaduwa and most of the way up to Bentota. Relatively few losses in Colombo, some at Negombo.
>
> However, here we are on the fifth day and still only news from Galle, despite the fact that for certain, there is complete devastation all the way up the east side including Batticaloa, Trinco and north

to Jaffna. The media haven't tried to cover these areas. The LTTE would surely cover media presence. Sky has just today got a man to Arugam Bay and the pics were frightful.

The response of the Sri Lankan locals has been wonderful. Within 24 hours there were collective centres set up all over town, with donations of food, medicines, clothing etc coming in. These supplies are being driven down in lorries and vans by volunteers —same story all over the island. Within two days, the local government had set up a "twinning" operation, local villages having stricken villages allocated to them with instructions to get emergency aid going immediately. This has been very successful. Thus it is that Nimal, my carpenter, is traveling down to Hambantota today with 4 lorries full and 20 other volunteers expecting to stay down there for 4 days, helping with first aid, cooking etc. The locals' generosity, given their own desperately impoverished state, is very striking.

People have said that a knee-jerk emotional response is not what is required. They are wrong. Instant whole-hearted and generous support is exactly what is required. Three days ago Sky proudly showed pics of "the first plane with relief aid leaving Gatwick bound for SL." Unfortunately, three days later foreign aid just hasn't turned up yet, even in the highly publicized places like Galle. The only aid that has been getting through so far is through locals like Nimal.

More sinister is the story just in from Janaka. He went to Trinco yesterday with Kandy Rotary—they had a big lorry stuffed full with food, water, and medicines. The Tigers had a road block on the way in, commandeered the lorry and sent the volunteers in a different direction to a village which apparently was not a priority area. There was furious frustration, and it is hard to avoid the obvious conclusion that the LTTE are simply pinching the supplies for their own purposes. Popular opinion before the tragedy was that the peace process would probably break down and that Sri Lanka would be back to war before the end of 2005. Now the dynamic has changed completely. Chandrika [Kumaratunga, the Sri Lankan president] has said all the right things about "putting enmity aside and all working together in the face of the shared disaster" etc. The LTTE have already complained to the world media that foreign aid is not getting through to the N and E areas under their control—but the aid isn't getting through anywhere else, and Janaka's most recent experience complicates the thing further.

The BBC and CNN had now established themselves down south in Galle. Dan Rather had managed a broadcast from Unawatuna Beach just a few kilometers south of Galle, but that was as far south as any of the news media made it. Nothing was coming in from the north or from the east. Alan's e-mail had gotten it exactly right; all normal means of communication with those areas had been completely cut off. Only the people like Sunil and his friends could find their way through back roads to the shore. As for the rest of us, we were left with only the muffled screams of people drowning, people who moments before had run excitedly down to the sea as it receded. They didn't understand what was happening.

From Alan, Sunday, January 2:

> There have been heavy rains down south these last 2 days—as if their misery were not already bad enough. There have been endless rallying cries in the press and from the politicians who are saying all the right things about "the time for enmity is past and we must set our differences aside." Some barriers do seem to be coming down and aid is now being allowed to cross into LTTE territory. Still Sinhala lorries tend to be southbound, Muslim lorries go east etc. There are white flags everywhere, on all the busses and roadsides—a symbol of mourning. It's like a whole nation funeral-house.

From Tissa Jayatilika, director of the U.S. Sri Lankan Fulbright Commission, Wednesday, January 5:

> Dear Adele
>
> The roads to Jaffna and Trincomalee are wide open. And there is much in the way of relief supplies that are being sent to the north and east (not only to Trinco) of Sri Lanka. The LTTE has been messy in the LTTE-controlled areas of the north from all that I am privy to. Several items that were sent up either by the government or civil society have been hijacked by the LTTE and then distributed as coming from them. There have been news items to the effect that the LTTE has torched a couple of refugee camps that the government had opened up to look after the needs of the civilians affected by the tidal wave so as to prevent the government receiving any credit or kudos for their good work in looking after ALL its citizens. Even adversity does not seem to have mellowed the Tiger. This is

not to whitewash the government of Sri Lanka which, on occasion, has also played politics with the conflict, but to highlight the challenges to a durable resolution of this senseless conflict that has been with us far too long. By contrast in the east where there is a marked split in the LTTE, there has reportedly been greater cooperation between the citizenry and the government institutions. As you may be aware, the eastern LTTE cadres and Prabhakaran have not seen eye to eye in the last several months, and so perhaps the usual LTTE intransigence is not in evidence in the east. US marines are here as well as several other international entities, and they, I am confident, won't be too worried about internecine conflict, as they seek to serve the citizens of Sri Lanka whether they be Tamils, Muslims, or Sinhalese. I am longing for the day when Sri Lanka can be its normal self again. If the LTTE and the government want genuine peace, this is as good a time as any to forge some solid settlement. In fairness to the President of Sri Lanka, she invited the LTTE to serve on a national committee for relief and reconstruction, an offer the LTTE, not surprisingly, turned down. As I understand it, the LTTE are fishing in troubled waters, hoping to get foreign governments to deal directly with them in disbursing aid and relief so that they can build further on their separatist agenda. So long as there remains this mutual distrust achieving a durable peace will remain a mirage. It is time for a leap of faith whereby the government of Sri Lanka offers a concrete political package that devolves power to the citizens of the north and east of the island regardless of the seeming intransigence of the LTTE.

All the best,
Tissa

From Alan, January 14:

The area just north of Kallar, on a spit of land, is cut off because both connecting bridges are down. The police told our group that no aid of any sort has yet reached the people there. Don't know how many are marooned—probably hundreds. Word was these people are in desperate need, and I cannot understand why the big agencies just down the road at Kalmunai have apparently not done anything. The Lynx helicopters—4 of them—were no good for ferrying supplies apparently. The police said all the agencies had done what we did—get as far as Kallar and then turn back since they couldn't get over to the stranded people.

I was appalled to see on Sky just now that, according to them, 40 pounds would keep a family supplied with drinking water "for a week"! In reality, through direct aid of the sort we can give, it would provide a family with drinking water for a year or more. We thought of sending gas cookers and bottles, or kerosene cookers and kerosene. However, gas and kerosene are restricted materials in LTTE controlled areas, so we wouldn't get through and it is clear that there is no shortage of firewood in the disaster areas—they are using the massive amount of debris from wrecked buildings. This is the kind of useful feedback which we are using to decide what to send.

Months after the tsunami I read that on December 26, 2004, 97 percent of the population of Sri Lanka had never heard the word *tsunami* before. I wondered to myself whether having a vocabulary for grief somehow makes it more palatable. I listened to the quiet sobbing on Jon's end of the phone line as waves carried away other lives on our TV screens. That the people had no word for the wave, that Jon had no explanation for what was happening in his life seemed immaterial to what they were feeling. Nalini would tell me when I returned in the fall that children yelled and screamed in delight, chasing the sea's trail, picking up seashells and fish in the process. "They screamed, 'The sea is drying up!'" Entire villages went down to watch the spectacle. It reminded me of stories I had heard about lemmings racing to the sea to their own death. A woman down south told me that her little boy had said to her, "Ammi, I'm going to go catch the sea." Instead, the sea came in and caught her son. She never saw him again.

> Mon 27 Dec 2004 21:56:57 +0600
> Consular Colombo
> !!!!!
> Sri Lanka and Maldives Public Announcement
> December 26, 2004
>
> This public announcement is being issued to urge American citizens to avoid travel to Sri Lanka and the Maldives due to the aftermath

of lethal tsunamis. The Government of Sri Lanka has declared a state of national disaster. The Government of the Maldives has declared a state of emergency.

In Sri Lanka, many hotels along the southern and eastern coastal areas were damaged and are not operating normally. Tourists in coastal areas have been evacuated to hotels in Colombo.

This public announcement expires on January 25, 2005.

CHAPTER 13

Home

It was early spring by the time I went out to see Jon in California. I was stuck in the classroom for all that semester and knew I wouldn't be able to get back to Sri Lanka until the fall. NGOs were quickly moving in to the affected areas in the southern part of the island while I was teaching nineteenth-century Russian literature to students who were complaining that the books were too long. What I was doing seemed completely irrelevant to my life and to this other life I had left half a world away. Tissa's hopes in his e-mail that a disaster of this magnitude might finally be the thing that could broker a peace were dashed as the Tigers began expropriating the aid that was sent north or blocking it altogether. The war seemed to be resuming its old, worn-out ways. Some things had changed, though—tourism, for one. The wave had stopped it dead in its tracks at the height of the season.

Jon had decided to go back to Sri Lanka that summer to do some consulting. It felt like the right thing for him to do for lots of reasons. He was alone now. In Sri Lanka his friends would look after him. Now, the two of us went to a little bodega by the sea in Aptos, got coffee and tea and sat on the beach for hours, talking about home and heartbreak. He thought he was going to have to sell the house. He wanted to dematerialize, yet something bothered me about the way he was doing it. I thought he was giving away too much.

"I don't know what to do with the memories," he told me. "I don't know what they mean anymore."

"You should keep some things; they were part of the memories,"
I told him. I wasn't sure that what was true for him now should
necessarily invalidate what was true in the past, but then again my
spouse of thirty-some years hadn't just left me, either.

We walked up the beach toward Capitola late one afternoon,
skirting a small RV park where people sat outside on their plastic
chairs on their plot of Astroturf with their dogs. We invented stories
about them. Perhaps, we thought, they had all reached a point in
their lives where they had thrown out the detritus and got it all down
to the basics: some pots and pans, the dog, the piece of fake grass, a
couple of chairs. And each other.

As I left for home several days later, Jon gave me a book called
Journeys of Simplicity. It begins with the story of a middle-aged man
named P'ang Yun who, twelve hundred years ago in China, loaded
everything he owned onto a boat and sank it all in the Tung-t'ing
Lake. After that, the story goes, "He lived like a single leaf." It was
the sort of wisdom that both of us aspired to, complicated only by
the fact that Jon was soon to be homeless from heartbreak and up-
wards of 35,000 people on a small island 9,600 miles away had died
or been rendered homeless by a wave.

"Go back to our beach at Mt. Lavinia," I reminded him just
before I left. "That at least is a sure memory."

A month later an e-mail came from him. Accompanied by
his group of friends, he had gone back to the beach to relive better times. The others stood on the shore while he stepped into the
ocean. The mother of a friend stood there, shaking her fist at
the sea as he tested the waters. The sand, the ocean, the grilled
fish, the ramadas, the chaises spread out beneath the palms—all of it
was as he remembered it. Only no one was eating grilled fish anymore, since they knew what the fish had dined on for several months
after the tsunami.

"I was alone in the ocean that day," he wrote me. "No one I
know will go to the beach anymore. Maybe only the people who
weren't here on Dec. 26 can swim in these waters."

"I couldn't refind the memories," he said at the end of his e-
mail.

By fall I had disengaged and was able to find my way back to the island. I had a book to finish, one that was going to be very different than the one I had envisioned. I felt impossibly torn. Should I not instead be helping with aid work? I had talked to people about this, but mostly the dialogue had been with myself. One voice said, "Writing changes the way people think; it changes people's lives." Then there was that other voice that told me that writing doesn't clear away rubble and build houses.

I wanted to walk the circumference of the island as much as I could. I needed to see things for myself. And from news reports, it looked possible to get up to Jaffna in the Tamil north. The cease-fire seemed still to be holding. Weeks prior to leaving Tucson, I woke up in the middle of the night with a phrase I couldn't recognize turning round upon itself in my head. A dry, hot, desert wind was blowing outside my window, the September reminder of the heat that refuses to relinquish its hold until mid-October. Samba stirred, and I lay there moving my lips silently to the sounds in my head. "*Vaessa vahinewa*," I repeated. Velu had taught it to me: "It's raining," or "The water is falling."

I left quietly on a morning in early October, zipping the last of the suitcases closed hours before dawn. Noah and I drove to the airport in silence and said a lingering good-bye. I was leaving him with a lot—school, the bills. "You have to do this, Mom," he told me. "You go." I watched him as I passed through security, and he watched me as everything I had so meticulously packed in my backpack got dumped out again for the random search. I gathered everything back up and turned to wave to Noah. He nodded. Everything was where it should be except my heart, which was in my throat.

Bandaranaike Airport at 7:00 a.m. was just beginning to stir when we touched down, its sole inhabitant, one lone plane, sitting in a hanger. A couple of shopgirls at the duty-free shops sat curled over white plastic chairs with their heads on the counters. The airport was heavy with sleep until I walked outside into the crowd of villagers who had come to see people off or to meet them. Nalini had told me that she didn't think that most of the people standing outside had ever seen an airplane before. I knew that they would drink toddy later that day to the stories of a world most would never see.

I made my way through the village on the sidewalk, grabbed a taxi, and headed into Colombo. In the fall of 2001, every conversation had its beginnings with 9/11. Now it was the wave, or, to put it in Sri Lankan terms, the story of the day the sea came to the land. We were not five minutes out from the airport when the cabdriver told me his own story. He asked if this was my first time back since the sea came to the land. "Madam," he said, "your word 'tsunami' was not known to our people before the sea came to the land. Now our people all know this word." As I watched South Asia stretch and yawn outside my taxi window, he told me that his family was okay but that his neighbor had gone missing. What was odd, he went on to say, was that the wave hadn't really hit Colombo. The water had risen; there was some flooding; but people who lived several city blocks inland didn't even know a tsunami had struck. "Madam," he went on, "I am not living near the sea. We're living in Nugegoda. The day after sea came to the land, I went over to my neighbor's house, and he wasn't there. And I am calling for him, but he is not coming. He just disappeared. He was going for a sea bath for the day, but he was not coming. And he was not telling anybody."

I looked out of the taxi window at the northern outskirts of a part of the city I had never seen in daylight before. We jockeyed with trucks for road space as we passed some nicer storefronts alongside makeshift *kades*. As we inched into the outskirts of Colombo, I watched a lithe young girl in a *sari* delicately deposit the day's garbage into the open sewer in front of her house. Men in checkered *sarongs* were still asleep on pieces of cardboard in doorways and on sidewalks, while the Muslim merchants in Colombo 11 began to raise the metal gratings in front of their shops in the Pettah district, where virtually anything can be purchased if one knows who to go to and where to look. We displaced a couple of dogs from the street and moved into the general flow of early-morning rush hour as we headed over to Colombo 6 and Nalini's house.

Mutto greeted me at the outside door, barely able to contain his astonishment at the amount of luggage I had brought with me.

Prolific apologies all the way around as a frame that carried thirty pounds less bulk than my own easily lifted the two duffle bags and swung them into the house.

Breakfast was on the table.

Nalini and Chitra appeared from upstairs. The cacophony of dog sounds began to compete with the morning traffic outside and Gamini, Nalini's brother, and Nimal came down to greet me. I stood still for a second to survey the bliss of sameness, places in a part of my life that had remained untouched. Sensing what I felt, Nalini came up, gave me a little squeeze, and said, "We are all still here, Adele."

It was a normal work day. Nimal went off to the tea board and Gamini to the shipping company while Nalini, Chitra, and I tended to home and talked while I moved in and out of a jet-lagged-induced fog throughout the day.

"It was so odd," Nalini told me as we sat upstairs later, just the two of us. "It was a normal day. Like today, really, except that it was a holiday. I don't know if I even told you this, but nothing happened here. You know this. You can walk to the ocean from here in twenty minutes, but we had no sign that anything was going on. They had flooding at the Galle Face Hotel and down on the esplanade but nothing here. We were just going on about our business. Really, it wasn't until one of Chitra's clients came to have her hair done that we found out what was happening. Then we started calling around and found out things, but we stayed put. What could we do?"

"Has anyone been back down the coast yet?" I asked.

"Only Gamini. Ask him tonight or tomorrow when you feel better. He's the only one. You know, he's always going down to Yala. He loves that park. I think he'll know more about the animals down there."

Two nights later, as I was in the process of painfully entering the correct time zone, Gamini told me over dinner what he knew.

"No one could get down there in those first few days. Everyone was worried over the elephants. But there were no roads. The east part of the island was a mess, and there was debris over all the roads going down there from the west. So we had to wait. And the human losses were so staggering we had to forget about the elephants for a while."

"You have no idea the chaos," Nalini added. "It was impossible to get any kind of good information. People were still looking for relatives, for loved ones. This went on for days, probably even weeks."

Before my return I had heard about a young biologist in Colombo, Prithviraj Fernando, who studies the elephants in Yala. When the tsunami hit he packed his bags as fast as he could and somehow managed to get to the park to check on the herd and the other animals. The small animals hadn't made it; their bodies were washed away and then redeposited on land with each successive wave. But the elephant herd was intact, all of it. They had run inland. Had they felt something in the early hours before the tsunami hit and started running, as some stories had it, or had they run only when the wave hit? The staff members who had survived at Yala told Fernando that the elephants had no prior knowledge of anything. They fled when everyone else did. All of them, including the babies, survived, miraculously—even the one herd that, for reasons known only to itself, had remained together and not run.

The next day I called Udaya in Peradeniya.

"When are you coming?" he asked. "We are all waiting for you."

"I'm coming. I'm just not doing it as fast as I wanted. It's partially jet lag, partially something else."

"Just let us know when you're coming. We're here," he said.

"Thanks. I know. It'll be just a day or two."

I needed to touch places and people I had known, to make sure everything was there in place. That night I went out on the esplanade and walked along the breakwater along Galle Face Green. It had rained almost incessantly since my arrival, but for the evening at least it seemed to have let up. The beach had long ago, even prior to the tsunami, been chiseled away to just a few yards of sand by the waves. It stretches the full length of the green, where kids fly kites, balloon sellers ply their trade, families picnic, and people just wander. Ten feet from the sea are identical booths selling popcorn and chili mangoes. I sat on a bench, ate some mangoes, and casually watched couples and families chase the waves in and out. Women's long black hair and *chalwa* scarves trailed behind them in the breeze.

The Galle Face Hotel was busy with traffic that night. I decided to go over, have a drink, and watch the sun set into Africa. We had stayed there when we initially came to Sri Lanka in our first and last days of colonialist luxury. I had early on christened the place a "she," a dowager much beyond her prime, a throwback to an era that was no more, yet still resplendent in her elegance. She looked as noble that night as she always had. I slowly made my way over there, where from one of the rooms on the second floor in those first weeks after 9/11, I had stared out to sea and Noah had watched the BBC. We had been the only guests back then and as such, the object of everyone's attention. Tourism had clearly recovered in the interim, at least here in Colombo. The outside portico was full of Europeans having drinks and the dining room seemed to be at capacity. A business center had sprung up, and I poked my head in to see lots of Anglos busily engaged with their e-mail.

"Excuse me, madam, is it you?" I heard a voice behind me say.

I turned and then smiled, almost in disbelief. It was the man from the travel desk. Somehow he remembered me.

"How can we not remember you, madam? You were the only guest. And your son? Is he here with you?"

"No, he is studying in America," I told him. Someone else, another hotel employee, joined us. We bowed and smiled, remembering each other.

"The wave. Are you all okay?"

"We are all okay, madam. We were lucky. The sea rose, and it came in over the seawall and flooded the grounds, but it didn't flood the hotel. We didn't really understand what was happening."

Fifty feet or less from where we were standing, the Indian Ocean was hitting the seawall with a force unusual for this time of year. The spray was sending people scattering. I felt my own unease. The three of us watched an ominous black cloud moving slowly in from the north, vying with the darkness that was quickly enveloping Co-lombo.

"We are having storms just now, madam."

"Yes, I've been noticing the rain, but the monsoon's over," I replied, vaguely remembering Udaya's comment when we first came to the island about monsoons and inter-monsoons and then just plain rain.

"Yes, madam, this is something else. This is a depression in the Bay of Bengal. As long as there is a depression, the rains will be coming."

"More problems from India," the second employee told me with a smile, rolled his eyes, and walked away to take an order from one of the British tourists.

The conversation quickly turned to our own problems with the sea in the United States. Everyone had heard of Katrina and asked me about it. I explained that it wasn't exactly a tsunami but a huge storm and that there was lots of flooding.

"Yes, we saw the water on television here," remarked a young man. "The sea came to your land too, no?"

People were also curious about something else. "Madam, why are all the poor people we see on our television sets black? We don't see white people, just black. We did not know there were so many poor people in America."

"Yes," I nodded and looked down. "We have many, many poor people."

The next morning I told Nalini and Chitra there was something I had to do. I went down to Mt. Lavinia Beach to try to refind a three-year-old memory. I paid my 400 rupees ($4.00) for a day pass to the beach. Minutes later I untied my *sarong* and tentatively followed in Jon's footsteps as I dipped into post-tsunami waters. I was alone in the water that day. I got out, dried myself, wrapped myself in my *sarong,* and walked down the beach past the "Proceed at your own risk" sign. A few huts lay on their sides. Wood lay randomly stacked here and there. Farther in from the beach I saw standing pools of water. And yet it was not altogether clear to me that what I was seeing was tsunami damage.

It wasn't long before some young men approached me, with stray dogs following on their heels, forming their own kind of entourage. They were fishermen and seemed eager to talk. One of them invited me inside his house, a hut containing a table covered with a plastic tablecloth and two chairs. The blue paint on the kitchen walls had for the most part peeled off, revealing plaster that had turned green from moisture and moss. A piece of material hung in the doorway, separating the kitchen from the family's sleeping quarters. The young man opened a net of shells.

"Will you buy one of these?" he asked me, while his daughter, age four, looked on, taking in the sight of me with liquid brown eyes. "This is now how we make our living. We lost a few old people from our village. We tried to reach them, but . . ." His voiced trailed off. "Mainly what we lost were the nets and the boats. Now we have boats but we have no nets. We are trying to get nets so that we can fish. People are giving us too much boats. Tell people to give us nets. So now we are diving for these shells. We call them tsunami shells.

"Those first few weeks," he continued, "you could not, madam, have believed this ocean. There were pots and wooden spoons floating on the waves. It was a kitchen, but we couldn't eat the food it prepared."

"Your house?" I asked him.

"We lost it. We live so near the sea. But we did not have so many things so we did not lose a lot. We did not lose each other. That is important thing. This house where I am now living with my family this we built after tsunami."

"Have you gotten aid?" I asked him. "Have the aid organizations been in here?"

"Not so much," he answered, "because we didn't suffer so much as they suffered in the south. Yes, in the first days we got food and tents. Yes, those things we got. But no building materials, no. Nothing. But then all aid organizations went south because that is where tourism is. So they had to be building again for tourists."

We walked back toward Mt. Lavinia Beach, past hastily constructed huts made of what wood could be thrown together. Chickens pecked for food in the sand. Laundry dried on top of wooden fences. The fisherman stopped at the breakwater and wouldn't go beyond the "No trespassing" sign dividing our two worlds. I motioned for him to follow, but he shook his head, indicating a firm "no." Not authorized," he told me. "This hotel will call the police."

Later I wrote to Jon that I couldn't refind the memories either.

The center of Peradeniya.

CHAPTER 14

Up and Down the Mountain

That Friday I took the afternoon train to Kandy out of Fort Station in Colombo. "Get off at Peradeniya," Udaya had told me. Don't go into Kandy. I'll meet you at the station."

Within minutes we had hit a blinding rainstorm. Water tore through the cars as we worked the windows, trying to keep ourselves and our baggage from getting soaked. Three of us finally got my window to close and then moved onto the next one. Half an hour later the rain stopped as suddenly as it had begun, and we had to reverse the process, which proved to be equally cumbersome. In the meantime, our car had metamorphosed into a steam bath, one immediately taken advantage of by a little girl in school whites who skipped from one end to the other, writing her name, Anuja, in English on all the steamed windows. She fastened her eyes on me for the duration of the journey as she carefully traced out the letters of her name. I smiled. By the time we were halfway up the mountain, and someone succeeded in disengaging one of the windows, Anuja's name was inscribed on every available pane of glass.

As we inched up, the humidity began to abate, and Anuja dissolved away from all the windows. Slowly the train folded itself in the jungle, whose green became more muted from the rain clouds overhead. I settled back in my seat, watching a land that for a time in my life had become our home. But there were other things about returning that were complicated. Back on U.S. shores I had once again become invisible and gently melted into the landscape of racial diversity. As I sat with the pair of small eyes fastened on me for the three-and-a-half hour ride up the mountains, I remembered that coming back to this island was also to shed my invisibility. If only it were just my red hair. However I try to negate it, I am still that complicated symbol of power and privilege that people both aspire to and yet are angry at, or just plain want to look at. There is nothing I can do about it. I wiped away the steam from the window and looked out at the island.

New foliage, and lots of it, obscured old familiar buildings; some new construction had cropped up. Memory was playing tricks on me. "Is this the right station?" I had to ask.

"Yes, Peradeniya Station," said someone, and I had about thirty seconds to disgorge myself, two oversized duffle bags, a backpack, and a computer from the train before it headed on into Kandy.

Udaya stood at the far end of this makeshift parking lot now filled with rainwater mixed with red soil. He looked hopelessly at my duffle bags. I shrugged my shoulders, and we picked up where we had left off two years ago. The family was there waiting for us as we drove up the hill overlooking the Hantana range. I fastened my eyes on them as I got out of the car. One quick turn of a van, providence—the "certain invisible powers," as Udaya termed them—were all that lay between these people waiting for me at the top of the hill and a very different fate altogether. Indu and her new husband, Sanjeewa, stood there radiant in their new marriage. Aruni, whose silence had been my most familiar memory of her, had gotten up out of her bed and planted a garden. She had put in a papaya tree, and had woven jasmine through an arbor. In half-thought-out rows, tendrils reached out with the casual indifference of nature's planting. The two of us toured the garden before heading into the kitchen to chop vegetables for the curry. We hugged each other. She was proud of what she had done. And she was sewing. For however long her health might hold, I think we all understood something about the fragility and gift of survival.

We ate dinner that night in the actual dining room, since Udaya and Aruni's son, Achala, had taken up what appeared to be permanent residence at the big table in the living room where we usually sat. He was facing his dreaded A levels in April and had four years of math and chemistry notebooks piled up in front of him, along with a large statue of the Buddha.

"Maybe it'll help," he told me.

"It's October, and the A levels are in April. There's time," I said hopefully.

After dinner that night we sat outside on the stoop, drank our milk tea, and looked over at the Hantana range while thick, black mosquitoes began launching their evening assault. We spoke only briefly about how the sea had come to the land. Udaya and his family were dealing with it by getting on with things. Like everyone else I knew who had been down south that day, they had not been back.

"I need to go back down there," he told me. "I want to see if I can find the man who saved us. I will revisit, just not now."

Udaya had been writing; he told me about a manuscript he had written. We talked for the first time about his past. I had heard from others that he had once been a *bhikkhu,* but I never mentioned it to him directly. I was waiting for him to tell me his own story.

"Well, I will tell you about it sometime. I think I wanted a family and a life in this world more than I wanted my world in saffron robes. This is part of what my book is about. Will you read it? It might help you understand some things, things about some of the monks, things about me."

I had spent the past few years peeling off layers of this man. His family had read parts of the manuscript. As I listened to him talk, I wasn't sure that he could get it published in Sri Lanka. It seemed much too controversial. He had said things about the mores of some of the monks that weren't encouraging.

We talked about Achala's A levels, and about how the whole system needed to be revamped. Aruni, meanwhile, went to get us some more tea. Below us in one of the small villages on the banks of the Mahaweli, the monks had begun their evening chant. I looked up at the moon.

"Remember this village?" prompted Udaya. "They're still at it. We can't get to sleep. It starts about five in the evening and goes on till dawn. This village seems to be always having festivals. I think they bought a PA system and are so happy to have it that they're organizing some celebrations every day."

Later I went up to the bedroom, where two twin beds had been pushed together to make one. I sorted through my stuff and untied the blue mosquito netting for the first time in three years. I waited until the mosquitoes had settled down for the night and then opened the windows wide to let in the air. Achala poked his head in the doorway and warned me not to leave them open too wide; they had seen a polecat on the roof not long ago. I tucked myself into the netting and listened to the monks below until the first stirrings of morning.

Two days later I moved over to our old compound on Mahamaya Mawatha. Kush, Nandana, their housekeeper Latha, and Velu, plus a couple of new canines, were there to meet me. Our old house had continued to reassert its identity as an actual lived-in place thanks to an Englishwoman who had taken it over for several years and fixed the place up brilliantly. It breathed again with life that looked as if it had not been forced upon it. I had often thought that this was a house that constantly needed to be jump-started in order to live. I was given a small room in the guesthouse this time so that I had something like a home to come back to in between my travels.

That night Kush, Nandana, and I talked until late over tea and rolls. They told me with much relief that Kiriya, the caged monkey, had finally and mercifully been given away to a research station for elderly monkeys where she would be able to live out her last days among other sick and wounded monkeys. Nandana reported that he and Velu still made weekly trips to see her.

In my absence Velu had lost his older brother. "A heart attack," Nandana told me. Velu had cried for days, inconsolable with grief, but was doing better now. Loku Menike came by now and then. She was without work the first six months after we left, but then was hired to do some sewing for a local merchant. For the first few months after I returned to the States, we had exchanged letters. Then hers stopped coming. The last one I received from her reported that she had run out of brown sugar. Our talk turned to the sea coming to the land. Nandana had gone down south and east, bringing supplies to the local villages while international aid was still sitting on the tarmac at the airport. I wasn't surprised. Born into a circle of hereditary privilege, both Kush and Nandana had spent much of their adult lives doing social service in addition to their work at the Alliance, keeping the guesthouse going, and Kush's work at the university.

"You have big hearts," I told them.

"The whole country helped," Nandana replied. "Everyone did it. We had to do it. There was no aid coming through. It took days. There was no water coming, no food coming, no medical supplies. Everyone did what they could."

I remembered Alan's e-mail to me a few days after the disaster. Immediate, spontaneous help, hand to hand from Sri Lankan to Sri Lankan, was what got this country through while cargo planes from Gatwick in London to Tokyo counted their boxes and waited for clearance to take off.

As we were finishing our rolls, Kush looked at me and said, "You are free now. You can come and go as you wish. Nothing is holding you back. You can sleep when you want, eat when you want. Your life is yours to live as you want."

I told them I'd leave the bulk of my belongings there but that I wanted to get back to Colombo, take the train down to Galle, and then walk as much of the shore as possible with my camera and my journal. I needed a day or two, though, before I set off. I wanted to catch up with Champika and needed to make a call up to Teldeniya to Alan.

I went over to Velu's shed later and showed him pictures of Samba. His fingers were still stained from the red of the betel leaves that he chewed. And I sensed that he noticed me trying to find the Sinhalese words that had once come, if never automatically, at least with greater ease. I wanted words I couldn't find to commiserate about his brother. Instead, the two of us did what we always did. We took the dogs out onto a small plot of grass nestled between the hedge and the shed and watched them dance. We mourned together through the continuity of evening ritual.

The next day, after a fitful night, I came down with a high fever, which worsened and then lingered for the next five days. I spent my time encased within my mosquito netting, with brief forays out onto the porch to drink tea and observe the life in the garden. I nodded off to the sound of rain landing on already saturated earth. Since we had left, Velu and Nandana had planted water lilies in the planters surrounding the porch. But the standing water had bred mosquitoes, so they had added goldfish to eat them. Then the kingfishers went after the goldfish, and now each planter was covered by a metal grating. From my rattan chair I listened to the ping of the raindrops in the planters.

At first these days were a hindrance to what I was here to do. This was not part of what I had envisioned for myself. This was the place where I was supposed to hang my hat, store my things, and come back to between trips. But I sat here, an unwilling pilgrim, burning up with fever. Then I remembered something Derek Wolcott had said in his poem *Omeros* about the right journey being motionless. I had traveled halfway around the world through thirteen time zones in order to sit still on this porch and contemplate the flutter of one leaf on a bush. I began to write obsessively in my journal, recording the daily movements of geckos and ant colonies, the feeding habits of hummingbirds and barbets, the subtle shifts in my own internal geography.

The rains continued unabated, unusual for this time of year, soaking themselves into our world in the hills. Kush and I decided it was a sign of the coming end of the world. I washed a few things out in the bucket behind the house as I began to feel better and put them on the line to dry. One week later they were still wet. The bread turned blue if I didn't eat it the day Velu bought it. At night I lay in bed and watched the reflection of the outdoor light filter through the frieze above my window, casting shapes that spread out onto my wall like the Sinhalese alphabet. Still the rains came. They choked the gutters, backed up the pipes, dislodged trees and rocks, and sent the monkey population into retreat. Velu came in one day to announce that the lake was at capacity.

During the day Latha brought me jackfruit cooked in coconut with orders to eat. Sometimes I went back with her to the kitchen and watched her preparing the meals for the family. Eggplant got molded into cubes; onion, garlic, and green chili got chopped; chili powder was sprinkled; *kahakuru,* or turmeric, turned everything a golden renaissance orange. I handed Latha the salt as she added the milk from the coconuts Nandana and I had fetched at the train station the evening I had arrived.

Latha looked up from her curry preparations one day, and I saw rain running down her cheeks. Only it wasn't rain. It was the husband who wouldn't give her a divorce because he wanted custody of their daughter and didn't want to work full-time. He had been showing up at the gate ever since we had first come to Kandy, needing money after a drinking bout. Her tears mixed themselves with chili and spice. We talked, but I didn't know what to say. I didn't know what to do. Divorce is not so easy here. I felt helpless.

Several days later I was beginning to feel as if my legs might carry me farther than the porch, and I set off for town to find Champika and do some banking. I found him sitting in his *tuk-tuk* down the street, as the drivers were no longer allowed to park in front of the grocery store. After enthusiastic greetings he announced his news that he and his girlfriend, Chamilla, were intending to marry. Much congratulation ensued. But then the conversation took a different turn.

"We will not marry now. No house, no place to live. Chamilla not wanting to live with my mother."

"I can understand that. In America newlyweds want to live separately."

"Not so easy here," came the reply. "No money for house or room."

The saga on other fronts was no better. His sister hadn't managed to pass her A levels and was looking for a job. Champika had been trying to get a car loan from a bank so that he could buy a van and take tourists around the island, but his application had been turned down. Reason given: he didn't make enough as a *tuk-tuk* driver. One thing, if just one thing had come through for them—but it hadn't, and the cycle continued. And the father still lay at home sick from something that Champika was unable to explain to me.

We promised to reconnect later, but for now I had a few things to attend to in the center of town. I walked over to the Hatton National Bank, where some of the bank employees remembered me. I needed to find the young woman who had helped me with my banking and through the morass of setting up an account when we had first arrived. I looked around for her but couldn't locate her behind the wall of people all pressing up against the tellers' windows.

I went over to the desk of one of the assistants and asked about her. Heads bowed.

"She was washed away, madam," an employee told me.

"Pardon?" I asked.

There were 35,322 versions of this same story, versions roughly equal to the number of people on this island alone who had been killed by the tsunami. The figures were still rising, as people continued to die from injuries sustained during the disaster. It was easy simply to get lost in a world of numbers. I wondered if I hadn't done that a little bit, at least until I walked into the bank that day. This was the first from among my acquaintances. I had initially calibrated it all wrong, thinking there would be fewer of these stories up here in the hills, but what happened to people that day defied geographic logic. This moment, 9:36 a.m., December 26, 2004, has become the reference point, etched in everyone's memory, as is 9/11 in the United States, yet directly impacting a much, much higher percentage of the population. It has brought with it a collective trauma that will be internalized by many on this island for years to come. And so, I found myself stopping short of probing too much and instead asked half questions and got half narratives.

By week's end I knew that it was something other than the flu that was keeping me from doing what I had come here to do. One morning I went down to the train station and bought my ticket south to Galle.

CHAPTER 15

The Story of a Wave

The sea has calmed down and wears an innocent look as if it never
committed any crime.

—*The Island,* January 14, 2005

November 1, 4:45 a.m.: The only sound around the lake was that of
Champika's *tuk-tuk,* which cut through the stillness of a town just
beginning to stir. The bats had not yet returned from their nightly
feed, and it was still too early for the warblers' morning oratory.
Even the cows and stray dogs had yet to emerge from their nightly
whereabouts. The train station, however, was at full throttle, with
lines of people buying tickets; others bestirring themselves on the
floor where they had spent the night. One ticket window was open
to accommodate commuters going to Colombo and some heading
further south.

"Sorry, madam, no change," the man at the ticket window apologized as I handed him a 500 rupee ($5.00) note for the train ticket to
Galle. I grumbled to myself as I boarded the train and planted myself
on a sticky seat next to a window that worked: why does no business,
no store, nobody in this country ever, but *ever* have change? This was
the tenor of my thinking as the train jolted out of the station and I
peeled myself a banana in the predawn mist.

As I sat looking out the train window, after several hours the
terrain began to change. Colombo was behind us now. I could see
more than I could several years ago, the wave having created an

unobstructed view. The fishermen's shacks had disappeared. Some small attempts at rebuilding were taking place. A few lean-tos had been constructed, but for the most part the beach had been reduced to masses of rubble: tin, wood, smashed pieces of concrete lay scattered everywhere. We passed along train tracks that at 9:36 on December 26, 2004, got refashioned in the space of ten minutes into a mass of twisted metal, as if they were so many children's toys. Outside of Beruwala, part of the train that had headed straight into the tsunami now stood rusted, with tracks wrapped around it, as an improbable memorial to the tsunami victims. On the sea side of our train, I saw other memorials, hastily constructed graveyards, their markers in white stone often embossed with pictures of the victims. Cardboard banners strung between two palm trees with photos of the deceased swung lazily in the sea breeze.

South of Kalutara, vegetation lay piled up everyplace. I saw the first temporary housing—cinderblock structures with tin roofing. Just north of the resort area around Hikkaduwa, standing black pools the color of oil came into view. The water was uncommonly thick and looked almost solid. Some Anglo aid workers were mixing cement and hauling it in wheelbarrows to a construction site in a palm grove otherwise surrounded by debris and trash.

The vista that opened before me was a mélange of devastation and parade ground. Every refugee camp, every temporary housing project, every water station, every reconstruction site sported the banners of the various international aid organizations, countries, and cities that had sent money or aid workers. I did a world tour through France, Italy, Japan, Kuwait, the Netherlands, and Portland, Oregon, on my way to Galle. Over the next few days the countries multiplied. There was no boat here, no piece of heavy machinery, no anything that was not embossed with the name of a city or a relief agency. And yet the evidence mounted that in those crucial initial days and weeks the real work was done by those who actually lived here.

Galle. I had steeled myself for this place. Here basically nothing stood between the wave and the bus station, people at market, and those just milling about. The Old Dutch Fort area, however, was spared for the most part because of the retaining wall around it. And so the wave took the other route, following the estuary, steamrolling into town, and taking just about everybody at the market and the bus station with it. This is the city that people who tuned into the BBC and CNN saw, since this was as far south as the reporters got. Dan Rather made it four kilometers further to Unawatuna. Beyond that, getting the power to broadcast was sporadic at best. Services of any sort were in the first days nonexistent.

I decided to look for a room in the Dutch Fort section and began the walk over, along with ten or so hawkers, what the Sri Lankans call totes, attached to me. It had been almost a year since the tsunami and still pictures were pinned to walls and poles of those who had gone missing the day that the sea came to the land. I went over to one and looked at a Xerox of a young woman's face. Below it read in Sinhalese and English: "Have you seen her? Missing. Chamudi Indupa Magedara Gamage. Last seen at Galle vegetable market on 26th Dec. 2004."

I rented a room in a Muslim household on a side street, presided over by an old matriarch who seemed eager to talk. As I checked in, I learned about the family's employment history over the past several years. The daughter and daughter-in-law, both dressed to the nines in their *saris,* were about to leave for the airport in Colombo to pick up the daughter's husband, who was returning home after working in Malaysia for two years as a gem dealer. I deposited my things in an upstairs room that looked out onto the lighthouse, told the old woman I would be back in several hours, grabbed a *samosa* and a cup of tea at a nearby café, and tried to find a local organization called Project Galle. Unlike many relief organizations, this one had concentrated its efforts just forty kilometers north and south of the city. Originally consisting of expats who wanted to help after the tsunami, the organization now numbered over six hundred volunteers from thirty different countries. Weeks later, with visits to countless refugee camps and relief organizations behind me, I remembered this one as unusually responsive to local needs. The people who lived here agreed with me.

It was lunchtime at Project Galle when I walked in. The Sri Lankans were eating in one room, the British and Americans in another. I introduced myself to a young man named Jake, who was head of the office, and the two of us sat in the inner courtyard and talked about how the work was progressing. I saw little on my trip down to suggest that reconstruction was progressing at anything beyond a snail's pace. I had seen any number of signs advertising the presence of international relief organizations, but hadn't actually seen many aid workers.

"You won't," Jake explained to me. "Enough time has passed now that they aren't as obvious a presence. They are still involved but more behind the scenes. There is actually a lot going on, it's just not as visible. The goal down here is gradually to turn over day-to-day operations to the Sri Lankans themselves.

"The problems were enormous," he continued. "There was machinery needed that we didn't have. Originally we were involved in putting together family packets for each affected family, but now we're focusing on housing construction, identifying areas through the use of a global information system [GIS] where water tanks should go, pumping out wells, and draining mosquito pools of standing water. We're doing a lot of hands-on community projects, from working with schoolchildren and planting vegetable gardens at the schools to introducing recycling programs. One aid worker jokingly referred to it as 'the 101 things you can do with plastic' course."

"For example?" I asked.

"Well, we're looking at things that can be done with plastic bottles, using them as planters for seedlings. We've got one business firm down here willing to start a recycling program. For every kilo of material that the school recycles, the school will get fifty rupees. It's not a lot, but it's a start. Sometimes the schools are incredibly welcoming and supportive. Other times we are frozen out. I don't know whether they are overwhelmed or tired of international aid or whether they don't see recycling as a real issue."

I didn't know either, but as a foreign resident of this island, I knew that it didn't take a tsunami to create a trash problem. Lunch packet wrappers newly augmented by Kentucky Fried Chicken bags spill out onto the sidewalk around the lake in Kandy where families come to picnic. Plastic cups and wrappers find their way along train tracks deep into the jungle. These are developing-country problems, but ones not solely due to a lack of environmental consciousness. There was a time when Ceylonese villages produced no trash because there was nothing to throw away: no paper, no plastic, or no tin. Villages lived and worked off of what they grew, and what they had. Things got recycled through replanting; people sat on floors on woven mats rather than the white plastic chairs that seem now to have proliferated all over the island. The country now produces and imports items that can neither be burned nor recycled: plastic bags, water bottles, and paper wrappers being cases in point. There is a movement afoot just to ban them altogether as they tend to end up on sidewalks, in lakes, and in the intestines of elephants. They also tend to end up in the ocean. When the tsunami slammed into the shore, people up and down the coast remember the wave as being black. Someone I know described it as a black cobra. What the wave brought with it was the bottom of the ocean, the silt, the sand, the plastic bottles, plastic lunch wrappers, pieces of metal, and everything that people had aimlessly thrown into the sea over the years. Everyone was furious at the sea. A friend of mine wondered to me if the sea, in turn, was not angry at having been turned into a dumping ground.

I asked Jake if there were enough money to fund all these different projects. Money, he told me, was not the problem. Quite the contrary. Initially there was such an outpouring of funds that no one knew what to do with the largess. There had been duplication and reduplication of effort. It took a couple of strong personalities to come in, take charge, and organize things. I saw what he meant. There were a bewildering number of organizations down here: Concern, Red Cross, United Nations High Commission for Refugees (UNHCR), CHF, World Vision, Caritas, Global Crossroads, International Organization for Migration (IOM), all in addition to Project Galle. And that was just the beginning.

"The problem," continued Jake, "is that most of them are in competition with each other. I call it 'competitive charity.'"

I was to see evidence of this problem up and down the coast in the next few weeks: brightly colored wooden fishing boats lining the beach in the southern town of Hambantota, while people two hundred meters away were living on concrete slabs on sites where their homes had stood before they were washed away. There were too many boats (all with organizations' and people's names on them), and not enough housing. Boat stories followed me all the way up and down the coast. Along the shore at Unawatuna, a pearl of a beach just south of Galle, a fiberglass boat factory had been constructed by an Austrian firm after the tsunami. The only problem was that the villagers in Unawatuna made their living through tourism, not fishing. Not only did they not need the boats, they didn't want them. Nor did they want the factory. The residents of the town suffered breathing problems for about four months because of the stench of the styrene used in the production process—a noxious, potentially poisonous chemical used in the sealing of fiberglass. The factory was finally pressured to shut down.

That night I shared a beer with an English aid worker, a young woman fresh from the University of Manchester with a degree in environmental protection. She told me about the Galle Photography Project—one of the first projects that Project Galle put into place. Among the casualties from the tsunami were people's personal effects—destroyed, washed away, or damaged, among them cherished family photos found amid the piles of rubble. Project Galle brought in a photographer who restored the photos when possible. The photos were then framed and presented to surviving family members. At first it seemed to me an all too cruel reminder of loss, but it also affirmed for people, many of whom had nothing else to hold onto, who they were and where they came from at a time when almost nothing of their past save memory remained.

The next evening in Galle the old matriarch of the Muslim family wanted to feed me. Stooped and wrapped in the white of widowhood that had turned an off shade of gray, she was insistent that I not leave town without eating her Ramazan fish cakes and macaroni. It was just the two of us. As I ate my fish cakes, she talked to me about Allah, her glaucoma, her servant's diabetes, and the sea that had come to the land. She asked me if I knew that Neil Armstrong had heard God speaking to him on the moon and had subsequently converted to Islam after arriving back on earth.

"No, I hadn't heard that," I told her.

"It is Allah's punishment for evil," she continued. "What do you think these floods, these storms, and the waves are? The end of the world is coming."

I took a walk later that night and got caught in the daily downpour. I ducked into a *kade* that was still open and waited it out along with several local men. They asked me if I could give them money for milk powder for their children. I had no money on me and apologized. When I went to bed that night I stared for awhile at the blinking light of the lighthouse. It still danced in my room, mingling with the blue of my mosquito net, as I listened to the Muslim call to prayer in the darkness of early morning.

At breakfast with the old woman I asked her about the photos I had seen all over town of missing persons.

"No one has found any of them. They were shopping. No one survived that shopping day," she murmured, returning to her food.

Later I said my good-byes to her and set out for the short walk to Unawatuna. I took the road since much of the shoreline between the two places was impassable. Along the way a couple of men stopped me and asked for money for milk powder. They had been walking as I was and looked to be in their late thirties. This time I had money on me and happily gave it, though I was curious why milk powder wouldn't be heavily subsidized by the government or just given outright by aid agencies.

In Unawatuna, with tourist season only a month away, reconstruction was proceeding at a fast clip. I turned down the lane to the beach, passing through the village, where some guesthouses had already reopened and others were in the process of being rebuilt. Gardens were being replanted, and small, locally owned restaurants and dive shops were beginning to show signs of life.

I swam in the ocean before the afternoon rains hit and lay on the sand drawing patterns in it with my fingers, letting my mind wander. Just to the north on a promontory sat a *stupa* the color of pearl overlooking translucent waters that bent into the bay and the beach. Sitting here staring out onto it all, one unwittingly becomes part of the paradox of this island: lying on these southern sands, one can all too willingly disengage from what happened here a year ago and from the paradise lost almost thirty years ago on the northern third of the island.

The next morning I found my way to the local refugee camp. Located less than two hundred meters inland from the beach, it was constructed and supported by money from the Japanese government and the JVP political party. The path leading into the camp was lined with fresh grave markers discreetly set back to the side near a stream. A middle-aged man in a *sarong* met me near the entrance, bowed, and introduced himself as the head of the camp. Some of the women looked up and smiled as they went about their daily chores. One was filling a jug of water; another leaving to take her child to school. Just another day on the island—except that these camps and these people were here to begin with. There was a greater sense of well-being here than I would encounter in the other camps I visited on the island. The women I met were earning a living with sewing machines and fabric donated by the government and relief organizations. Some were employed by the local hotels, making linens; others sewed *sarongs* and blouses that were then sold on the beach to tourists. There was an internal organization in this camp not always in evidence elsewhere. I spoke to a woman who had been designated the camp accountant. I had brought pencils, magic markers, stickers, and crayons, all of which she carefully recorded in a logbook so that the supplies could be carefully apportioned out to each child in the camp. As I moved down the coast in the days that followed, it was easy to predict how well a camp was fairing by whether it was adjacent to a tourist area or not. In an area between Matara and the blowhole at Dikwella, where there is little tourist traffic, villages seemed to have been discarded altogether. The farther south from beach tourism, the starker was the damage, the less the attempt made at reconstruction.

There were complaints in the camp, mainly over the heat and the lack of ventilation. Constructed in connecting rows made out of cinderblock, or in some cases wood, of two rooms each, the houses had roofs of corrugated tin that heated up terribly during the day. I could feel it already, as a woman with six children invited me into her house. She showed me the gas burner that the government had supplied each family. Her husband had just woken and was lying on a mat in the next room. This was one of the few intact families I saw in my travels around the coast. I wondered why the children weren't in school. The oldest, I was told, hadn't felt well that day, and the other three of school age stayed home with her. "They are too much afraid, madam," one of the women in the camp translated for me. I could not ask this woman what her children remembered of the tsunami. Some things I just turned and walked away from.

I gave the kids some play dough, and we talked for awhile about the housing situation. It had been almost a year since the tsunami, and I was beginning to wonder why so many families were still in temporary housing. In every camp I visited, data were posted at the entrance regarding the number of people living there, the break-down in terms of age and gender, and the percentage of permanent houses that had been completed and handed over versus the number promised. Sometimes I saw building materials stacked up, with only five out of fifty promised houses completed in an area. It remained a source of puzzlement, not only to me but, more especially, to the people living in the camps. I wasn't sure that there was one overarching explanation for it. Invariably, there was criticism of the government for not moving fast enough. In many cases, the cost of rebuilding was shared by the relief organization and the government. But too many factors intervened to impede progress: bureaucracy; delivery of supplies; training the local population to help in the re-building; replication of effort, with too many people trying to do good and stumbling over each other in the process.

That night I sat on the beach and called Noah on my cell phone. It was his birthday. November 3. From thirteen time zones away came a voice that sounded uncertain. School wasn't going well. None of the courses made any sense. He was feeling depressed. We talked a long time about the situation and what he might do. I asked if he had any plans that night. "None," came the answer. After we finished talking, I remained on the beach and thought about the price I had paid for the choice to come back here. I had initially uprooted Noah from the school he knew and the friends he had and had brought him to the other side of the world, thinking that the experience would in some way be a defining one for him. When we

returned late in 2002, he entered a new high school where he knew
no one. Most of the students there hadn't heard of Sri Lanka. Those
who had seemed from Noah's perspective little interested in either
him or the life he had led. In some ways coming back to a world
that had once been familiar seemed as foreign to him as the one I
had dragged him into on the other side of the globe. And now there
was college. It was too big. He just couldn't find his way. And I was
over here. I was as full of self-doubt as he was.

I wrote in my journal that night that you don't always get the
story that you think you are writing and that you construct for yourself. Stories go their own way, make their own plots. Perhaps we are
the guest on the page. Noah was writing his own story, his own life.
I had left him alone at another fragile transition period in his life for
the sake of a story that ultimately perhaps would have less value than
the wells that Jake and his cohorts were digging in Galle.

I walked most of the next day from Unawatuna to Weligama and
then took the last five kilometers to Matara by bus. The town square
looked somewhat more prosperous than the one I had left earlier in
the day in Galle, which was surprising since it wasn't a tourist area.
Late in the day I boarded another bus for Hambantota. Tired from
the day, I watched thick tropical vegetation begin to thin out onto
flattened plains. The air here shimmered from the rising heat from
the wetlands. Not far beyond Hambantota lie bird sanctuaries where
winter visitors from India and Siberia come to wait out the cold, to
plume and preen. And from there it's only kilometers to Yala, elephant country. Jungle gives way to dry zone. I could see for miles.

Hambantota was one of the areas hardest hit by the tsunami.
More died here than in any other place in Sri Lanka. Two waves
took ten thousand people with them in the space of ten minutes. It
is not hard to see how this happened. The center of town lies only
feet from the sea. There were no mangroves, no palms, no dunes
to protect the place and its people from the wave. As the bus jolted
down the hill into town, I saw the old clock tower that Udaya had
described in the e-mail he wrote me just after the tsunami. The wave
had come rolling into town at somewhere between thirty to forty
miles an hour. I had heard that it was as high as seventy to eighty feet

over in Banda Aceh in Indonesia. It was beyond anyone's ability to imagine. Udaya and his family must have arrived just after the wave hit the shore and was in the process of displacing houses and sucking everything else back into its maw before the next onslaught. I could see where they had sought shelter up on top of the hill. It was one of the few shoreline areas in the entire south that had a well-defined hill above the water. When I saw the topography, I realized that it was only this incline that had saved them.

That night I found a government rest house to stay in on top of that same hill. These modest hotels with restaurants attached were originally established in colonial times as way stations to break up the journey into the mountains and into hill country. When the British left, the rest houses remained and now provide decent accommodations, though they are not nearly as well appointed as they were under the British. I was the only guest except for a Japanese gentleman who, I took it, was here in connection with one of the NGOs. Our rooms opened onto outside terraces overlooking the sea. Just down from me a family had moved in and constructed a clothesline and a tetherball set on the balcony. The kids and I exchanged "Hellos" and "How are yous?" while the mother took down the laundry. For reasons all too easy to imagine, this place had simply become the family's home.

It was early evening by the time I dealt with a plumbing problem in the bathroom and got myself settled. I opened the window to the outside and discovered that it wouldn't shut. The door handle to my room was jerry-rigged. A pink mosquito net hung from the ceiling over, mysteriously, an empty space, so I set about repositioning two of the three twin beds in my room, the size of a small dormitory, into the middle of the floor in order to avoid the nightly mosquito raid.

I ate in the restaurant alone that evening, my only company a family of cats that was much more interested in the fresh seer fish than I was. I had lost my taste for it after the cook had taken me back into the kitchen just before dinner, with much hand waving, and proudly shown me how the fish's heart was still beating even as it was being filleted. Something began to rise from my stomach as I remembered the stories I had heard from countless fishermen about how their business had been off for four or five months after the tsunami because people were afraid to eat fish. Now business was back.

That night the cats got the fish, and I went out with my evening tea to sit on a bench overlooking the Indian Ocean. I called Udaya and Aruni to report on what I had seen thus far. I had told his story to some shopkeepers sitting outside their stores on their white plastic chairs earlier in the day to see if somehow I could find the man who had helped them.

"Many people helping many people," one of the men had told me in reply. What he said struck a chord. It was a newspaper article I had read in the Kandy Municipal Library reprinted from the *Guardian,* written by Jeremy Seabrook. I had Xeroxed it and kept it: "The Sri Lankans, the Thais," he had written, "who saved western tourists from drowning are, when they appear in the West, regarded as interlopers, as unwanted migrants, as asylum seekers who should go back to where they belong. The locals who saved the tourists earn less in a year than the price the privileged pay for a night's stay in a five-star hotel on a South Asian beach." He went on to talk about security and what that term ultimately means. "We are always at the mercy of nature, and yet we inhabit systems of social and economic injustice that exacerbate the insecurity of the poor. . . . We in the west are prepared to lay waste towers and cities in distant lands in the name of something called security that in the end eludes us all."

I had read so many articles in the press about Sri Lankans saving tourists. There was a harsh truth for the West in what Seabrook said. I had been thinking lately about what sustains people in times like these. Religion? Memory? In the days immediately after the tsunami, the churches and temples in this country opened their doors to as many as they could accommodate, probably even more. Monks took the food and money that had been given their temples as *dana* and used it to feed and shelter the survivors. From there, slowly, the people were transferred into tent camps and then gradually into the temporary housing that I see now. But in those initial days the *bhikkhus* and the priests on this island lived out their values.

People told me that the Buddhist *stupas,* the Hindu *kovils,* and the Christian churches were the only structures to have survived the wave. I had walked along shorelines where nothing at all remained but a *dagoba,* housing an image of the Buddha watching serenely over the shells of people's lives. But in the coming weeks I would also walk on beaches where the temples and *kovils* were smashed as indiscriminately as the other structures that lay beside them, as the bright blue and rose colored figures of Krishna, Ganesh, and Lakshmi danced, extending their signs of peace from toppled towers. It was easier to take solace in these structures of belief. If nothing else, this thinking provided a vocabulary within which people here sought refuge. Without it, they were left in a world of plate tectonics.

The next morning I set out to walk the wave's path. I headed down the street away from the center of town. I had seen two temporary camps down there and wanted to get a closer look at how post-tsunami life was unfolding in a place that had taken a direct hit. For all the bravado in the press about housing reconstruction, Hambantota was essentially a place that hadn't recovered. Less than a hundred feet from the shore people still lived on the sites of their former dwellings, squatters in what used to be their homes. Some had tents; some nothing more than blocks of concrete. An aid worker told me later that many of the people here had simply refused to be relocated so they took the tents they were living in, pulled up stakes, and repitched them back onto the rubble where their original huts had stood. I was taken aback by how little had been done down here. The destruction was on an order of magnitude much greater than any other place I would visit in Sri Lanka before or afterward. But would this not seem to argue for more effort being put into reconstruction? Even though the place isn't a tourist site, it is an area of the country where the man who was about to be elected president, Mahinda Rajapakse, comes from. As I left town, preparations were being made for a Mahinda rally later that day. When I got back to Colombo, Nalini told me that several thousand people had been bused in from farther north for the rally because they couldn't find enough local people to fill the park where the rally was to be held. Small wonder.

With the loudspeakers blaring in the background, gearing up for the rally, I followed the road for awhile away from the center of town, and then headed in toward the shore. Just south of Hambantota the land splays out into flat shoreline punctuated by dunes whose softness conceals a mass of sharp undergrowth and prickly pear. I interrupted a couple of sea turtles that were busy digging themselves into the prickly ground cover that lay on top of the sand. I had asked the man at the rest house if there was a place to swim down here, and he gave me a firm no. I took a long look at the ocean and understood why. The waves on this southern edge of the island on a completely calm day pound the shore with the fury matched in my own experience only by post-hurricane waters. I walked down the beach, pondering the shape of this shore. According to statistics, 75 percent of seashore vegetation in this area was destroyed. What survived were areas shielded by tall sand dunes, broad beaches, forest strands, and large mangrove patches. The tsunami also created new dunes—temporary graves to cover the bodies of the victims—while survivors became impromptu gravediggers. It is hard to know as one walks along the shore here whether what lies beneath is the foot of an old dune or a new grave. I paused to pick up a few delicate shells, and as I bent over, I came upon the heel of a woman's shoe. Did someone lose it yesterday from one of the nearby villages or was it something else? All along every shore it was like this—a button, a child's toy, a pen. I remembered the fisherman whose village stood just south of the Mt. Lavinia beach who told me that in the days immediately after the tsunami, his village had acquired new items courtesy of the sea: fishing boats, pots and pans that randomly floated north and came in with the tide.

There was something about the impact of these waves upon the southern shoreline that still eluded me. Villages just meters from one another sustained very different kinds of damage. Some were demolished entirely; others survived almost intact. I remembered something Alan had said about the waves being "wanton." There seemed sometimes to be no pattern to what survived and what did not. I knew that much was due to the presence of estuaries or protective stands of mangroves, but I had also heard that the marine geology of this part of the island had dealt it a particularly devastating blow. I wanted to talk to someone when I got back to Colombo about the geology of what had happened.

As I stood on the beach watching the waves slam into the shore, a woman's cry pierced the air. "Tsunami, tsunami!" she shrieked, using the actual word in English. I turned and froze. Was she trying to warn me about something? There was nobody else on the beach. Had an announcement been broadcast throughout the town? I started to move quickly back up onto the dunes. In the weeks and months immediately after the tsunami, I had read in the paper about any number of false alarms, of towns being evacuated because word had gone out that a tsunami was coming. Everyone was on edge. People were ready to flee in a heartbeat. With my back to the water I saw a small woman of indeterminate age run up onto one of the dunes in a *sarong* and bare feet. Her hair had come unbraided, and her high-pitched cries rent the air. "Tsunami, tsunami!" the word most villagers had never heard a year ago. She yelled repeatedly at me, waving her hands over her head. Something inside me told me that the ocean was okay. The cries came from someplace deep down inside this woman. This wasn't a plea for charity. Or was it? I couldn't decipher it. It felt like something else, something that I feared I could not help her with. I turned toward her, the two of us facing each other alone on a beach. Suddenly a male figure appeared on the dune where she stood, said something to her, and gently led her away. He turned back to me and motioned that everything was okay.

I spent most of my walk that day unhinged from the incident. Aid signs, the ubiquitous white SUVs that moved around the island now courtesy of the NGOs, people drying fish on mats beside the ocean, quietly talking to each other belied the full extent of this tragedy and the process by which a twenty-minute trauma can become internalized for a lifetime. I thought as I walked that I knew where that howl had come from.

The heat rose from dry, flat roads as I headed south. There were no aid signs to be seen. Only a truck passed from time to time, sometimes stopping as the driver asked if I wanted a ride. The land was flat and sparse; structures lay abandoned; a few scattered boats sat similarly on the sand; proprietors of hastily erected *kades* sold juice along the road. One of the merchants told me that a tour van bringing people to Yala passes by once or twice a day. Life lay dry and desiccated. My mouth was thick with sand and dust. By evening I turned back. A local truck driver gave me a lift back to Hambantota, where I spent the night next to the family with the tetherball set.

The local bus to Galle and from there to Colombo the next day had about twenty more people on it than it could comfortably hold. I was one of them. Wedged in the back with others with similar travel plans, I watched in despair as a young boy flagged us down on the road and maneuvered his way onto the bus with several huge burlap bags. Everyone did the Sri Lankan squeeze, and the boy and his bags finally fetched up next to me, which was also on me. A quick readjustment gave me an automatic seat from Galle to Colombo; I rode back up the coast on two bags stuffed with something soft.

CHAPTER 16

Early Warning System

Back in Colombo, I went over to Nalini's. Mutto had dinner and tea ready for us. He listened as I told what I had seen, Nalini translating for him. We talked late into the night about the state of the damage down south. Nalini, as always, gave me the political context against which I could better understand what had and had not been done in terms of cleanup and reconstruction. Of the entire family, only Gamini had been down the coast since the wave hit. The rest of the family had stayed away. I thought about it as I was pulling the windows shut for the night and realized that no one else I knew, no one, had been back.

The next morning I managed to secure an appointment with the assistant director of the Bureau of Geology and Mines, an organization that is now the nerve center for monitoring seismic activity that could potentially affect Sri Lanka. In the days immediately following the tsunami, this place became the center of controversy over whether Sri Lanka had a functioning early warning system or not prior to the disaster. I was eager to talk to someone there about the science of what happened and what kind of monitoring system might help get the word out in something approximating a timely fashion should this, God forbid, ever happen again.

As the *tuk-tuk* maneuvered its way down Galle Road to the bureau, the humidity from the night's rain mingled with the bus fumes, providing me with all the incentive I needed not to breathe.

"*Rata? Oyage rata?*" (Your country?) the driver yelled over the blaring of horns.

"America," I yelled back, and he threw up both hands, stood up from his seat, and shouted, "America rule the world!"

"*Mokkada?*" (What?) I said.

"America rule the world. America is king. You are king."

I didn't say anything and waited for him to deposit himself back into the seat. The driver finally left me off on the sidewalk in front of an unmarked building that sat innocuously next to an enormous statue of Buddha under an equally imposing bo tree, another unlikely moment of calm in a part of the city gone mad with traffic, horns, and the general cacophony of street life.

"Going and coming, madam?" he asked me.

"Just going," I told him. I decided to walk home after the meeting.

The bureau consisted of an enormous room rimmed by glass-enclosed offices with typewriters and computers on wooden desks that had seen better days. When I arrived, the place was completely empty, save for the sound of voices from down the hall. It was lunchtime. No doubt every one was just finishing up their curry packets. The assistant director, Mr. Preme, I was told, would be with me in a minute and wouldn't I take a seat outside his office?

I sat waiting, making a few notes in my notebook and generally taking in the detail of the room. It looked to be badly in need of an infusion of technology since it was presumably from here that any sort of monitoring of seismic events takes place. Row upon row of cubicles lined a singularly empty space that seemed to have gone unused far longer than the lunch hour. Mr. Preme arrived and ushered me into his office. I was given fair warning that we had only an hour since the bureau was about to be descended on by hundreds of schoolkids on a tsunami informational field trip. I cut right to the chase and asked him if there had been any system in place that could have predicted what happened.

"Do you mean was there an early warning system?" he asked. "Many people are asking this. Well, the answer is both yes and no. We have a system up in Pallekele near Teldeniya. It's an information-processing center, but it doesn't require a staff. All it does is transmit the information it gathers to California Research Headquarters in San Diego where it is processed. But the information we receive there doesn't tell us anything about whether a tsunami is approaching. It tells us about seismic activity. Unfortunately, a seismograph can only measure an earthquake, not a tsunami. So we had no way of knowing what was coming towards us, at least not from any of the instrumentation available to us. There is no warning system for tsunamis," Mr. Preme clarified, looking straight at me. "There is one for the Pacific but nothing for the Indian Ocean."

I told him that none of this made any sense to me given the nature and the size of the tectonic plates in the Indian Ocean and the Bay of Bengal.

"The will surprise you," he answered, "but only a few tsunamis have ever been generated in the Indian Ocean, at least according to written record. The Japanese have been much better at keeping good data than we have. The monks there have been recording deaths, including tsunami-related deaths, since roughly 600 AD. There are a few mentions in our chronicle *The Mahavamsa,* but it is unclear whether they were tsunamis or just sea surges. One was recorded around 200 BC near what is now Colombo. There was another recorded in 1883 that was definitely tsunami related, and then there was a volcanic eruption on Krakatau Island in Indonesia, but we have no casualty figures for it. A lot of our tsunami stories come out of the oral histories of coastal tribes. We do not know if they were elaborated or if they merged with other local legends. We need to start keeping better records. Right after the tsunami we went with an international team all over the island between January 10th and 14th to try and get measurements. We needed the degree of destruction, the distance of inundation, the wave heights. We were able to get into most places, but not all. We had problems with security near Kalkudah over on the northeast coast. We didn't get up to Jaffna because of the war and the LTTE. Before you go today I'll give you a copy of the report. Just be sure to bring it back."

As I listened to Mr. Preme, I remembered reading about a man named Stuart Weinstein, who happened to be on duty in Honolulu at the Pacific Tsunami Warning Center the morning of December 26. Sitting in front of his computer, he had watched the data pour in on the earthquake. Realizing the enormity of the seismic event, he and another seismologist, Barry Hirshorn, spent the next several hours revising upward their original estimates of the quake's magnitude. They sent out advisories to twenty-six Pacific countries. None of the countries in the Indian Ocean, however, could receive them because they weren't part of the Pacific Warning System. By the time Weinstein realized that they were dealing with a tsunami, it was already too late to get word to Thailand, Indonesia, and Sri Lanka, so he and his fellow scientists attempted to contact Mauritius and Madagascar in the western Indian Ocean, which lay directly in the path of the wave. Partially because they were able to warn those areas, there were many fewer casualties there. The distance of these two islands from the epicenter and the fact that some of the energy of the waves was dissipated by shallow banks in the Indian Ocean mitigated the force of the tsunami for them, as it did for the eastern coast of Africa, where Tanzania reported only thirteen deaths.

Several months later I spoke with Stuart Weinstein over the phone, asking him to go back to that day in 2004. It was not a pleasant memory, particularly if you were sitting in front of a computer with data pouring in and no way to get information to the countries that lay directly in the tsunami's path. Weinstein called the earthquake "pathological" because it took almost ten minutes to rupture. This was three times as long as any known earthquake had ever taken, he told me. The longest earthquake anyone knew about prior to that was recorded in 1960 and took 270 seconds. This one took 600 seconds before rupture. "We initially thought it was an 8.1 and that if there was a tsunami it would be restricted to Thailand," he told me. Thirty-five minutes later, using other techniques, he and Barry Hirshorn upgraded it to an 8.5. There were earthquakes after this, measuring 8.0–8.5, one in Badung, Indonesia, in 2006, and another in Peru in August 2007, but the tsunamis they generated were confined locally. Even as Weinstein and his colleagues were revising their original estimates upward the day after Christmas, there were no sea-level instruments in the Indian Ocean that could relay information on what was actually transpiring. Only four hours later did they understand the magnitude of the event. By the time the day was over, the earthquake measured somewhere between a 9.1

and a 9.3 on the Richter scale. The State Department had somehow managed to get news from the U.S. Embassy in Sri Lanka and called Dr. Weinstein in Hawaii. Thus it was that I was able to get e-mails from the U.S. Embassy in Sri Lanka since I was on their Listserv, while people who were living on the island next to the shore got no warning at all. There was just no system in place that could warn the Sri Lankan population that a tsunami was on the way. Nothing. Nothing at all.

"People died," said Dr. Weinstein, "because there was no warning system in the Indian Ocean, and we could not just invent one. The earthquake struck the earth where a warning system was not operating. If it had happened in the Pacific, a warning would have gone out in fifteen minutes. We would have known much earlier about what was going on, and hundreds of thousands of people would not have died."

"What to do?" one old man whom I had met down in Hambantota said, throwing up his arms to the heavens. "We are a poor nation."

Back at Geology and Mines, Mr. Preme took out a sheet of paper and proceeded to draw diagrams of tsunami waves for me. I asked him if it was true that the geomorphology of the shore had changed in some places because of the waves.

"No, from satellite photographs the shoreline still looks the same even with all the destruction it sustained. But the wave hit at different velocities in different places. Here, look. A tsunami wave occurs when there is a sudden release of energy in the sea. An earthquake can cause it, or a volcanic eruption below sea level, or even a landslide on a seamount. It's not water that's moving but energy."

I sat looking at his diagrams, remembering something Jon had told me. We were standing on the pier at Santa Cruz, the two of us looking down at the ocean, watching waves tumble over surfers. "Do you see that wave?" he said as I leaned precariously over the railing, trying to take a picture of a recalcitrant sea lion hiding under the pier. "It's not really the water molecules traveling in, it's energy. The wave carries the energy."

Mr. Preme went on to explain how a tsunami travels. "In deep sea the height of a tsunami is less than one meter, but the wave length is about a hundred kilometers, or a little over sixty-four miles. Tsunamis are long gravity waves. The actual wave length shortens as the wave approaches the shore and slows down. But because of the long wave length, the rest of that wave is still traveling fast out in deep water. So, you see, the leading edge slows down while the trailing edge catches up with it and the water in the middle is squeezed. That's what causes the wall of water, or what we call amplitude, to hit the shore. The reason tsunamis are so destructive is that while they are traveling in a deep ocean, they retain most of their energy, which they bring to the coastal shores with them. This is why ships out at sea or even those waiting in the shipping lanes outside Colombo for a berth were not affected. In most cases they didn't even know there was a tsunami."

"So this is why the people who were scuba diving off a boat down near Hikkaduwa said that they didn't know there was a tsunami even though they were right in the middle of it?" I asked him.

"That's right," he said, nodding. "I read that interview. They felt some strong current underwater, but it wasn't until the depth of the ocean decreased sharply near the shore that the full energy of the wave was released. The farther out one went, the safer one was. You see, some places were more severely damaged than others because of the differences in the strip of shore that the wave hit. The worst damage took place on the coastline around Ampara-Kalmunai because the flat beach allowed the waves to move in at heights that reached from eight to ten meters. Marudamunai, Kalmunai, and Saintamaruthu were also heavily damaged, more so than any other place on the island. Those are all on the eastern side of the island."

Another sheet of paper emerged from the drawer, and Mr. Preme began to sketch something else. "Here, these are tectonic plates. These are the two plates here: the Indian and the Asian. I'm not very good at drawing, so you'll please pardon. This is an enormously volatile area. The Indian plate moves northeast at about 6 centimeters (2.36 inches) a year at an oblique angle to the Java Trench. Sumatra slides over the top of the subducting Indian oceanic plate. On any given day there can be an earthquake in this part of the world, but not all earthquakes generate a tsunami. For example, since December 26, 2004, there have been approximately a thousand earthquakes in Indonesia alone. We're now in February 2006. We actually had a national response to one of them here in Sri Lanka because we thought it was going to generate another tsunami. Come, let me show you."

I followed him down the hall to a small room where a young woman sat, monitoring a seismograph.

"You see, we now have round-the-clock monitoring. I just came off my own night shift two nights ago. We are plugged into the California Integrative Seismic Network out of the University of California, San Diego, U.S. Geological Survey, and the Japan Meteorological Agency. Now within ten minutes of an event happening, we can get the information on it. We get the exact place and magnitude."

I looked at the screen and noticed that it was color coded to reflect areas of greater or lesser seismic activity. "But this tells you about the earthquakes. How does it help you predict the tsunamis?"

"We figure that anything over a 5.0 on the Richter scale contains the possibility to generate a tsunami. This is also generally the figure they use in Japan."

I glanced up at the white board on the wall. It listed all the seismic events over 5.0. that had taken place recently. On February 13 at 3:40 p.m. one had taken place in Simuele, Indonesia, and another in Banda Aceh.

A light suddenly flashed up on the West Coast of the United States. All three pairs of eyes in the room shifted focus onto the screen.

"California just had an earthquake. It looks to be someplace south of San Francisco. We'll know in a minute."

The woods behind Jon's house skirt the San Andreas fault. After the divorce he couldn't afford to keep the house and had to sell it. He was worried that having a major fault line running through his backyard would deter potential buyers. Someone bought it anyway, redwoods and the sea having the greater allure.

"You had an earthquake today," I e-mailed him later. "Did you feel it? It was three something on the Richter scale."

"No," came an e-mail back. "No tremors today. No more than I already feel."

I turned to Mr. Preme and asked him what sort of plan is in place should one of these earthquakes generate another tsunami. How does one really test for a tsunami? And how do you get the word out if there is one coming?

"There is a system. It works with buoys. We don't have it yet. It's extremely expensive. It works like this. You have two Geigers, one on the sea bottom that measures wave pressure. This bottom detector sends signals to a floating buoy that has another Geiger in it. This, in turn, sends signals up to a satellite, which then communicates back to earth. It's a very expensive system. The German, Chinese, and Japanese governments are all interested in helping us out financially with this. Or we may piggyback on India's program."

"And if the system confirms that you have a tsunami on your hands, what then?"

"Well, we call the Department of Meteorology. They are the ones who are supposed to get the word out. They take it from there."

"What sort of plan do they have in place?"

"You'll have to ask them that."

Stuart Weinstein of the Pacific Tsunami Warning Center in Hawaii would tell me some months later that setting up warning centers for tsunamis is the easy part. Much more difficult is the emergency management system, which involves getting warnings out to the population through whatever means are necessary.

We left the monitoring room and were surrounded by waves of a different sort—little kids in blue shorts and oversized backpacks who began to hail the white woman with "Hellos" and "How are yous?" We all smiled and laughed; some of the little girls hid behind their giggles. Outside the early-afternoon sun was sending midafternoon silver sparkles dancing upon a slow sea. I looked out the window at this body of water that informed my life here. I thought that if I didn't get to its shores once a day, I would feel as if I had lost my compass. Was it the pull of someone who lives in the desert toward all things water, or are there just some people who, like sea turtles, are always trying to find their way back home into it? It seemed impossible that this ocean could ever have been different than my experience of it, and yet something tapped on my shoulder continually, reminding me that it could all change in a heartbeat.

Mr. Preme handed me the bureau's final report. "I think you'll be interested in this. It will tell you a lot. I hope I've helped."

"You've helped a lot," I said, thanking him and bowing. Something made me turn, though, as I said my good-byes. "By the way, do you mind me asking where you were on the day of the tsunami?"

"I was driving down this coast with my family. We were on the road that goes along the shore. We are lucky to be alive. That's all I can say."

I nodded, sighed, and left him surrounded by squeals and backpacks. I walked out onto Galle Road, bought a paper, and headed back to Nalini's after a quick stop at a fruit stand in Wellawatte. Mutto had tea ready for me, and Chitra, Nalini, and I broke into a package of lemon biscuits I had bought the night before. The paper was full that day of the upcoming cease-fire talks between the LTTE and the central government that were to take place the next week in Geneva. I lay in bed that night and thought about the geology of heartbreak and early warning systems. And about war and plate tectonics. Twenty-three years of intractable plates pushing against one another in this country.

A couple from Pottuvil in their new house, handed over to them by the Sri Lankan Lion's Club.

CHAPTER 17

Arugam Bay

"Aren't you going to take a sea bath?" asked Richard, the cook at the Stardust, a small beach hotel on the southeast coast of the island run by a Danish lady named Merete who came here in the early 1980s with her husband and stayed. She now ran the place by herself.

"Not on your life," I said to Richard, pointing at the waves hitting the shore with something like the energy force of the elephant herd down the road in Yala. "I vote to live." I proceeded to remind him of newspaper reports of two boys off Pottuvil who had been washed away only a few weeks before by one of these waves.

"They were swimming in the wrong place," Richard told me.

Is there a right place? I wondered.

He stood on the shore and gallantly gestured. "Ladies first."

We went back and forth on this for about twenty minutes until I took the plunge. Richard followed me. After another twenty minutes of being hammered, I was ejected from the Indian Ocean and rolled up on its shores.

"What's the matter with the surf today?" I queried Richard.

"Normal surf, madam. Normal surf."

I have read weekly stories in the papers about people drowning. Irrespective of monsoon season, there are simply areas of the country where the waves are stronger. Mr. Preme had explained to me that down south the geological formations of the underwater rock shelves cause the waves to hit the shore at ninety-degree angles, thus substantially increasing the force of the wave. Still in all, it felt to me as if there were an unwarranted number of fatalities in the water. And I knew only about the ones that got reported.

Perhaps we expect too much that island nations be seafaring nations, for it often happens that they are not. For all that water is the defining factor of life here, this is not in essence a seafaring nation. It all seems so counterintuitive to me—the silt-driven rivers that wind their way lazily to the sea, the winds that gather moisture from the ocean's waters, releasing it back onto the land, all this fundamentally on an island historically with little relation to the sea. The first settlers who arrived here from northwest India in the fifth century BC may originally have come as traders but quickly began to take up agriculture, predominantly the cultivation of rice. Onto the southern shores the sea deposited the Arab traders who came searching for trade routes to the east in the tenth century, long before the first Europeans plied the waters looking for spice and then empire. *The Mahavamsa* reports little about the ancient Ceylonese setting out on ships to other lands. For the most part, the island did what islands tend to do: sat still while the waters brought boats, merchants, and ultimately new rulers to its shores. Nor am I really sure that Sri Lankans are great swimmers, this despite the fact that the sports section of the daily newspapers is routinely filled with headlines about swimming, second only to cricket as the sport of preference here. The fancy private schools on the island either have their own pools or have access to pools and organize interschool swim meets. But most of Sri Lanka's children attend government schools with no pools. And many of the people on this island, including the ones who live near the shore, can't swim.

Fishermen who can't swim go out in boats every day. Villagers who can't swim do their laundry on fragile rocks in the midst of racing rapids on the Mahaweli near where we lived. It reminded me of stories I had heard over the years of the Seri Indians on the island of Tiburon in the Sea of Cortez in Mexico. They travel by canoe to the shores near Kino Bay to sell their fish and their wood carvings, the women in their long skirts, often with several layers of petticoats underneath. And when the storms come up and the seas are rough, the boats have been known to capsize, and they drown. Here, in the wake of the tsunami, people who can't swim are rebuilding their huts on some parts of the beach less than fifty feet from the ocean. When CNN and the BBC talked to survivors of the wave down in Galle and Matara, many of the stories they heard from distraught family members still looking for their loved ones was "She couldn't swim." As if swimming would have helped.

Arugam Bay is a tiny slip of a place just northeast of Yala National Park and across the lagoon from the Muslim town of Pottuvil. It took a direct hit the day the sea came to the land. Pottuvil, on the other hand, was spared much of the destruction thanks to the presence of sand dunes and the lagoon. The location of these two places—long, difficult hours from the major tourist centers, bordering on territory that has gone back and forth between government and Tiger control—has left it unsullied by the worst of beach tourism that has overrun the southwestern part of the island. It is still possible to feel sand between one's toes down here that doesn't belong to a hotel conglomerate.

When I first set out to track this wave, I had visions of walking the circumference of the island, stopping at villages along the way for a night's rest. I thought I could understand better what happened by putting my feet on the soil and walking every inch of the shoreline. I had just finished Rory Stewart's book *The Places in Between,* a chronicle of his walk across Afghanistan. He spoke about how we tend to romanticize the act of walking. Imaginatively, we recall the wanderings of the dervishes, *sadhus,* and friars who approached God on foot; or the Buddha, who meditated by walking; or Wordsworth, who composed sonnets while striding beside the lakes. He recalled Bruce Chatwin saying that we would "think and live better and be closer to our purposes as humans if we moved continually on foot across the surface of the earth." "I was not sure," said Stewart, "that I was living or thinking any better." The reality that he came to understand was that his life as a walker across Afghanistan was quickly shorn of anything resembling the romantic. Two armed soldiers attached themselves to him at the beginning of his journey; he suffered from dysentery most of the way; and the best he could say about some of the villages he passed through was that the local population didn't kill him.

I didn't have to contend with the same things Stewart did. I had

a different load, obviously a much easier one. My imaginary map—
one long ribbon of road wrapped around the island—gave way to
hawkers on the road, hawkers by the sea, roads that ended at elephant reserves, and, perhaps most importantly, the shifting boundaries of territory in a stubborn civil war. Like many things here, maps
tell only half the story. The other half is the route I actually ended up
taking. "I don't think you're going to be able to do what you want to
do," Nandana had said on my first night back at his house in Kandy.
"There's Yala down south. You can get down the west coast a way.
After Hambantota I would say it's difficult. The east is not secure.
We don't even know anymore which part is controlled by the Tigers
and which part by the military. When you get back from the south,
we'll have Dulip come over. He's a professional driver. He takes
people all over in his van. He's good, he's reliable. He'll know which
roads are in Tiger hands. "This isn't a choice," he added. "You're
not going to get there any other way. And you'll be safe."

Nandana was right. Nalini had also warned me in Colombo.
Roads in the eastern part of the island ended in roadblocks, were
washed out, sandbagged, bunkered, skirted areas where land mines
were still active, fell under the control of government forces one
week, and Tigers the next. It was like a ribbon with knots. Working around the knots, I took the bus back north up to Kandy from
Colombo and waited for Dulip to arrive to plot our course.

The night before we left for the east Dulip came over in his van.
Very young, very good-looking, and a little shy, he arrived with
map in hand and several pens. The two of us sat with our tea at the
dining-room table in the big house, and I explained to him what I
was trying to do. Together we poured over several maps. I wanted
to head straight east and then down the shore to Pottuvil. I showed
Dulip the route. Suddenly his shyness vanished. He wouldn't hear
of it.

"It's Ampara district, madam. Too dangerous."

He reminded me of incidents there of late, none of them encouraging. He took a pencil and drew another route, bending like a
snake's tail across, down, up, and through terrain that he knew to be
safe. Whether he was right or wrong about the Ampara Road was

immaterial. What was true one day could easily change the next. We agreed on a price, but I understood after he left that the two of us had signed on for something other than driving. I was not just his passenger; I was his charge. He would see to my safety, and by agreeing to his route, I would see to his. And so the following morning the two of us cut across tanks and mountain ranges, tea and rubber estates, and forest and came straight at Pottuvil from the southwest.

The Ampara area, of which Pottuvil is a part, was hammered unlike any other on December 26. This is the area to which my friend Alan up in Teldeniya had organized a massive food and aid delivery. He had opened up a special account at his bank in Kandy. Money poured in from friends all over the world. He and his crew—people from the school where he had been headmaster; Tamils and Sinhalese from the neighboring villages; the stonecutter who was working for him; Sunil, who helped him manage his guesthouse—all pitched in loading up the trucks with pots, pans, candles, matches, kettles, buckets, plastic bottles, rice, *dhal,* dried fish, coconuts, and medical supplies for the trip over to the east coast. Before they set out a Sri Lankan friend had warned them to take one white person with them in case there was trouble. White skin, a Western voice would bring order out of the chaos. Later Alan told me, "There was trouble. People grabbed at the lorries for supplies. It was complete mayhem. Then the white guy we had gotten to go along stood up in the back of the lorry and yelled for restraint and order. Everybody obeyed immediately."

Now I took a close look at Dulip behind the steering wheel. "How old are you?" I asked him.

"Twenty-six, madam. Always war, madam, in my life. Since I was little, war."

Reason enough to be cautious. Perhaps there was something else as well. We had talked a little bit the night before about the tsunami. He told me very quietly that he had taken a group of tourists down to the Yala Preserve in the south. He had been waiting in his van somewhere outside its borders when the wave hit. The group he had brought down was inside the preserve. I listened as he spoke and wanted to ask him more but stopped when he told me that he never saw them again.

———

In her late fifties or early sixties, Merete wears her red hair pinned up and tends to the daily business of running the Stardust Hotel. Open aired, with clear architectural lines that pay homage to the sea, the tiny hotel sits directly on the beach at Arugam Bay. Merete's training as an architect shows in the play of line and color, the way she has planted a young palm next to a building, the design of the windows at bed level so that one can turn over at night, push the portal open, and look out onto the sea. On the day the wave hit, she was in the kitchen with the employees. Her husband was outside. They found his body washed inland several hours after the last wave receded. For days afterward she and her employees all carried rocks that had been part of the rubble the wave had left in its wake. Together they cleared a path leading down to the ocean again.

"It was our therapy," she told me. "It helped us in our grief. It gave us something to do."

Eleven months later she continued slowly to rebuild, hut by hut, room by room.

I had asked if I could spend some time with her. She invited me up one morning to her room cum office. She curled up on her twin bed, her legs tucked under her, framed by a wall of pictures: art, photography, grandchildren. I looked but saw no pictures of her husband. We sat and talked for an hour. I sometimes forgot that I was not the first person to ask people down the coast about the wave and realized only later the toll that the telling and retelling must take upon people. But Merete was gracious all the same.

She lost only two employees that morning—something of a miracle considering the force with which the wave hit. But the employees lost family members. One lost all his children. We talked about the aftermath. Only one employee didn't return to work after the tragedy.

"He is Muslim," Merete told me. "All his children died. I remember he went to some Muslim camps where they were praying. For a long time he moved between camps and from family to family. He is supposed to come back tomorrow. I am praying that that happens. It will help him.

"Do you see that structure over there?" she pointed. "We got it up rather quickly to shelter the people who came and helped us re-build. A lot of our former guests, especially from Denmark, donated their time. Some of the guests who had known our employees put up the money for their houses, so they were the first in this area to get decent housing."

What had been just a cloud to the north several minutes ago had now engulfed the entire sky and let loose with a volley of rain that sent Merete stepping out through the window sill to her balcony to close the shutters.

We continued our conversation with an adjustment up in deci-bel level. I asked her about what, if anything, the government was doing down here in the event there should be another tsunami. The area was so terrifyingly and beautifully isolated. I would stand on the beach and to the south saw the beginnings of Yala. To the north wild dunes. "Is there some sort of early warning system in place?" I asked dubiously.

She laughed. "In a manner of speaking. Not long ago I was vis-ited by the STF."

"What's that?" I interrupted.

"It's the Special Task Force. It's government. They came down and told me about the early warning system that they had put into place in this area. They said that if there was a tsunami warning at night, they would set off flares and explosive devices; during the day bombs and grenades. We haven't had any flares or bombs go off, but we've had tsunami warnings during the past year. Actually, I received one not so very long ago from Denmark where friends are looking after me. Somebody picked up a high level of seismic activity over here and relayed the news to me. This always happens at nighttime. I took all my guests up to the second story of the main house here, got on the computer, and after two hours saw that any danger of a tsunami had passed. Everyone went back to their rooms."

"Have you had any problems with the Tigers?" I asked.

"Some but not many. We came here initially in 1982. We started off by exporting red rice to Denmark, but that same year we also began work on these buildings. Our business opened in 1984, and then around Christmas in 1986 we had our first robbery. The Tigers 'borrowed' some jeeps. The second incident was more dangerous, so we went back to Denmark for one year, in 1987–88. But then we came back, and since 1992 everything has been fine.

"This part of the island is like a string of pearls," she continued. "One village is a Tamil pearl, the next a Muslim pearl, all strung on the same string."

I thought to myself as I listened to Merete that to be Muslim in this country is as much an ethnic identity as it is a religion.

"You see," she continued, adjusting her *sarong,* "most of the people down here are Muslim: 85 percent, to be exact. And they speak Tamil. Before the war there was a much greater mixture of peoples, but the war began, and the Sinhalese left. Then some, but not all, of the Tamils left."

Later that day I went over to see one of the Muslim pearls on the string—a group of houses that was being handed over to the tsunami survivors by the Sri Lankan Lion's Club. The families moving in were all Muslim save one Sinhalese family. I arrived in the middle of the ceremony amid much speech giving and free soft drinks. Some of the local children were playing on a seesaw, the girls in new frocks, the boys in freshly ironed shorts. Rows of blue concrete houses were being presented with much fanfare. I asked a young man, an official of the camp with excellent English, if I could see one of the houses. The two of us were welcomed inside by one of the Muslim families. The place smelled like fresh paint over freshly laid concrete. In the front room some men sat on white plastic chairs, talking among themselves. There was no other furniture. A few scattered possessions—amounting essentially to bundles—and a floor mat lay in the two side rooms. I walked back through the front room to what was presumably the kitchen. There four women were sitting on the floor over a small gas burner, boiling eggs. There was no sink, no stove, no counter on which to chop. As I left the house, I was surrounded by a group of young men. Some had driven up on motorcycles; others had cell phones that kept ringing. They were eager to talk to me.

"You see what they gave us. We get houses delivered to us without even the basics. No electricity, no plumbing, no running water. We still have to use outhouses. Somebody in Colombo needs to know about the sanitation in this camp. The conditions are impossible. If they are going to give us houses, they need to give us something we can live in. The relief organizations need to monitor better where their money is going."

This was a familiar refrain. I would hear it many, many more times.

Someone pushed through the crowd and asked the young man to translate something for me to hear. He wanted me to know that the location of the housing units made no sense. All the men here, he told me, were fishermen. This meant that they couldn't walk to work; they were too far away. These houses were five kilometers from the beach. The bus came in the morning and took them all to work. The children were bused to school as well. That left a village of women here alone all day, defenseless. The bus brought the men back in the evening. There was no one to watch the nets or the boats. These houses, he told me, were irrelevant to people's lives here.

I wandered back through some of the temporary housing to see how people were faring in some of the first houses to be handed over. One lone wire ran electricity into some of the homes. I was invited into several of them, where I saw some toilets and running water.

It is impossible to understand completely what is going on in these new housing communities, though its very complexity is perhaps the best lesson one can take away regarding the economics of disaster relief. While they are in temporary housing, the survivors receive aid; once in permanent housing, however, their aid is cut off. For some, having that permanent roof over their head is more important than aid; for others, the monetary and material support they receive takes precedence.

Merete had told me that since the tsunami she had seen the material quality of people's lives improve significantly. I saw it myself; materially, people seemed to be doing better here due to the amount of aid that came pouring in. Food and clothing were donated. Outright gifts of cash went in many cases to buy the cell phones and motorcycles I was seeing.

That night I had a beer on the beach with a smart young Danish woman, an aid worker who had been working out of Batticaloa for six months.

"Have you run into the powdered milk scam yet?" she asked me.

"Only about every day," I laughed.

"Well this seems to be the scam of the month. Before that there were other scams. What people are doing now is getting money from tourists or whomever and buying up boxes of powdered milk. They are then hiking up the price and selling them to the hotels but still well under what the hotels would normally pay. Everyone comes out ahead."

There were other scams as well. People were taking the rice donated by the aid organizations and selling it to the tourist hotels for much less than the tourist hotel would ordinarily pay. Everyone made a profit, and tourists unwittingly ended up eating aid rice and drinking aid powdered milk in their tea. And yet, I wondered increasingly if "scam" was the proper word for what was going on. Was it not something else, whose bottom line rested with the fact that the tsunami devastated the local economy? This wasn't a moral or a criminal issue but rather the natural functioning of a population trying to make ends meet in desperate times. It was a form of survival. People did what they had to do.

I wrote, slept, ate, and walked my way through the next day. I ate imported Danish butter on homemade bread—this just days before the Muslim world erupted in a spate of anti-Danish frenzy over some political cartoons that had appeared in a Danish newspaper denigrating the Prophet Mohammed. I took some time to gather my thoughts in my journal. Toward sunset the ocean turned orange and vermillion, and an enormous anvil cloud, black like ebony, moved in and hovered over Yala. Later that night I tucked my mosquito netting tightly into the four corners of my bed, slid under it, and maneuvered my hand out just far enough to push open the small screen window in my thatched hut. Less than fifty feet from where I lay the waves were hammering the shore. I thought about how mortality slams up against us as we are buttering our bread in the morning. You turn to call your husband to breakfast, and the place where he stood is now the wall of a wave.

That night I counted the seconds between waves, remembering Richard's comment: "Normal surf, madam."

CHAPTER 18

Batti

There were over one hundred thousand people sitting in refugee camps in and around Batticaloa. Some had been there for years as the area had slid back and forth between government and Tiger control. People ran from their homes when they heard shelling in the distance and took refuge in the camps. Others ended up there when word went out that the Sinhalese Army was about to embark on a major advance in the north. And so, since the nineties, the population of Batti, as the locals call it, had gradually decreased while that of the camps had burgeoned. Then the wave came, creating new refugee camps.

I had said a reluctant good-bye to Merete's carefully tended patch of coast in order to go back to Kandy and over to Batticaloa. Dulip and I agreed to take a few days to tend to our other lives before we headed over to Batti. He would come and get me in three or four days.

I wanted to touch base with Alan, though, and called up to see if I could come up for a night or two. I was told to "come along," and grabbed a few bottles of wine at Food City before the bus ride into tea country. An hour later, freshly deposited by a fruit stand in Teldeniya, I looked up and saw Alan standing there, a slightly quizzical expression on his face. We gave each other hugs. It was good to see him.

"Don't mind if I've got some errands to do, do you?" he said, as we made our way along the street in his car. He apologized for what he considered his foul humor, explaining that he had just returned from a "soul-destroying trip" to Colombo to get his residency visa extended. "I ended up at the bloody Defense Department," he said, narrowly missing a dog.

"I didn't know you were a security risk," I joked.

"Don't even ask," he countered. "I went from office to office trying to get the silly thing renewed. Seems that I needed some sort of stamp, and the bloke who was supposed to stamp the visa application was in the Defense Department. I wasted three bloody days down in Colombo in the stinking heat over all of this."

We looked blankly at each other.

That night we sat on the back porch as purple mist rose between the ranges. In the distance I heard the muted tones of music coming from a village in the valley below. Conversation turned back to last December. I nursed my wine as Alan sipped his scotch and told me more of the story.

"I think we made about ten relief trips to the east in all. I basically stayed back at base raising the funds needed to buy all the supplies. Sunil and about six others would usually take a large Tata lorry with wooden sides and pack it up with the ration bags that he and his buddies had assembled. First there was the buying, then the packing everything in the bags. When everything was ready they'd usually set off around 3:00 a.m. It took Sunil and his crew about six hours to get over to the coast. Usually they'd stop at a roadside place for a rice and curry breakfast. Mobile phone connection was hideous in most areas and signals just faded. It was always a worry of mine back at base that any number of groups might hold them up at gun point and embezzle the lot, but it never happened. Everyone—police, local relief groups, even LTTE groups, though the LTTE bit depended on where Sunil went—were unfailingly helpful and never any hassle. The funny thing was the coming back. A bunch of them would get into the back of the lorry, which was empty now. They'd take an old washing-up bowl and a couple of toothbrushes that served as drum sticks, a bottle or two of arrack [an immensely popular local alcoholic drink made from the sap of the coconut palm] for six hours of singing on the return journey."

We talked late into the night, did a little singing of our own, though minus the toothbrushes, and played with the cat. The next morning I wrapped my *sarong* around me and brought my laptop out onto the porch in an effort to do some writing. But it was hill country, the air was dense with birdsong, and anytime was teatime. I spent the day following Alan around, swimming in the pool, sleeping, and devolving into my own kind of *nikan innawa*.

I said good-bye to Alan the next day and took the bus back to Kandy. I did my laundry with Kush on the back porch that afternoon and chatted as always about this and that. Kush called it "natting."

"I'm heading out again in two days," I told her. "Do you think the laundry will be dry by then?"

She turned, stared at me, and then looked up at the sky.

Later that night it rained . . . again.

Two days later, along with a canvas bag of wet clothes, I got into Dulip's van and the two of us made our way over on the Peradeniya Road to the spot where we would meet Ambi, a biology student at Peradeniya University recommended to me by my student Kanchuka. In addition to fluent Sinhalese and English, Ambi speaks her native Tamil, the language I would need for the next leg of the trip to the east. She and her father were standing there alongside the road, her father in his *sarong* and long white shirt, Ambi in a pair of slacks and an Indian top. Her father watched while we loaded everything into the van. I had heard that he is a retired professor of history from Peradeniya University and that Ambi is his only child. I bowed to him, introduced myself, and assured him that Ambi would be fine.

On the way east the two of us got to know each other a bit. Ambi had brought her bird book, *samosas* that her mother had carefully made, and a thermos of tea. As Dulip maneuvered the van over the mountains, Ambi and I set about identifying a large percentage of the population in the bird book: Indian rollers, brahminy kites, fishing eagles, egrets, and peacocks.

We were meanwhile starting to run the gauntlet of bunkers on the side of the road, then roadblocks. We passed abandoned houses, shells of schools and churches now occupied by the Sri Lankan military. Sometimes government soldiers waved us through; more often, though, we were stopped and then stopped again. Sometimes we were pulled over, and Dulip dutifully produced identification and paperwork. At times the procedure dragged on long enough that Ambi and I got out, stretched our legs, and broke out the fruit and *samosas,* aware of fifteen or more pairs of military eyes trained on us.

Tsunami damage has a disconcerting way of looking the same no matter where one goes. Houses are toppled, concrete displaced, trees uprooted, and stairs ascend to nowhere. I started seeing this miles from the water's edge, too far for even this wave to have made its way inland. And then I did a double take. The houses here were different—riddled with holes—while trees black from decay stood alongside, punctured with the same outlines of gunfire. Solitary frames of former dwellings were all that remained of areas once populated. There was no wave here, just war. Dulip pointed to where the bullets had landed. And as we moved closer in to the shore, the war and the wave began to blend indiscriminately into one another. At first I tried to find the telltale marks of difference between the two. I kept wanting to label it, to categorize it, to make the mess in front of me neat. Then I realized it didn't matter. Maybe the war just made it easier for the waves to roll through and do cleanup.

Had it not been for the minor distractions of one civil war and two very large waves, Batti could well have been one of the gems of this island. Woven with lagoons whose waters empty into an ocean scarcely a mile from the center of town, it is known as the city of singing fish. If you walk along the lagoon at night, local legend has it that you can hear the fish sing. We made mental notes to try it.

Sitting in the canals of Batti were beautiful, spanking-new fiberglass boats, most of them red, shining examples, so I thought, of international aid. Several days later a Sri Lankan aid worker explained that in the aftermath of the tsunami, everyone wanted to donate in any way they could. International donors wanted to help get the fishermen back to work as soon as possible, and so they gave boats. I had already seen this down south in Unawatuna and Hambantota. The difference here is that people actually do fish for a living. In the weeks following the tsunami, everyone who was registered as a fisherman in Batti was told to sign up for a new boat. People who weren't fishermen forged documents in order to get a free boat, which they then planned to sell at a markup. But who was going to buy them? The fishermen already had the boats they needed, and had gotten them for free. Whether the ersatz fishermen actually succeeded in selling these boats remains unclear. They sat in the lagoon, shiny and unused.

I had forgotten before we set out for Batti that we were just days away from the presidential election. Almost every available room in the town was taken up by the UN Election Monitoring Commission. We finally settled ourselves in the last room available at a small hotel-cum-guesthouse-cum-restaurant a scarce block from one of the lagoons. The owner, a middle-aged man in glasses with gray hair, looked to have his hands full as he stood behind a desk fielding questions, seeing to the needs of the Monitoring Commission, and trying to accommodate the three of us. Ambi and I were given one small room furnished with two army-type beds and a ceiling fan that clicked with each rotation. There was no mosquito netting.

"Are you going to be alright here?" I asked her as we took turns peering into the bathroom.

"Yes, yes, really, it's okay," she assured me.

There was no room for Dulip in the area where drivers usually stay, but after some negotiations the owner came back and announced that he had found something. Normally when one is traveling with a driver, the guesthouse or hotel provides some sort of accommodation for the driver, but I was never sure where. As we signed ourselves into the hotel logbook, the proprietor leaned over and said quietly that there wasn't much food and that he wasn't sure what he could do for us. "The Monitoring Commission, you know," he said with raised eyebrows and a slight smile. "Would rice be alright?"

"Rice would be just fine," we told him.

Later that night I learned something about the hotel's owner. He was Joseph Pararajasingham, a member of Parliament and the Tamil National Alliance in Batticaloa. "He's a huge defender of human rights on this part of the island," one of the guests informed me.

"Is he a Tiger?" I asked.

"I think not. I just think he is very aligned with the Tamil cause and is trying to protect people's rights here."

The next day the representatives from England, France, Italy, and Japan checked out. Two weeks later the election was co-opted by both the Tigers and the JVP. Most of the Tamil population in the north was strong-armed by the Tigers into not voting, thus depriving Prime Minister Ranil Wickramasinghe of enough votes to easily win the presidency. Rumors started circulating that Rajapakse's party had actually hijacked the election by paying the Tigers to prohibit voting in the north. It was just rumor, but I filed it. There were other election irregularities down south. The day after the election, in an extraordinary move, the Sri Lankan election commissioner resigned, claiming he was tired and begging to be released from his job—a resignation timed, according to many accounts, to avoid being indicted as a party to election rigging. I kept wondering what exactly the Monitoring Commission had done here.

The next morning Dulip, Ambi, and I set out for the local refugee camps. We went north from Batti into an area just on the edge of Tiger-controlled territory. The road we took had all but disintegrated into a sand path. We stopped and asked if this was, in fact, the road to the refugee camps. Some men on bicycles told us that what we were on was simply a passable track cleared by the army in order to get supplies through to tsunami survivors. This was the only way people could get into Kalkudah. The rest of the area was thick with land mines. If we followed this one lane dug into the sand, we were likely to be alright.

The heat had already moved in for the day by the time we found our way to the camps where survivors from Pasikudah and Kalkudah were resettled after the tsunami. These were two of the largest camps in the northeast part of the island and sat on opposite sides of the road from one another. They also sat on the edge of LTTE territory. We walked in past stacks of building material—concrete blocks, wood, metal siding—but saw only five or six permanent houses amid row upon row of temporary dwellings. It was a relatively quiet place—perhaps, I thought, because most of the men were still busy with the day's catch and hadn't returned yet. Ambi and I walked around and soon had a trail of little kids on bicycles behind us. Here, in this place where people had almost nothing, no one asked for anything. Here, to be white was not to be a tourist but an NGO worker.

"Come, madams, you want to drink?" two young women asked us in Tamil. We politely declined but were led just the same to a thatched hut where, in the slit of a window, stood bottles of soda layered in dust. Someone had opened a small *kade,* whose offerings consisted of four bottles of soda (now down to two after our visit) and two packages of cream crackers and lemon puffs. The storefront also served as the kitchen and eating area. "Come, come," one of the young women offered. I ducked down into the hut and saw, off in a corner, a darker room with several sleeping mats made from thatched palm scattered about. I went outside and joined Ambi, sipping at what was offered while the camp looked on.

Ambi spoke to the women in Tamil. One young woman knew Sinhalese, and together we managed to piece together a conversation. From my time down south I had learned not to ask about relationships, about who was related to whom. It opened too many doors to loss, particularly when it came to children. And so we indulged in a bit of girl talk. I told the young woman how beautiful her gold necklace and earrings were.

"*Thali,*" someone said.

"*Thali?* What is *thali?*" I asked.

Ambi translated for me. "It's the thick, gold necklace women receive as their wedding gift from their husbands. Some people believe that you need to wear it all the time."

"It was what we had left," a young woman, who looked to be pregnant, said. "When the sea came to the land, many of us had our saris on. Do you know how to wrap a sari?" she asked me with laughing eyes.

"Don't test me on it," I replied, "but kind of. With help. With pins."

They all laughed.

The one who was all smiles continued. "We lost our saris in the wave. The sea unwrapped them from us. When we came out of the sea, we were nearly naked. Some of us had slips on. Some of us had nothing. But we had our jewelry," she said, fingering her *thali* lightly.

I remembered Richard in Arugam Bay telling me how the wave reminded him of a black cobra. I imagined rich gold and red saris floating out to sea, entangled and holding onto each other on the back of the sea serpent. We walked for a bit; kids came over to listen and look. There was a schoolgirl in the group improbably attired in a houndstooth suit two or three sizes too big for her. People walked about wearing clothes from other nations, other lifestyles, other lives. It was one of the stranger disconnects I saw repeatedly in all the camps: that between the poverty of the survivors' living conditions and their attire. After weeks of this, I reached the point where seeing someone in clothes that didn't fit or were unmatched was all I needed in order to reconstruct the story of their past year. It was also in these camps, talking to survivors, that I was able to piece together my own experience, riding on the burlap bags in the bus down south, with the economics of post-tsunami survival. While most of the clothes that people were wearing in the camps were donated by local and foreign aid organizations, the survivors had started a kind of grassroots clothing business by packing up the clothes and taking them to the larger cities such as Colombo, Kandy, or Galle, where they could sell them for a good price. The irony here was that many of the items from France, Italy, and the United States were originally made in Sri Lanka and so had come home again, not just as clothing but as barter. I believed that's what I was sitting on that day in the bus.

As we walked around the camp, I remembered the photography project that Project Galle had begun during tsunami cleanup, and I asked if I could take some pictures. I stood in front of the group that had gathered round, my camera pointed at them. Joined improbably at the hip by loss, dressed in clothes from countries they would never see as they sought to understand what was essentially incomprehensible, they smiled at my camera. There were no old people among them. Young men and women surrounded by a few children stared into my lens. One woman held a baby five months old. She told me that her husband had been killed after the tsunami by LTTE forces in this very camp. "He survived the wave but not the Tigers," she continued, with a smile that seemed disconcerting given the story. "The Tigers shot him at night."

The children wanted to show us the small gardens they had planted—flowers and trees donated by other countries, Germany mostly. After a while I asked the women about more neutral things, forgetting that there was nothing that was neutral in all of this.

"Are you working?" I asked them.

"No, but we want to. There is nothing to do here. There just aren't any jobs. No one has found any for us. The men are back at fishing [I noticed that none of them used the word "husbands"], but even with them it took some months."

"We are scared to live in these shacks," one said. "The wind at night makes them shake."

"Since February we are here," another added. "Before that we were in churches. Now we just wait for the houses."

A man in a checked *sarong,* who had been standing to the side, listening, explained that the reason there were not more houses was that middlemen had started intervening, charging each family 7,500 rupees (roughly $75.00) before construction could begin on each house. "Where to find this money? Some people have paid it, and so they have gotten houses. They want to train us in construction so that we can work on the houses. But then they are not building the houses for us. And we are not wanting to do the construction. We are fishermen; we want to go back to fishing."

Sometimes the locals themselves were reluctant to move into the houses that were being built because they were too far from the sea. "We need to live where we work," was the refrain I heard often, this from people who were deeply divided over whether they even wanted to return to the sea's edge. But it was the only work they knew, and so they wanted to go back to it.

The young woman with the five-month-old baby told me that the aid organizations really had helped. The entire camp, it seemed, was supported by funds from the German government. "We got a lot of clothes just at first when we were in the churches but nothing since we've been resettled to the camps. We've got bicycles. This is how we get our food. We go in to Valachchenai. At first we had health care. People were coming a lot because there were many problems. There were problems with suicide."

"And now?" I asked hesitantly.

She told me about an incident just the week before in which a young woman had tried to poison herself. "The counselors don't come so much anymore."

I had heard this before, and I would hear it later in Jaffna. There just weren't enough people on the island among the local population trained in trauma counseling and those that were didn't speak Tamil.

On our way back into town, I thought about reports I had read that stated that four times as many women as men were killed in Indonesia, Sri Lanka, and India. Women had stayed behind to look for children. That much I knew. Many were unable to swim or climb trees, which had saved some men. Somehow what I had seen around the island thus far didn't suggest that more women had died. What I saw instead were women who had run naked in order to save their children. There were things I saw that I could not explain.

Later Ambi, Dulip, and I went over to GTZ, the German aid organization involved in much of the reconstruction and relief effort here. They had been in the Batticaloa area for some time, working with refugees from the war, and thus already had solid on-site experience before the tsunami hit. Under hibiscus and bougainvillea in the garden, an elegant, middle-aged man, his hair streaked with gray, named Mr. Gunaretnam sat with me and Ambi. He was the only one in the office willing to talk to us. Sitting there with a pile of folders and his cell phone, he dispensed with formalities and got right down to business. We wanted to know more about what we had seen in Pasikudah and Kalkudah. We asked him about the middlemen seemingly extorting money from tsunami survivors before construction could begin.

"To my knowledge, none of this is happening," Mr. Gunaretnam told us. "But such things are always possible. This is a very difficult area. Part of it is geography. We are right on the edge of Tiger territory. There has been a lot of violence here. At night what happens is that the LTTE moves in against the Sri Lankan military. Some of the residents of the camp have gotten caught in the crossfire. There have been sixty killings in the past three months. Not all of them were military. And there is still the problem of land mines here. Not all of them have been cleared. And when they are cleared the Tigers plant new ones."

The day before, Dulip, usually soft-spoken, began shouting at me as I wandered off on foot into a graveyard set back from the road. I wanted, if possible, to see whether these were graves of war or tsunami victims. Perhaps, I thought at first, he found it inauspicious to walk among the graves of the recently departed. His concern was, it turned out, the land mines.

We asked Mr. Gunaretnam why the building wasn't proceeding more quickly. It had been a year already.

"Many, many reasons. Some of it is plain bureaucracy. The government is basically sharing the cost of these houses with the aid organizations. Sometimes the government is not providing the money quickly. We are also trying to train the local people to help build their own houses. Some don't want to live in the area that has been designated for them. There are people all over the island who are rebuilding their huts and thatched-covered restaurants directly on the beach. This is a clear violation of government mandate to build no closer than two hundred meters. But people are doing it, and the government isn't saying anything. Chandrika [Kumaratunga] temporarily relaxed the prohibition because she needed votes for her party in the last election. We will see now what happens."

"What about the suicide rate?" I asked him.

"There were lots of problems at first. Yes, lots of suicides. It was because of the loss and the trauma. It is still about loss, but now we have other factors. There is a high incidence of domestic violence here. The men drink; they come back to the shacks they are living in and they beat up these women."

"So is the suicide rate higher among the women?" I asked.

"Yes, I suppose that is natural," he replied. "The problem is that we don't have trained counselors who speak Tamil who can go in and counsel and work with these people on a sustained basis. Listen, I'm out in the field with the Tigers today. Do you want to come? We can talk more there."

Ambi and I looked at each other, remembering that Dulip had told us he needed to get back to Kandy for another driving job he had contracted.

"I'll come back," I told Mr. Gunaretnam. "I'd like to join you in the field next week if I may."

That night, just before sunset, Ambi and I went to the beach and stepped between houses, buildings, and lives on our way to dip our feet in the Bay of Bengal. Several hundred yards down the beach, three men were working on a boat. Closer in, a few people had begun to use the beach again. A young couple, leaning against a concrete gazebo that had fallen completely over on its side, tentatively embraced. Two older men, deep in conversation, walked on the sand, lending an air of near normality to life on the sea's edge. Two cows further up, separated from the herd, had together walked to the shoreline, vacantly watching the waves until they grew tired and turned toward home. Ambi and I collected shells, sharing the filigree designs with one another.

I walked alone down the beach a little way, alternately looking for shells and sidestepping the surf. Back toward the line of palm and palmyra were the remnants of discarded lives such as I had seen down south—heels of women's shoes, a comb, a pencil, some pieces of things whose form was no longer recognizable. Had people taken their shoes off before they began running or did the sea throw the heels back after claiming their owners? I thought of the saris, the *chalwas,* the sarongs—with or without their owners in them—floating out to sea and turned back to where Ambi and Dulip were waiting.

We never did hear the singing fish of Batticaloa though we tried. We listened at night from the bridge near our hotel as the local fishermen silently pulled small silver fish and prawns from the lagoon by flashlight. We left early the next morning.

The next month on Christmas Eve in Batti, Joseph Pararajasingham, member of Parliament, kind owner of the hotel where he had found rooms where there were no rooms, went to St. Mary's Cathedral for the Christmas Eve service. The bishop of Batticaloa, Kingley Swampillai, was there to officiate. Just after he received Communion, Pararajasingham got up from the Communion rail and was gunned down by two assassins who had entered the church by a side door. He died immediately. His wife, who had thrown herself over his body to protect him from more bullets, was critically wounded and rushed to the hospital. The usual rumors began to circulate. Word moved throughout the northeast of the island that he was assassinated by the Tigers for failing to pay his taxes; others said he was a Tiger and that it was a government job. A journalist told me months later that he was killed by a breakaway faction of the Tigers in the east, led by a former Tiger general named Karuna. When Karuna split with Prabhakaran, ultimately aligning himself with the Sri Lankan government, Pararajasingham had sided with Prabha-karan and become a target for Karuna and his men. This murder on early Christmas morning—a man gunned down while kneeling at prayer—struck a place deep inside everyone in Batti and beyond. The knots that tied this fragile peace together were starting to come undone. And everyone knew it.

Cows on the beach outside of Batticaloa.

CHAPTER 19

The Road to Jaffna

For many on this island, Jaffna is a memory of summer holidays spent at the beaches: long lazy days and the succulent sweetness of Jaffna mangoes, by anybody's standards the best on the island. It's been twenty years since they've been available anywhere in the central and southern part of the country, war having extracted its toll on the general ability of people and things to move about. The seeds of those summer mangoes were transported to Anuradhapura some years back in the hope that they might flourish elsewhere on the island. They took root and the mangoes grew, but the taste wasn't quite the same. Then Elephant House Ice Cream Company came up with a mango ice cream whose flavor calls forth memories of better times as we spoon it out down south. I asked my friends what they wanted me to bring them as I prepared to go to Jaffna just after the elections in late November. "Mangoes" was the universal reply. But when I got to Jaffna, the orange fruits with the green skin were still small green nodules on the tree. It would be June before they were ripe. It had been too long since anyone had been up north. People had remembered June and forgotten December. The sweet and cruel tricks of memory.

When I arrived back to Kandy from Batticaloa with Ambi, there was a call from Udaya. He had found a person willing to put me up in Jaffna. I reached the number the next night. "Can I come?" "Yes, come now," the voice on the other end of the phone replied. "It is relatively calm here." I did my laundry, forgetting that it was never ever going to dry in Kandy, stuffed it the next day into my backpack, and headed down to Colombo again to catch the bus to Jaffna, the place that the Tamils call Yalpanam, the heart of Sri Lankan Tamil culture.

The next evening, I stood outside Atlas Van Lines in Wella-watte, waiting for the Jaffna bus. I watched people threading their way in and out of an odd assortment of nondescript *kades* that sold houseware items, ladies' housedresses, and fruits; their displays spilled out onto the sidewalk. Across the street were sari shops, still open after 9:00 at night and to all appearances still doing a brisk business, proffering silks and cottons from India. But not everything glitters on this street. Some shops, even in daylight, stand unoccupied, with one or two uninviting pieces of jewelry in need of a good dusting displayed in a window also in need of the same. Rumor has it that these are shops in name only and actually serve as fronts for the LTTE where taxes are collected from the local Tamil merchants to support Tiger operations in the north and east. The Colombo Tamil population is not forthcoming on what they do and do not pay, and so rumor and hearsay make the usual rounds. But looking at these shops is also an object lesson in things not always being what they appear. This is a country of middlemen. Thus it is possible to be a gem dealer but have no gems in one's shop. A buyer comes, places an order, and the gem dealer procures the gems through his contacts. Hence the phenomenon of the storefront advertising the very thing that isn't inside. Sometimes a store is just a store, even in wartime.

I looked at my watch. The rain still had not let up. Cars, trishaws, and buses honked their way down Galle Road through the humidity and mud. Some of the waiting passengers sat on the outside steps of the van line office, reorganizing the contents of their baggage now and then as they looked south along the road. It was 9:30. The bus had been due at 9:00. We would not leave until at least 10:00. People sat there on the outside stoop of the van lines, patiently soaked. I sat inhaling the aroma of fried chickpeas from the vat several doors up, wishing I had brought more food for the trip with me. I reached inside my backpack and felt wet clothes.

There is talk here and there that Atlas Travel is owned by the Tamil Tigers, or at least dominated by them. The massive revenues that the LTTE have accrued to support its twenty-three-year-plus war effort are partially the product of taxes paid them, voluntarily and otherwise, from everyone from the Tamil community abroad to the bus line that I was about to take up north. From Switzerland, Canada, and Britain, where the Tamil diaspora is the largest, comes revenue given either voluntarily or by force, estimated to be as high as $2 million a month to support Tiger operations. Tamil friends had told me that a percentage of my bus fare tonight (that is, if the bus ever comes) was indirectly going to support an organization that three U.S. presidents and the European Union have labeled terrorist. Once a month the bus pays a certain amount to the Tigers as tax. I paid 1,200 rupees for a one-way ticket to Jaffna, roughly the equivalent of $12.00, high by Sri Lankan standards. Per trip, Atlas Van Lines pays 1,500 rupees to the driver, who is always Sinhalese, and a somewhat lesser amount for his assistant, always Tamil, that all-important number-two man on buses in Sri Lanka who helps navigate and deals with whatever comes up. And road travel being what it is here, things always come up. Having both Sinhalese and Tamil at the helm keeps the balance right as the bus travels to the north through invisible and constantly shifting political terrain.

Two decades of war have brought travel jitters to this country. I had been trying to make this trip since February 2002, always with the same result: "Not just yet. It's a little tense up here; just wait a bit." Someone had made a contact for me up in Jaffna several months prior to this. I needed a place to stay since there were no hotels. At first the woman agreed and then backed out. It had also been impossible to calibrate just when to go. Theoretically, it had been possible since the cease-fire agreement of February 2002 when the roads opened between Colombo and points north to Jaffna and Trincomalee. In the 1980s people still went back and forth between north and south. Even in the early 1990s one could still move between Jaffna and Colombo by train or by plane. But after the Tigers brought down a civilian plane, killing all on board in 1998, the only way one could fly up north was on military aircraft. The problem, however, was that the Soviet-made Antonov planes with their distinctive markings became Tiger targets as well. The situation was such that people ended up traveling to Jaffna by sea, which meant that they first had to get across the island by road to Trincomalee, then book passage on one of the ships leaving for Jaffna, with no guarantee that they could get on the first or even the second boat. By 1995 even rail and air travel to Trinco and Batticaloa had been halted out of fear that the airport runway was too close to Tiger territory and that the rails were similarly in danger of being bombed. And yet people, somewhat miraculously, continued to travel. They had business and family in the south and vice versa. An acquaintance of mine told me this: "It is impossible to imagine what it was like getting from Jaffna to Colombo. But we had to do it because life went on. First of all we had to start off in the evening for fear of military or Tiger attack. We'd take a van to the Kilali Lagoon just southeast of Jaffna. Then we'd get in a fisherman's boat; a motorized one would have made too much noise. We rowed the boat all the way to Elephant's Pass. Then we used to get into tractors and cross the paddy fields. All this at night. Then we'd get a van again, which would take us to the Tiger checkpoint at Omanthai. The security checkpoint there closed at night but reopened early in the morning. From there it was by van to Colombo. We'd get there late in the afternoon of the same day. I remember once I was with my son. It was dark outside, and we had just put our feet in the boat that would take us across the lagoon. A helicopter appeared out of nowhere and started firing at us. We dove into the bushes and stayed there for hours. That was how we traveled."

This war has seeped down into Colombo, into Ratnapura, into Kandy. The Tigers, I am told, move south by concealing themselves in vegetable trucks and vans. "This is what I have heard," said a Tamil acquaintance. "They construct false sides on the trucks. The trucks come into, say, the Pettah district, unload their vegetables and whatever else they are carrying."

It is now almost four years since the cease-fire went into effect, and travel between north and south still retains the feel of a war that will not go away. To be sure, there have been some improvements. For one thing, the noxious pass system is no longer in effect. Formerly, if a Tamil in the north wanted to go to Colombo, he or she would have to get a letter of sponsorship from a permanent resident of Colombo. Address and identity would have to be checked and verified; then the police in Vavuniya or Jaffna would issue the travel pass. This process could often take weeks and effectively eliminated spur-of-the-moment travel. Flights have resumed between Colombo and Jaffna, though rail service to the north is still a thing of the past. Automobile travel is once again possible, though.

My journey up, like the north itself, was punctuated by unpredictability. That night in Wellawatte just before the bus pulled up, I got a frantic call from Nalini who told me she had just heard something on the radio and that I should turn back. It is hard to know what to do, but it is just as hard to get straight reporting from the press. The bias in the media is huge, the anger on both sides over the atrocities committed enormous. Twenty-some years of virtual noncommunication between north and south have generated their own peculiar fictions that overpower memory. The only narrative that everyone can agree on is that the war, thus far, has not been won by either side and may, in fact, be ultimately unwinnable. The cease-fire hangs by a thread and by the end of 2005 continues to exist in name only. Months later someone in Jaffna would tell me, "We are not at peace. We are in postwar. There you have the difference."

On this particular November night, my feet were tired; the rain was coming; the bus wasn't; and visions of creature comforts were dancing in my head. I could take a *tuk-tuk* and be back at Nalini's in ten minutes. Mutto would make me tea. But I also knew that my life here had been lived south of an invisible line that cuts through this island just north of Anuradhapura and that anything I write, any story I tell about this place, is a story whose vision breaks off at that line. This war had seeped into my everyday. Somehow a lot of emotion, both for me and for the people I know here, had coalesced around this trip. I remained sitting on the steps in the rain.

By 10:00 we were on the road out of Colombo.

This was not the usual bus ride that I had taken all over this island, with music blaring and flashing images of Lord Buddha in the front by the driver's seat. This was a businesslike bus ride. Someplace between Colombo and Negombo, about thirty minutes north of the city, maybe less, a fight broke out between three men in the back who had gotten on the bus drunk. One was unceremoniously ushered off; the remaining two given a serious reprimand by the driver's assistant; the women were all moved up front; and we settled in for a night of silence.

Our route took us up the coast to Puttalam and then inland toward Anuradhapura. From there we headed straight north through an area of Tiger-controlled territory called the Wanni and finally over Elephant Pass, the isthmus that links the northern mainland, or Wanni, with the peninsula itself and finally back into government-controlled territory on the Jaffna Peninsula. From Vavuniya, north of Anuradhapura, the road turns into the A9, linking Kandy in the central highlands to Jaffna in the north. The highway now goes by another name—the Highway of Death—so called because in 1998, during Operation Jaya Sekurui, 1,418 soldiers were killed and approximately 10,000 wounded as the army attempted to open the A9 up to Jaffna. The government needed to reclaim this seventy-five-kilometer swath from the Tigers so that they could move military and civilian supplies between north and south. But since 1995, when they retook Jaffna, the Sri Lankan military has had to deliver supplies and food to the north by air and sea since the Wanni linking the two areas has been under Tiger control. And in April 2000 the LTTE recaptured Elephant Pass, the vital link from the south to the Jaffna Peninsula.

Looking out the window, I thought to myself that the return trip would be less arduous. Someone had told me that the bus sometimes takes the straighter, shorter route following the coast down to Colombo skirting Wilpattu National Park. There are problems taking this shorter route at night so the driver avoids it as well as the area north of Puttalam. I had heard that by the mid-1990s Sinhalese soldiers had begun deserting the army, as things were not going well, and the military was suffering one grueling setback after another. Some simply returned to their villages and lived obscurely; others vanished into areas such as Wilpattu, where they became poachers and robbers. Their hunting, evidently, was not confined exclusively to animals. The park had just recently reopened, and by all accounts, it was not only the animals that were posing the problems there. But I saw none of this in the darkness. My sightseeing was confined to four security checkpoints—two government and two Tiger—which turned a 250-kilometer ride (155 miles), a two-and-one-half hour trip in the United States and a seven-hour trip on these roads under ideal conditions, into a fifteen-hour marathon.

"You know," a Tamil friend told me, "there was a time here when you could take the seven thirty a.m. train from Jaffna and be in Colombo by noon; or the two o'clock from Colombo and be in Jaffna by evening tea."

I was awake for most of the night. An hour or two out of Colombo I looked out the window and thought that we were probably near Mannar. From there you can look over Adam's Bridge toward Dhanushkod at the southern tip of Tamil Nadu. It's the place where Sita in the Indian epic *The Ramayana* was captured by Ravana and saved by Rama, the incarnation of the god Vishnu. You can see the lights of India from Mannar, but it would be awhile before anyone can go there. It hadn't been de-mined yet.

It was around midnight when the driver's assistant collected our passports and identity cards. First it was foreign passports—i.e., mine —then Sri Lankan identity cards, then foreign passports held by Tamils. He clearly had done this before, lots of times. He put them into discrete piles, started filling out forms, and we waited.

1:00 a.m., military checkpoint one. Thandikulam. We had moved into a border area just north of Vavuniya on the outskirts of the Wanni that is under Tiger control. This was the last government military checkpoint until the Jaffna Peninsula. We moved silently down from the bus through a series of sheds under tin roofs. I had one shoe on; the other had skidded beneath several rows of seats in the darkness when the bus driver had slammed on the brakes to avoid something crossing the road an hour ago. The women proceeded to one shed, the men to another to be body searched. The luggage ended up in yet a third shed, where it, too, was searched. We were then separated into other areas depending on the kinds of passports we held. No one was quite sure where to go. Or what line to get in. The place was badly marked and had a familiar air of lassitude about it, populated by soldiers who, I suspected, were as fed up with this war as was the rest of the country. We stood listening to the drizzle, watching the soldiers inspect inside and underneath the bus. One of the Tamil women and I nodded to each other.

Once we were back on the bus, it seemed only minutes before we arrived at yet another checkpoint. This was the first Tiger checkpoint at Omanthai. The man sitting next to me, a tall Tamil in his mid-forties, spoke to me for the first time. "This is an LTTE checkpoint. You must get down here. You must get down at each checkpoint." Someone handed me my other shoe.

This place had an altogether different feel to it. Signs were every-where, telling us where to go. The people processing us all seemed to be under the age of twenty. I saw no soldiers at the tables, only civilians—teenagers, dressed in starched red and white. Behind the open-air processing center stood soldiers who were clearly LTTE cadres. There was no mistaking them. They had their eyes trained on us. Someone in Jaffna had told me over the phone to be prepared for anything here and to remain cool when I am interviewed. I was not interviewed. In fact, I was seemingly of no interest whatsoever to the young women checking documents. Of more interest were the Tamils with foreign passports, who were siphoned off into an-other line where they *were* interviewed. Only two English words were uttered to me the entire time: "Laptop?" "Yes," I answered to the inquiry. "DVDs?" I answered in the negative. I was told later they were looking primarily for pornography. From here I passed through the women's cubicle, separated from the rest of the line by a muslin curtain, for the routine body search. With my back to her I stood as a young woman with her hair pinned behind her cap did the obligatory body check top to bottom. It was businesslike and nothing more. She never turned me around, never met my eyes. I stepped out into the night and into an open-air building resembling a ramada.

We sat on wooden benches in an open-air shed while another young woman handed out forms to the passengers, all except me, in Tamil and Sinhalese, listing the duty owed on various items be-ing brought into Tiger territory. Anything that is potentially sellable and not for one's personal use is taxed by the Tigers. Both sides are cautious about the importation of items that can be construed as military. During the war one couldn't bring chocolate and instant noodles into Tiger territory since they were part of a soldier's stan-dard military ration. But things change from week to week. There was a time when the government wouldn't allow batteries through security for fear they would be appropriated by the Tigers. Now, as it happened, the peninsula was under the control of the Sri Lankan government, the lights were on, and no one at the checkpoints seemed to have much interest in whether we were carrying batteries or not. Electronic equipment is another matter altogether, since their component parts can be used by either side to build military hardware. I had also heard it said that the Sri Lankan Army would expressly forbid precisely those items that Jaffna residents were in need of so that they could expect bribes. When electricity was at a premium, Jaffna needed matches. Businessmen and private citizens would pack them in their luggage knowing they were forbidden but also knowing that they could get them through government security checkpoints by slipping a guard some money under the table.

Above our heads in the shed were colored posters of Tiger martyrs with inscriptions under them I couldn't read. But I could read the pictures. Girls in pigtails with their necks slashed in half. Women and children whose bodies lay in the middle of a road. Men in uniform, dead. Alongside them posters of the leader of the LTTE, Vellupillai Prabhakaran, in camouflage suit: pudgy and determined with uncommonly small, beady eyes staring out from under his army cap. This is the man who has given his followers permission to kill him should he lay down his arms or desert the cause one moment before liberation is achieved in his lifetime. Born in the north of the Jaffna Peninsula, he has been at the helm of the LTTE since 1973, amassing weaponry to rival that of a state army. As I thought about the organization he has assembled—the cadres of suicide bombers, the assassinations, the millions of dollars raised in taxes from Sri Lankan Tamils both here and abroad, and the kidnapping of young children to serve in his Baby Brigade—I remembered something that a friend at Peradeniya once said to me. "He is a monster, but he is one of our own making. The kidnapping of the kids, some of them in broad daylight. How do you think this happened? The Tamils in the north all fled to escape the violence. They went to India, Canada, Australia, the UK—wherever they could find other Tamils. There was a population problem. He needed soldiers. I think he himself was a child soldier."

After we were on our way again, I spent most of the night looking out the window of the bus. The darkness outside was illuminated by patches of wet moonlight, and I watched jungle disappear off the map into brush, as the terrain gradually flattened. Just at daylight we made yet another stop.

"Tiger or military?" I asked my neighbor.

"Neither. Sacred water stone. Murikandy Pillayar Shrine."

I looked out and saw people washing themselves and drinking water from what looked like a cistern. The bus emptied quickly as the passengers hurried to make offerings and pray in front of a modest little shrine, some breaking coconuts as a sign of good fortune. I got off the bus and wandered around, knowing I was in the middle of something important, yet not understanding what it was. This was not a bathroom stop. I watched people scooping up ladles of water either to drink or to splash themselves with as a kind of symbolic bath. They lit incense and intoned their prayers at this small shrine so deeply reflective of Hindu culture.

"This place," explained my neighbor when we had all gotten back on the bus, "is auspicious. When they were building the road up here from Kandy under the British, there was a big problem with finding water. They had to push a cart with oxen all the way up to Murikandy to get water and then bring it back for the laborers. The man who was in charge of the road building had a dream. In his dream it was told to him that he would be able to dig a well with water along this road but that first he had to go find the body of a holy man who had died in the jungle around Murikandy. He was to give him proper funeral rites and find the special stone that the holy man used to take with him wherever he went. And so the man in charge went with his workers in search of the body of the holy man. They found it, gave it the proper burial, and put the stone inside a shed that they built. They came back to their road project and immediately found water. Now we are in the dry area so this shrine and the water commemorates this auspicious event of finding water when there was none. You see the north has not only bad stories. It also has some very good ones."

I smiled and thanked him for the tale. I complimented him on his English, and he smiled unassumingly. I sat half in daydream, thinking about the competing stories between north and south as the first real light of day hit the land hard. I saw fields left idle, punctuated some-times by palmyra trees and dried bramble that obscured the view for miles. The tin roofs of the south and central part of the island were replaced here by thatched roofs woven over thatched huts. We passed twenty years of war—the contours of charred houses we saw in Batticaloa multiplied, with vines growing in the spaces between the stones, the roads increasingly delineated by sandbags, barricades, and barbed wire.

"First time in Jaffna?" my Tamil neighbor asked me.

"Yes, first time in Jaffna," I replied.

He told me he did this commute once a week between his two businesses, one in Colombo, one in Jaffna. I asked him how he man-aged a soul-destroying trip like this so often.

"You get used to it. I sleep through most of it. We're almost there."

We shared a little food. I looked out the window at the land as we moved over kilometers of vast, unoccupied space, not terribly dry by Arizona standards but certainly such by standards here. The northeast monsoon season had settled in, so the land was as fertile as it would be all year. There were no paddy fields, no tangle of jungle, just miles of flat earth dotted with a makeshift hut every so often. Sometimes I saw a sapling of a palmyra growing in the sand in front of these dwellings, something oddly out of place where so little else seemed to be cultivated. This inconsequential image of the one palm in front of a hut would return to me the next Sunday in the Tigers' Heroes' Cemetery. But for now I watched a woman and her four children walking along the road, the woman with a water jug on her head, the stuff of which tourist pictures are made.

"Where are they going?" I asked my neighbor.

"To the well. They have about a six-kilometer walk."

"And then back home?"

"Then back home."

I asked him what these people were doing out here. There was no village, no community, no agriculture, nothing. He told me that possibly they were refugees from the war. "A lot of people lost their homes and came out here. They had nowhere else to go."

"Is your family okay?" I asked.

"Most of them."

I didn't pursue this. Our talk was careful and restrained. We were quiet for awhile.

"What about food?" I asked him as we passed more huts woven together from the debris of war.

"They get bags of rice and *dhal* delivered to a central point, and they pick them up there." Foreseeing my question, he continued: "They carry them home."

One more Tiger checkpoint, this at Elephant Pass, seized by the Tigers in 2000, thereby shifting the military balance in this area. There was no vegetation on either side of the road anymore. It was barren save for barbed wire and the water in the lagoon. I had read that in the eighteenth century the Dutch, in order to consolidate their trade monopoly in the country, added elephants to their already-flourishing export business of areca palms, chanks (spindle-shaped shells), and pearls. Captured on the mainland of the island, the elephants were driven up to the Jaffna Peninsula, where they crossed the lagoon at the area that became known as Elephant Pass and were put into stalls to await export to other countries. But now Elephant Pass conjures up images no longer of elephants but of war. This was the military stronghold that everyone thought was impenetrable, and it came as a decided setback to the Sri Lankan Army that the Tigers, numbering only five thousand strong, were able to take it from fifteen thousand government troops. Most feel that what Prabhakaran was able to accomplish was the result of brilliant military strategy, the lessons he had managed to extract from previous Tiger losses, and the demoralization of the Sri Lankan troops due to the constant shift in military leadership. The taking of this part of the island was anything but sudden. The LTTE had been making gradual inroads into this area since 1998 in a series of maneuvers that for propaganda reasons had gone unreported in the Colombo press. To celebrate, groups of Tiger cadres and some civilians had walked from the Jaffna Peninsula south into the Wanni along the Elephant Pass causeway while others walked from south to north. For many of these people, this was the first time in living memory that they were able to cross to and from the peninsula. For the Tigers, and even for Tamils in the north with no Tiger affiliation, it was a defining moment.

There was a kind of perverse silence to these roads as we inched toward Jaffna. Oddly, they breathed a peace and calm so absent in Kandy. But it was a peace that belied a much different reality, and I knew it. It was a weekday and there were virtually no cars on the roads, mainly due to the government's practice of severely rationing delivery of gasoline to the north so as to strangle the Tigers' hold. For most of the war, the only cars in Jaffna had been a few Austins, relics of the early part of the twentieth century. By the mid-1980s, the central government had set up a "fuel control plan," which limited the number of liters each vehicle owner could purchase in a month. Motorcycle owners were allowed fifteen liters, car owners thirty or sometimes less. And so the population of Jaffna became a bike-riding one, with the addition more recently of the motor scooter. Between 1990 and 1996, the gas situation in the north spiraled completely out of control from government fear that the Tigers would use the fuel for their own vehicles. People in Jaffna adapted their cars to run on kerosene, which was in plentiful supply because it was used primarily for cooking. Later, a new Jaffna acquaintance would tell me how he would put just enough kerosene under the hood of his car near the carburetor to allow the engine to "smell it." This was enough to get the engine started.

"One more checkpoint," my neighbor informed me. "This one's government. This is the easy one."

There was a noticeable feeling of relaxation on the bus as people pulled out fish patties and egg sandwiches. Somebody handed me a patty and a *samosa*. I thought to myself that I was going to have to stock up better with food for the return trip.

We arrived in Jaffna at 2:00 in the afternoon. For a final time Atlas Van Lines unloaded us and our bags. I stepped out of the bus onto the sand-lined streets near Jaffna University bustling with students who seemed impervious to the war. For the moment at least, I preferred not to think about the return ride in front of me in several weeks.

Fishermen on Jaffna Peninsula.

CHAPTER 20

In Jaffna

Jaffna carries thirty years of war lightly on its shoulders. In a town where nothing has been normal for far longer than many local residents have been alive, cobbling together something approaching everyday life is a way both of surviving the present and of recouping the past. Ads for cell phones hang on banners across the street, announcing in English, "We've got you covered, Jaffna." Signs and ads in English appear up here as more than a passing nod to English as the bridge language between Tamil and Sinhalese. Many here know English. One of the odder features of modern hi-tech life is that residents find themselves in a place where basic foodstuffs cannot get through, where movement between geographical and political zones is severely restricted, yet they can receive a call from someone half a world away who is putting dinner on the table. Tamils in Toronto talk to Tamils in Jaffna who talk to their relatives in Australia.

I was lulled by the comfort of the daily ritual up here. I was staying at a guesthouse on Chetty Street Lane where I seemed to be the only guest. The day blasted into my room at 4:00 a.m. with the roosters crowing, followed by the antics of two tomcats in the back yard. Only minutes later the bell from St. Martin's Monastery down the road announced Matins, followed by a different bell ringing from nearby Nallur Temple, announcing the morning *pooja*. There are as many monasteries and churches up here as Hindu temples due to the Portuguese, Dutch, and English presence, dating from the seventeenth century. By 6:00 the first stirrings had commenced in the kitchen, with something that sounded like the Tamil hit parade playing in the background. I disentangled myself from the mosquito netting, careful not to create another point of entry for Jaffna's mosquito population, and headed into the bathroom, where I showered in water whose temperature was that of the weather that day. Once dressed, I wandered out into the front courtyard to survey the day's beginnings. I passed the gentleman at the makeshift front desk, who in the first few days seemed distressed that a guest had arrived. But after two weeks his chill began to thaw slightly as he realized I was not going away anytime soon.

Most mornings I wandered out with my tea and watched the woman next door picking delicate white jasmine blossoms from the trees in front of the guesthouse. She nodded and smiled at me. We shared no language, but I gathered that the jasmine was for the Hindu temple down the street. Outside the gate the neighborhood goats had already installed themselves in the middle of the road, and the cows, for their part, had begun their daily saunter, helping themselves to what grew along the road's edge. The milkman moved up and down the street on his bicycle, threading his way between the animal population until he stopped at our gate and announced himself with the beep of the bicycle horn. Our kitchen staff of two emerged with their empty milk bottles, which the milkman proceeded to fill from the metal canister attached to the back of his bicycle. In twenty minutes I was drinking milk tea that tasted like onion grass eaten by the cows just hours before.

I had been given the loan of a bicycle and moved with others along sand-swept roads past temples, cows, and goats and past people who never asked me where I was going or what country I was from or whether I wanted a *tuk-tuk* ride. Over the years, I suspected, people had learned, as a means of survival, to go quietly about their business.

I took long bike rides down roads lined in the blue and rose pastel of Hindu temples, as the figures of Rama, Sita, Ganesh, and Shiva oversaw the progression of cyclists from their station on the outer walls of the temples. Outside Nallur Temple, just blocks from where I was staying, the local peanut and popcorn lady sold her wares in the evening. If the wind was blowing right, I could sometimes smell the proximity of the sea.

But enough of this. I catch myself beginning to wax romantic about it. Except for the central downtown market area, where beans, onions, and over twenty different kinds of bananas shared loud, raucous space with buses and *sari* shops, the city for the most part moved quietly. It was the first thing I noticed, but I also knew that city streets are rarely silent of their own accord. Just down the street from the guesthouse were dwellings essentially reduced to shells, relieved of everything that made them livable. Outside walls had been obliterated, exposing all the rooms, where goats had now taken up residence. Spaces were filled in by vines that threaded their way in and out of grenade wounds and bullet scars. It was this way everywhere, on every street. There was no section of this city that did not contain the traces of something now razed to the ground. The eye of my camera was not able to take in this war and give it focus because there was no focal point. It was impossible to bring any visual integrity to this rubble.

Someone called me from Colombo to see how I was doing and asked if I had seen any Tigers yet. I hadn't, and I wouldn't. The fact that the city itself has been under government military control here since 1996 has all but forced Tamil Tiger operations underground, turning the conflict into a shadow war. But for those who live here, they are very much a presence even though they are not visible on a day-to-day basis. I had been told that I could identify them by the red motorcycles they ride.

A local Tamil told me a story that he thought would give me the best sense of how the Tigers function. Several months ago his house had been broken into.

"Was this a Tiger operation?" I asked him, remembering Udaya's stories of the JVP breaking into people's bungalows at the university during the student insurrections.

"No, no, they do not do these things. These things are done by our own local robbers. The Tigers are very strict. They are the ones who keep the order in this town. When things like that happen, we are supposed to call the military, the Sri Lankan military, I mean. In our case, they came and did a report. But then someone, maybe a neighbor, saw something and reported something, and suddenly two men arrived on motorcycles. The Tigers are almost always driving these motorcycles. They arrived at our house after the military left and looked around. One left us his number and told us to call if we have some problems again. So that is how it all works. There is no building that says 'Tiger Headquarters,' but they are there and actually they can be of help. They do not tolerate any breaking of laws or any disorder. They are very, very disciplined. But the thing is that we don't see them."

I thought about what he said later. Life up here is strictly circumscribed by a group that one rarely sees, but when it comes to the struggle for the homeland, the laws bend to accommodate this group's activities. Neither side in this war views the violence perpetrated by its own side as anything other than self-defense.

"One wants to see people in tiger stripes up here," a woman I met told me jokingly. "That's just not the way it is. You have to remember that so much is hidden beneath what you actually see."

Home and homelessness are another one of those topics that sits just under the surface of the everyday as the foundation of people's lives continues to shift. I was introduced to a young woman who, over tea, told me that she and her family had moved fifteen times in twenty years. "There would be a vacant house or a piece of property next door and someone would move in, either the government forces or the Tigers. They would be using it as a storage area for arms or whatever. So we knew we couldn't stay, and we moved on to the next place. Finally, we decided to shift ourselves out to Delft Island off the northeast coast here. It's the place with the wild ponies. So we went there, thinking we would be safe. Then the government forces attacked it. I think I am still feeling the trauma of this. I don't know if I will ever be able to settle and have a home. War and homelessness have been the norm ever since I was born."

What, I wonder, constitutes the norm in a war zone? Normal life, a professor at the university told me, was no electricity in the city of Jaffna for ten years and severely rationed gas. The young woman who had moved so many times recounted what it was like trying to get schooling throughout all this. She told me that for her entire education up to university she did her homework in the faint illumination of wick soaked in coconut oil and then lit in a small clay pot. One sees row upon row of these small, delicate vessels, lighting the entrances to *kovils* and temples. They diffuse a soft light appropriate for meditation and prayer, but reading by them is out of the question.

"This is all the oil we could afford," she explained. "My eyes are ruined. My brother was trying to study for his A levels during all of this. There was only one light in the city at night and that was the street lamp outside the International Red Cross. I guess they had a generator. My brother went there every night with his books and sat on the street underneath that lamp to study for the exams. He passed; he did very well. But this was our norm. I missed my childhood."

Several days later I was invited to go up to the northern part of the Jaffna Peninsula to see what the tsunami had left in its wake. The area is located in the high-security zone, heavily guarded by the Sri Lankan military because of its proximity to the sea and the all-too-real threat of arms and other contraband coming in over these waters to supply the Tigers. Six of us piled into a van and headed up to Point Pedro, the area on the Jaffna Peninsula closest to India. At the security checkpoint we handed over cell phones, passports, and identity cards to military police and picked up two extra passengers, young Sinhalese soldiers whose rifles rested casually on their knees. Not much older than twenty, they silently accompanied us up to the northern shore, partially to watch us, partially to protect us. There were areas up here that had not yet been de-mined. We drove where we were told, passing fields thick with birdlife and war's decay. We stopped at the Keerimali Baths, where the land reaches out to touch the Palk Straits. A legend about this place says that a *sadhu,* a wandering holy man from India named Nagulaswami, with a face like a mongoose, came to bathe in these springs. The miraculous powers of the waters transformed his face into a human one. People come here to bathe because of the healing powers of the waters, but I saw no evidence that anyone had been here in a long, long time. Inside the building, which has separate entrances for men and women, the walls sprouted mold of decay and neglect.

We stood and looked out to sea. Waters the color of light turquoise and pristine white sands put the tired southern beaches to shame. But they were also largely inaccessible, sequestered behind the same old barbed wire, military posts, and sandbags that were probably as sick of this war as the people who lived here.

One man pointed out onto the water. "I used to go to the movies over there."

"You're pointing toward India," I reminded him.

"Yes, yes, quite right. We would all take a boat over to Valvettithurai. It is just—I don't know the miles—maybe it is twenty-five from here to there. So, we would see the Hindi movies and come back that same evening. This was in the 1960 and 1970s. Have you seen Hindi movies?"

I explained about the monkeys taking the TV antennas in Kandy, a problem that limited our TV viewing. But yes, I had seen a few.

"Our Tigers here were forbidding the movie magazines to come in from India. Maybe they thought they were not sufficiently serious. Maybe too much women's flesh. So here in Jaffna Town there was a big outcry. People were really angry, so the Tigers said alright, we will allow Bollywood magazines in again. But now our situation is very bad, and we have the magazines but we can't afford to buy them. They are four times here what they are in India. What to do?"

"But you can get the Hindi movies here?" I asked him.

"Yes, direct from India. We are also now seeing American movies on our television sets."

I was afraid to ask which ones, judging by the sort of grade D films that Hollywood has a bad habit of exporting to developing countries.

"John Wayne, Chuck Norris, Rambo. We see these."

I noticed that the soldiers standing over on the side suddenly came to life hearing the names of Norris and Rambo.

"Our kids in Jaffna," he went on, "have been joining the Tigers without thinking of the consequences of their actions. They see these films and they get the impression that carrying a gun is wonderful. Carrying a gun is not wonderful."

"I know," I replied. "We have the same problems in America. Our children are brought up on violence from the toy stores to the

TV sets to the movie theaters. It's a complete disgrace. But isn't Prabhakaran also insisting that each family give one child to the cause?"

"It is mainly in the Wanni that this is happening. But children from Jaffna are joining because they want to be heroes."

"The Tigers have earned the reputation of a terrorist group mainly because of the child kidnappings," I told him. "From what I hear, these kidnappings are taking place all over Tiger territory."

"Look." He turned to me. "Why would the Tigers kidnap children up here? They need our support. Everyone who is supporting the Tigers will turn away if the Tigers are taking their children. Yes, there are kidnappings, but it is not by the Tigers. It is Karuna's men. They are a splinter group from the Tigers. Colonel Karuna is operating out of Trincomalee. He also has government support because he is against Prabhakaran. You must believe me. These are the people doing the kidnappings. The Tigers up here need the support of the people who live here. The press down south, the press everywhere, says it's the Tigers. It's not; it's Karuna's men."

I was thinking about what the man had said as we moved over to Naguleswaram, a temple sacred to Shiva in another area devoid of human activity—no houses, no worshippers, only a few soldiers over on the side of the temple, their eyes trained on us.

We walked into the musical frenzy of a *pooja*. To the sound of bells ringing, cymbals clashing, and drums beating, I watched an elderly Hindu priest tending to the gods, setting offerings before them and lighting incense. I was gently led around and told what to do, understanding nothing. The priest looked at me to ask my permission to tie the string of blessings and prayers around my wrist. I nodded and bowed. His *sarong* wrapped carefully around him, his chest bare, his body cleansed before the gods, this priest conducts most of these *poojas* alone, his own people having left the area. Cut off from everything and everyone but his own faith, he continues his rituals. I was deeply moved.

A kilometer or two further on lay a small fishing village where twenty or so young men in their *sarongs* followed us as we walked down a road dusted in sand.

"Come. I want to show you something." One of the young men in our group turned to me. And he led me to Prabhakaran's house.

The sign in front identified the place in Tamil, Sinhalese, and English. It was a small, unimposing structure with blue paint peeling from its inside and outside walls. Nobody had bothered to turn it into a museum or even some sort of historical landmark. "This isn't Prabhakaran's way," the young man told me. But it was decorated with streamers and balloons, since Prabhakaran's birthday was coming up. From all appearances the house had been left to fend for itself, letting time and the work of graffiti mongers do with it what they would. But this was a different kind of graffiti, one that paid homage to the cause. Someone had written in chalk, "Pongu Thamiz 2005," a festival that celebrates the unity of the Tamil people. Pro-Tiger slogans were scratched or painted onto the walls, sharing space with events and dates in the conflict.

As I turned to leave the house, I noticed that the group of men that had followed us down the road was waiting outside the shell of what used to be the front door. "Why does America call the Tamil Tigers a terrorist organization?" asked one of them in Tamil. A young woman in our group translated for me.

I answered that I didn't know but added that I didn't support the policies of the Bush administration. "But we're not the only ones," I continued. "There are eleven other countries that call the Tigers a terrorist organization."

I couldn't tell if they knew that or not. Their attention was focused on the United States because of me. But it quickly shifted to what we were doing there and what I was doing in Jaffna. The people in Point Pedro don't get many visitors these days.

I asked the men if they were fishermen and they nodded. "This is the caste that Prabhakaran came from," one of them told me.

"You have to understand," a member of our group explained to me, "that to be a fisherman is both a profession and a caste. We say that the person belongs to the fisherman caste."

"But I read that Prabhakaran's father worked for the postal service."

"It doesn't matter. If you are born into a caste, you stay in that caste even if you do some other kind of work. Sometimes there are exceptions. There is a man very high up in the Tigers whom Prabhakaran helped move up in the caste system, but generally one dies in the caste into which one was born."

"So this is then the lowest caste?" I asked, noticing that the local men were still gathered round trying to get the gist of the conversation.

"No, no. This fisherman caste can be very educated. The castes under them are the *ambatan*. These are the barbers; then one down are the toddy tappers. Our lowest are the drumbeaters, the *paraiyar*. For example, my daughter will marry soon. We are trying to find the right person for her, but he must be within our caste. We are looking all over with my wife. We are members of a high caste so there will be no problem. My daughter will have the best education and a good comfortable life and good status. But look here at these people. They are fisherman caste. For them there is no opportunity. Prabhakaran wants to change that. There are people up here who do not like his methods. He was behind the assassination of Rajiv Gandhi in 1991. Gandhi hadn't wanted to pull the Indian Peace Keeping Forces out. It was a female suicide bomber who detonated the bomb that killed Gandhi, herself, and I think about eleven others, but it was Prabhakaran who was behind it. This was a terrible blunder. We have not forgotten this. It was a terrible, terrible blunder. But one of the reasons Prabhakaran is popular up here is that he wants to do away with the caste system. People are supporting that a lot. He also wants to do away with the dowry system. People cannot afford these things. I am buying a house for my daughter as a dowry. And people are marrying based on how much dowry there is. There are many reasons why people up here would support the Tiger cause. But not the Tigers' methods. There is a difference."

"Are these fishermen we've been talking to Tigers?" I asked as we left Prabhakaran's house behind and headed back to the van.

"No, not Tigers," he answered. "Just people who live here. They want their lives to be better. Let's go."

That afternoon we found a portion of shore that was accessible near the Point Pedro lighthouse. The barricades had lifted to allow the fishing boats that lined the shore to come and go. We walked along the water's edge just feet from the refuse that the war and the wave had deposited on the shore. There were no structures here that one could really call houses, just shells, just frames. People were living in fragments of doorways, on concrete slabs that once were walls. As I walked along what had once been a road by the shore, villagers looked up, and then went back to what they were doing. No one approached to tell us their story. An old woman was busy laying small fish out on a piece of material to dry. Fishermen were repairing their nets.

People are a lot more circumspect up here about whom they will talk to. Small wonder. For my part, I was still trying to draw some sort of visual and perhaps useless distinction between what the war and tsunami had left in their wake. The detritus looked as if it had been created yesterday. The Marines had come in and done major cleanup on the beaches along the western and southern coasts in the immediate aftermath of the catastrophe. Not so in the north. I remembered that Alan and Tissa, in their e-mails to me right after the tsunami, had told me that the consensus was that the Tigers had appropriated the aid coming up from the south and redistributed it in their own name to tsunami victims. Whatever happened, two facts remained indisputable: the Marines never set foot up here; and significantly less aid got delivered to the Jaffna Peninsula than to other parts of this island. Beyond that, one gets caught up in the different narratives of what did and didn't happen and why.

I walked down to the shore past the usual lineup of UN boats and waded into the water. Three small boys were swimming and splashing, and I asked them if they wanted to have their pictures taken. A minute later I showed them their instant selves on the camera, and they struck picture-perfect poses for ten more shots while the fishermen readied their nets for the next day. One of the young men in our group approached a fisherman to ask him how the fishing has been since the tsunami. There was really no difference, he told us. The fishing was good enough. The problem was that every time he went out he needed military permission to fish the waters. He didn't have to pay, but he had to get the piece of paper, get it stamped, and take it with him.

"And if you don't get the permission paper?" I ventured.

"If I don't, there is a fine to pay, and I have no more permission to fish. Big problem."

There is much worry about what lies out in these blue pastel waters, particularly beyond the government-controlled area. Almost every week stories appear in the press about the government seizing trawlers loaded with material that could be used for making explosive devices. Many of them come from Tamil Nadu in southern India, but even that fact is deceptive. There is no one country that is supplying arms to the Tigers—but rather arms dealers. Kalashnikov rifles seized by the military point the finger less at Russia than at a proliferating arms trade in Pakistan, India, and China that makes it possible for the Tigers to purchase what they need either already assembled or in component parts. The government's goal is to strangle the flow of arms and materials to the north through heightened security in and around these waters. The Tiger response, and one consistent with their aims, is to blow up the ships, and often themselves as well, rather than allow their cargo to fall into enemy hands.

There is geological evidence that Sri Lanka, some 200 million years ago, was part of the immense supercontinent of Gondwanaland linking India, Antarctica, Australia, and the Malagasy Republic. There are those who believe that India may be wishing to politically reattach the piece that broke off its southern coast in the Late Jurassic era. Geology, however, seems to be working on Sri Lanka's behalf, as scientific evidence suggests that the island continues to move away from the Indian subcontinent in a counterclockwise rotational movement as a miniplate. Geology aside, many see India's participation in Sri Lankan politics as overly meddlesome. India has been a powerful player in the civil war. Not only are Sri Lanka's Tamils racially, linguistically, and culturally linked to the Tamils in India's most southern state, but during the worst days of the war in the 1990s and again in 2005, many fled back to India for safety, waiting for sufficient peace to be restored in their country before returning to the Jaffna Peninsula. Aid in the form of armaments has been funneled to the Tamil Tigers through the southern Indian state of Tamil Nadu as well as through Tamil communities abroad. Between 1987 and 1990, relations with India were complicated by the fact that India was brought in as peacekeeper to try to resolve the conflict between the LTTE and the government. Many, quite rightly, saw India's presence as disingenuous since Tamil militants had been training covertly in India since at least 1983. The first group of Tamil Tigers was trained in India's Utar Pradesh, its second in Himachal Pradesh by instructors from the Indian Army. By 1989 the Indian Peace Keeping Force was asked to leave, at which point war broke out again between the LTTE and the central Sinhalese government. It would not be an exaggeration to say that for many Sri Lankans, irrespective of where one is on the island, India is far too close . . . and perhaps too meddlesome.

I watched the fisherman repairing his nets with calloused fingers. He had told us that his house was washed away by the wave. "Do you have plans to rebuild?" I asked him.

"This is my village," he said, waving his hand over the entire area of stone. "I have lived here my whole life. My house was shelled in 1983, and so I moved. I moved lots of times. Then the sea came to the land and the house was broken again." He pointed to a pile of rock next to another pile along what used to be a street or an alleyway. "No, I have no plans to rebuild. I am living with relatives. Why should I rebuild? First it was the war, now the tsunami. Now it looks as if we may have war again. Do you know why I don't want war?" he continued. "Well, when I was young I had strong legs and they could carry me. Now I am an old man, and I know I can't run fast enough to escape it anymore."

There was something else I learned from him, something I had heard in the refugee camps outside Batticaloa. Oddly, it came less as a complaint than as an observation on the part of those who had been displaced already by the war. He added that more help was coming to tsunami victims than to those who had suffered in the war. There were some people in the north, according to him, whose homes had been demolished by the war but who were now living better since the tsunami because their houses had been located next to the shore.

"There's another thing," said one of our group who had been translating for me. "There's no concrete up here. It's like this. Some of the NGOs have tried to help rebuild, but the government is not allowing that much cement up here to the north. They are afraid the Tigers might use it to make bunkers. Look, here's an example: cement in the south costs 650 rupees for fifty kilograms; up here it's 2,250 for the same amount. You see what we're dealing with. These problems all come from Colombo. They won't allow the development of any industry up here. They are choking us. We can't move freely; we can't develop economically; we can't get the same access to education as the Sinhalese students in the south. You don't need to support the Tigers to feel these things."

It is not only industry and cement that stand in the way of rebuilding homes on the Jaffna Peninsula. I had read about a psychiatrist in Jaffna, Daya Somasundaram, who studies war trauma and how the mass exodus of Tamils from Jaffna in 1995 during the government's seizure of the Jaffna Peninsula had affected those who were forced to leave. Somasundaram had compared the concept of home for a Tamil to a womb. When people returned to Jaffna after the exodus, they no longer had any relationship with their homes. They couldn't be bothered with repairs, or even cleanliness. It seemed hardly worth it. Among those who came back, there were many who believed that their homes had come to be haunted by evil spirits.

I thought about what the fisherman had said as I walked that afternoon on a beach strewn with concrete, rock, and pieces of scrap metal. In an odd way, there was more security to be found in remaining homeless, less to lose and mourn over. I imagined Jon on the San Jose Freeway with his possessions in the back of his car as he had recently been forced to sell his house. Ninety degrees of separation, tremors of a different sort. I watched the fisherman carefully tie the knots in his net and thought of Jon designing computer models—the ways we keep the fabric of our life together in times stricken by the waves of misfortune; the things we do to keep the evil spirits at bay.

It was Prabhakaran's birthday, November 26, to be exact. Jaffna was draped in streamers, and my pockets were full of uneaten hard candies that had been proffered at every intersection by young Tigers in honor of the day. Music was being piped through every public address system in the city. It was also the Day of Remembrance in the Tamil north. People were simultaneously celebrating and mourning.

Later in the day the families who had lost someone in the war would gather at the various cemeteries where the war dead are buried. At 6:00 in the evening Prabhakaran would give his yearly address to the people. In Jaffna, in Killinochchi, in Chavakachcheri, the northern Tamil population would ride out to the cemeteries on their bikes and scooters to find out if they were going to war again.

I hitched a ride on his motorcycle with an acquaintance to whom I'd been given an introduction by some colleagues from Peradeniya. "Will you be coming with us?" I had asked his wife as we took our tea before setting out. I received a definite no, accompanied by a smile and a wave. We headed out through the monsoon mud and potholes to Sudalai Cemetery, known locally as Mavirar Thijilum Illam, or the Heroes' Sleeping House. Some of his friends accompanied us on their own motorcycles. We parked the bikes and walked across a mud-soaked field toward the cemetery with thousands of other Tamil families who had come to grieve, pay their respects, and listen to the speech.

The gravestones here were separated by year. Some lay horizontally, replicating the length of a human body; others, roughly hewn, stood upright, squeezed together by war. I asked why the stones were of such different sizes and was told that in the first days of the war the bodies of the victims had actually been brought here to be buried. As the years wore on, people disappeared, bodies were not recovered, mass graves were dug, and tombs were replaced by simple gravestones on which the name and dates of the deceased were recorded. Over on the side stood a glass case containing fragments of gravestones recovered after the cemetery was razed by the Sinhalese Army in October 1995.

Under a light rain, thousands of families sat in vigil by the graves. For the most part, they sat quietly, lost in thought and meditation. Some had brought the favorite foods of the deceased—small cookies, coconuts, *waddi* (a Tamil cracker made from *dhal* and chickpea). Alongside a marker an old woman lay prostrate, wailing, her arms wrapped around the gravestone. Some of the stones stood alone, unmourned. Perhaps, I thought to myself, there was no one left in the family to come visit. But I was told later that there are those who stay away from these events because not everyone approves of their sons and daughters joining the LTTE, since to do so is often tantamount to a suicide mission. Some kept their distance from such events because they do not want to brush up against the LTTE any more than is absolutely necessary.

Not everyone in the north is a member of the LTTE. Most, in fact, are not, which is not to say that they aren't sympathetic to the Tamil cause. This is a hugely important distinction which, sadly, not all Sinhalese in the south appreciate. Many Tamils feel strongly that they do not enjoy equal rights with the Sinhalese. Many, though not all, argue for a separate homeland. But Prabhakaran's tactics—recruitment of the young, the murder of those who fail to carry out his wishes, the suicide bombers—have alienated many. And then there is the simple exhaustion caused by years of war that transcends politics. Twenty-five years of bombs, mines, displacement, and homelessness have left their own indelible marks on this population. But to want the same access to education, to government jobs, to the same opportunities the Sinhalese have is far different than being a member of the LTTE. As someone told me, "To be a Tiger is very much to be a Tamil, but to be a Tamil is not at all the same as being a Tiger."

I watched from a distance as young men and women—college-age kids, with the same crisp uniforms I had seen at security checkpoint two—moved in tandem, finalizing preparations for the ceremony. Banners had been hung; meals were being prepared for the families of the deceased. Alongside each grave stood a young starter palm tree, its roots wrapped to protect it, donated by the LTTE. At the end of the remembrance ceremony, each family would carry a starter home and plant it, in symbolic recognition of rebirth and hope. That night I remembered the small palmyra I had seen from the bus window on my way up to Jaffna. Sometimes, I was told, the LTTE donates a palmyra instead of palm to the families of the deceased, and I understood now what it was doing there. A family had lost someone in the war. These trees are so deeply intertwined with the martyrology and notion of the *Eelam,* or homeland, at whose core lies the belief that the heroes buried here have not died but are only sleeping. Some maintain that there are no bodies inside the graves, only seeds, and that once the dream of an *Eelam* is achieved, the seeds will sprout and rise up as trees. In the meantime, the families sit and weep.

As a Tiger, one does not kill oneself as a suicide bomber but rather gives oneself to the cause, even in death. Suicide missions are part of the ethos of this organization. The rationale behind them is that the bombers can inflict a maximum amount of damage with a minimum loss of life, this with close to two thousand civilians dead, most of whom just happened to be passing by when a Tiger detonated him- or herself in over 245 suicide attacks thus far. There is fierce competition among potential suicide bombers, known as the Black Tigers, for the honor of going on such a mission. These are not randomly chosen people but individuals named on a list that is reviewed carefully by Prabhakaran himself. Once selected, the men and women are put through rigorous physical and psychological tests, often lasting for months. The day before the mission, the Black Tiger is invited to take his or her last dinner with Prabhakaran. "There was a time," a Tamil friend told me, "when pictures of each suicide bomber enjoying his or her last meal with Prabhakaran were published in our local papers in the north. But now they are stopped. I don't know why. Perhaps for security reasons."

The culture of martyrology is fundamental to the philosophy of this organization. There are special camps that train the cadres who will be actively involved in the fighting both on land and sea. At the end of a three-month intensive period of training, each Tiger is presented with a glass vial containing cyanide, which they are supposed to wear around their necks. Women are given two, according to Prabhakaran, although the logic of this eludes me. If captured, the Tigers bite into the glass, which cuts the skin on the inside of the mouth. In approximately seven seconds, they die, death being preferable to capture. "It protects the organization," I was told.

It was close to 6:00. A light drizzle continued to fall while people moved forward to the raised platform and the eternal flame to listen to Prabhakaran's speech. It was usually broadcast from his military headquarters in Killinochchi. There were repeated reports in the Sinhalese and foreign press immediately after the tsunami that Prabhakaran had not survived the wave. In the days after the disaster, rumor had it that the Tigers had ordered an expensive coffin from

abroad shipped up north. The fact that he was the only political figure in South Asia who failed to make an appearance to address his
people also fueled speculation for months that he had died. But on
this night, for the five thousand or so who stood quietly, listening
to the voice over the public address system, whether Prabhakaran
was alive or not was less important than whether this war was going to continue. Some at the cemetery undoubtedly were aligned
with the LTTE. Many more, though, had simply lost someone in
the war and had come to hear whether their lives were going to be
uprooted again. Others had come to grieve collectively. I told my
friends not to translate for me. They could tell me later what had
been said. I stood and listened to the measured rhythms of a speech
in a language I didn't understand and saw from the expressions on
people's faces that there would be no war tomorrow, nor the day
after. Prabhakaran had given the new president, Mahinda Rajapakse,
some time. Just how much time was unclear. No one knew. Someone speculated that it might be several months. Prabhakaran had
intimated as much.

It was dark when we left. One of the people in our party glanced
up at the sky and announced that he would have to take a bath immediately when he got home. "I stayed at the cemetery after nightfall. We have this belief that being here after nightfall puts me into
contact with the dead. My wife will make me take a bath in order
to purify myself. These customs are fading a bit, but my wife still
keeps to them. It is also a custom here, perhaps not so much Hindu
as Tamil, that women should not go to the cemetery. That's why
my wife didn't come. That custom, too, is fading, but she still holds
to it. You saw Tamil women today at the cemetery. But still I will
have to take a bath. I was in contact with the dead."

We rode back into town through wet streamers and lights.

The next day the violence began.

Downtown Jaffna.

CHAPTER 21

Reading the Classics

Gerard Robouchon wears at least two hats in Jaffna, maybe more. In addition to teaching literature in the English department at the University of Jaffna, he simultaneously runs the Jaffna branch of the Alliance française, yet another casualty of this war, having been left to fend virtually for itself by the French Embassy. I am amazed at the way Gerard seems to move through all of this. Through peace and war, cease-fires and broken crease-fires, he placidly walks from the Alliance to the university, stopping at the vegetarian shop where he likes to eat. The mines and the gunfire seem as much a part of his everyday as teaching literature and giving French lessons. I was grateful for his company. We ate rice or noodles together some evenings at my guesthouse. Going back and forth between French and English, he gave me his take on life on the Jaffna Peninsula.

Gerard had asked me to give several lectures to his literature class at the university. I jumped at the chance because it was the only way I was really going to meet the students here. On a warm December afternoon I biked over to meet him at the Alliance, threading my way between the usual barriers, sandbags, and young Sinhalese soldiers. I was obviously not a threat to them. They shouted something with a wave, and I waved back. It was all very pleasant, except that the entire scene could turn on a dime.

Like most places in Jaffna, the building that houses the Alliance has somewhat gone to seed, yet it still sports a certain grace and charm reminiscent of better times. It is also the center of cultural life up here, this thanks to Gerard. When everything else is closed down, Gerard continues to show films, hold classes, and organize talks here on a daily basis. And it is not just the students who come. It is anyone interested in European culture.

On my initial arrival Gerard gave me the grand tour. He showed me the photocopy machine that didn't work (donated by the French Embassy, he noted), the computer that didn't work (donated by the French Embassy, he again noted), and the refrigerator that worked occasionally (French Embassy again). The supply of books was impressive—everything from Voltaire to the latest in detective fiction. The only problem was that there was just one of everything. "I can't teach with one copy of a book," he told me. "Somebody forgot that we have more than one student."

Over tea we decided that I'd be teaching Dostoyevsky's *Crime and Punishment,* some poems of Emily Dickinson, and Virginia Woolf's *To the Lighthouse,* all favorites of mine. We then embarked on sorting out the ever-present problem of texts. My problems with texts at Peradeniya pale in comparison to what confronted me here. Like Peradeniya, Jaffna is a campus without a bookstore but, unlike Kandy, it is also a town without an English-language bookstore. The one bookstore in the center of the city carries no foreign literature, including that of the people who happen to live 150 kilometers to the south. When books are assigned, one or two lucky people check out the library's copies. We discovered one copy of *To the Lighthouse* in Jaffna, and no anthologies of Emily Dickinson. Gerard was used to this and knew what to do. We downloaded Emily. In the meantime, a student was dispatched over to the university library to find *The Norton Anthology of American Poetry.* Success. This supplemented what we couldn't find of Dickinson's poetry on the Web. We were less successful with *Crime and Punishment.* No one had a copy. I would teach Dostoyevsky with no text.

Having solved the text problem, Gerard proceeded to make his way through a stack of videos. He had the movie *The Hours,* based on the book by Woolf, which he wanted to show the students in conjunction with *To the Lighthouse.* I thought it would be wonderful if the students could see it. It would give them a fine sense of Woolf as well as the issues women struggled with in the UK and the States in the 1950s. But there was a problem. Gerard was not permitted to show any films with overt sexual content. Even implicit sexual content is suspect.

"Is this a Hindu law?" I asked him, having seen some fairly racy films coming out of Bollywood over the years.

"No, it's Tiger," he told me. "No premarital sex, no alcohol, nothing that will distract you from the goal."

The issue with *The Hours* is that it shows two women embracing. He has to preview each movie. If it's a gray area, he leaves the decision in the hands of the students. Gerard took it before them and got the go-ahead. *The Hours* was on for next week.

"You show a movie that isn't approved," someone told me a few days later, "and then in a few days suddenly you have a visit from the Tigers. They ask you some questions. They warn you. How did they know? They infiltrate. People talk. All I know is that they know."

Several days later I went over to the Alliance and walked in to the strains of *Around the World in 80 Days*. The caretaker was watching the movie, transfixed, as Cantinflas, alias Passepartout, was rescuing Shirley MacLaine, alias Indian princess, from *sati* on the pyre. "Not to worry," I told Gerard and the caretaker. "No overt sexual content here. There may be one chaste kiss between David Niven and Shirley MacLaine at the end, but that's about it."

I had two days before my lecture and decided to squeeze in a trip to Delft Island, a place known for its wild ponies, introduced by the Portuguese in the 1600s. I arranged with the gentleman at the front desk, who was just beginning to say a few words to me, to order a *tuk-tuk* before dawn the next morning to take me down to the central bus station. From there I'd catch the bus to Jaffna port and then take the ferry for the hour-ride across the Delft Channel to the island. I had the name of someone whose farmhouse I could stay in since there were no guesthouses over there.

"Just hire a tractor. They'll get you there," I was told.

At 5:00 the next morning, I woke up the night watchman to unlock the gate, and the *tuk-tuk* driver and I set out for the bus station. As we arrived, a crowd was milling about and there was a heavy presence of military. There were no buses going anyplace that day. We heard that there had been two murders up the road. My driver and I tried to piece together the information. It seemed that two men unloading a truck had been gunned down an hour earlier. The first question everyone asks in situations such as this is whether the victims were military. If so, it means they were Sinhalese and thus the murder had probably been carried out by the Tigers. In this case, however, the victims were civilians, local Tamils, which complicated the problem. Whether they were Tigers or not became less clear. One of the first lessons of living here is that one doesn't have to be an active member of the Tigers to become a war casualty. No more information was forthcoming, however, and we were advised to turn back in case this was the beginning of something more serious. I arrived back at the guesthouse at the first light of day. The jasmine lady from next door was already out picking blossoms from the tree in our yard. She left, the day began, and the town shut down in protest. I learned a new word, *hartal,* a word used here and in India to describe the closing of shops and businesses in protest. I was struck by how this city communicated with itself. A murder at 4:00 a.m.; the city was shut down by 7:00, or earlier. This wasn't military ordered. These were shopkeepers and business owners waging their own collective strike against the violence here.

Technology has brought a new form of communication to Jaffna. The banner I had seen flying over the town—"We've got you covered, Jaffna"—no longer seemed superfluous. I text-messaged to Gerard to find out about the murders and to tell him what I knew.

"*Meutres normales*" (normal murders) was the message that came back.

Curfews and *hartals* have an odd effect upon the psyche if one is not used to them. I had discovered this early on in Kandy with the imposed curfews. Under normal conditions, one might choose to spend the day at home anyway, reading and puttering. But when one is forced to stay within the confines of home, it becomes a different thing altogether. The men at the guesthouse were used to it. I was not. I couldn't concentrate on anything. I set up my laptop in the dining room and tried to write up my notes. Failing at this, I took a book outside and tried to read on one of the plastic chairs. Failure again. I walked over to the iron gate and looked out between the gratings. I felt caged. Just before sunset the *hartal* was lifted for an hour before the curfew. I heard the clanging of iron and chains being loosened on gates up and down the street as parents and children came out and milled about, talking to neighbors. I took a short walk down Chetty Lane and wandered over to the storage yard where the Halo Corporation, in charge of de-mining here, kept their equipment. I got myself back in time for curfew.

The next morning I sent another text message to find out if the university was open and whether we were still on for Dostoyevsky. "Dostoyevsky is on," came the reply. I biked over and found an auditorium filled for the lecture on Dostoyevsky. I looked out on my audience and saw Tamil students, some Muslim women students, nuns of varying ages, a few priests, and, as I learned later, four or five Sinhalese students. They were poised with pen and notebook in hand, and I was about to talk to them about murder.

For the next two hours plus, we wound in and out of the streets of nineteenth-century St. Petersburg, in and out of the mind of Dostoyevsky's young protagonist, Raskolnikov, no older than most of the students in the auditorium today, a young man who, as the novel opens, is trying to decide whether he should kill an old woman pawnbroker or not, ostensibly with a view to improving his lot in life.

"Raskolnikov has a theory," I told the students. "He calls it the extraordinary man theory. He believes that there are certain people who can commit crimes for the benefit of humanity and that such people, precisely because they are extraordinary, differ from the rest of us in that they feel no guilt." I tossed a ball to the auditorium. "Are there conditions under which murder can be justified? What do you think?"

Silence. Then the ball got tossed back. "I have a question," a smart, young male student asked. "Doesn't this have something to do with the revolution? The Russian Revolution is in 1917. This is written in the 1860s. You said that the seeds of the revolution were planted as early as the 1860s. Isn't Dostoyevsky giving his characters permission to do what is necessary because of social injustice?"

"Yes, I think he is, but Dostoyevsky thought that when we commit crimes we are not only pitting ourselves against the legal system but we are transgressing God's law as well. So, the crime becomes twofold, against both man and God."

"Yes, but how binding are the laws if they are not adhered to by the rulers?"

I threw it back. "If you live in a society in which the ruler rules by divine mandate, what does that do to notions of legality? What do you all think?"

The auditorium was silent. I was not entirely comfortable with what I was discussing. The students were clearly smart. They had raised important questions. I suspected there wasn't one student in this class who hadn't drawn the obvious parallel between what Dostoyevsky was talking about and the political situation they were living in today. I felt that there was a limit to certain kinds of dialogues up here, but I was not yet sure where that limit was. I hadn't been here long enough. Did one know any more about where that line was if one had lived here far longer? I didn't know, but Gerard kept reminding me that there are boundaries one cannot cross.

He also reminded me of something else. "They got what you said, philosophically they got it," he told me later over tea. "But, you see, there are things about Dostoyevsky that are completely alien to these students. The idea of a young student living alone, for instance, is very difficult for them to understand. People live in groups here or they live in extended families. And there's another thing: the cold and how that contributes to isolation. Life here is outside. After class, the students sit under the trees or walk up the street to get something to eat. The idea of running between home and class and having to stay inside because of the cold doesn't compute here."

I bought some but not all of what he said. I am not sure that loneliness is always a function of being physically alone. I don't think that the experience Dostoyevsky is talking about is a uniquely Russian one. I thought this was something that I might be able to open up for discussion with the students, but it is also a sensitive topic. Sri Lanka has one of the highest suicide rates in the world—and not exclusively among suicide bombers; nor is it just a post-tsunami phenomenon. I thought of the statistics I had read on self-poisoning on the island as I headed back to the guesthouse for the day.

Word was now out on the street that the two men killed near the bus station had been part of the team decorating the cemetery, readying it for Remembrance Day. Evidently, according to what I had been able to gather, the military had infiltrated the ceremony, marked these two men, and gunned them down the next day, perhaps as a warning. Most people I talked to felt that there would almost certainly be reprisals. "There always are," someone said. "One murder up here gives birth to five or six more."

The next day two government soldiers stepped on a claymore mine at the junction I had passed the day before on the way to the Alliance. *Hartal* again. A text message came from Gerard. He was okay. Toward evening I felt that it was safe to go out and biked over to the house of a family I'd met. They were businesspeople who had spent their entire lives on the Jaffna Peninsula. They wanted me to meet a friend of theirs who got through the war by reading the complete works of Dostoyevsky, Tolstoy, and Turgenev in Tamil translation. I biked down quiet, jasmine-laced lanes to a modest, yet beautifully appointed, house, a treasured home for these people. I didn't even need to go inside to sense that. I was met at the door, however, by a thick haze of something that looked like smoke that almost totally obscured the people sitting just feet from where I was standing.

"We don't want you to be bothered by the mosquitoes," the owner of the house said, "so we lit a coil."

The coil was a deterrent to more than mosquitoes. But I was given a chair, handed a cup of tea, and plied with sweets, and the mosquitoes all vaporized into a conversation about the Russians.

"Yes, I have read all of Tolstoy, all but *Anna Karenina,* that is," the white-haired gentleman told me. I thought to myself that there was something decidedly patrician about his bearing and mannerisms. That translation was just now out, he went on, and he was waiting for it to appear up in Jaffna. He had a job here, a good one. Through times of war and peace he and his wife had continued to live in Jaffna. And somewhere along the line he became passionate about the Russians. "I just read them; they calmed me. While the bombs were dropping outside, I sat and read *War and Peace.*"

"I wanted you to meet this man," my friend said, smiling at the gentleman, "because this is how we survived the war. Yes, of course we survived physically by not going out, by being careful, by building shelters, by taking cover when we had to. But we also survived spiritually. My children couldn't go out to get culture, so we brought culture to them. We brought people like this to them. Culture was not outside the home; it was inside. I wrote nine books during the war. What else could I do?"

On my way back to my quarters on my bicycle, I decided to stop at the one functioning Internet café, near the university. It sat just across the street from the Hindu *kovil*. One could send e-mail to the ringing of bells for the evening *pooja* in the background. It had been a busy day at the café, which functioned as one of the collection points for applications for the U.S. State Department's annual green card lottery. The year before, three of the applications submitted from this point had been successful among the thousands that the State Department had received from Sri Lanka. The Internet café had thus been declared an auspicious site by half the population of Jaffna, resulting in three times the number of applications being submitted here this year than last. I stood on the third-floor balcony with the young woman who, along with her husband, ran the business. Trained as a doctor, she quit her job to help him. Tonight the two of us took in the evening air and listened to the chants and prayers intoned by the Hindu priest below as crowds arrived en masse, some with flowers and honey cakes to offer with their applications for a coveted green card.

After a time, I suddenly realized that the only lights left on the street were the small flickerings from the oil lamps in the *kovil*. The shutters of the vegetarian snack shops had rolled down for the night, and the people hoping for a chance at the American way of life had all cycled home. I remembered the injunction I had gotten from just about everybody—"Don't go out after dark"—said some quick good-byes, and set off for the guesthouse. I cycled past *kovils,* over bumps and potholes, mistaking the shapes of dogs sleeping on the road for something more sinister, past the banana stalls that had folded up their shutters for the night. As I turned into Chetty Lane,

I saw three figures, including the cook, standing in the road waiting for me. They took my bicycle and locked the tall gate behind me. It was 7:00.

Being in by dark carries more than war reverberations with it. I remembered my friend's remark at the cemetery about being in contact with the dead after nightfall. Nalini had told me stories about people on the beach at Hikkaduwa on the southwest coast hearing and seeing the ghosts of those whom they had lost in the tsunami. Merete in Arugam Bay had told me that her employees wouldn't ride their motor scooters alone after dark. Someone must be with them. I asked her why.

"Ghosts," was the answer.

Local fishermen gather in front of Prabhakaran's house on Point Pedro to have their photo taken.

CHAPTER 22

Leaving Jaffna

Things had deteriorated badly up here. There were seventeen people dead in Jaffna, this since the incident near the bus station several days ago. Most had run over claymore mines. Gerard's comment to me about "normal murders" stuck in my stomach.

I had all but moved into the dining room at the guest quarters, since it was the only place where there was semi-sufficient light and I was able to work. I was thinking tonight about all that I had heard today as I sat at the table with my plate of noodles and tea. The day had started out with a conversation near the Jaffna Library. Something had been bothering me about what I was told about the child kidnappings being done solely by Karuna's men. A man I spoke to over at the university had a very different take on the kidnapping stories. It felt like an unusually open conversation for a city that holds its information close. He said this to me: "There are many kinds of kidnappings all over this country. People confuse them. For example, there have been roughly fifteen hundred to two thousand young Tamil men abducted and killed by the Sri Lankan government. We know this up here in Jaffna. They are saying Karuna and his men do the abductions. That is one kind of kidnapping. The Tigers have their own ways. They don't do official recruiting. They simply move in closer to schools and randomly catch students and take them away. Then some time later the parents find that the kids have not come home. That is how it happens. Is it more prevalent in the Wanni than in Jaffna, you ask me? I think not. No, when the

LTTE had control of Jaffna, the kidnappings happened a lot here. Now that they have been pushed back to the Wanni there are more kidnappings there. Here, I will tell you something that perhaps you do not know. There are many, many more young people getting married up here than there used to be. They thought that if they got married the Tigers would not kidnap them. But now the Tigers have started kidnapping the young couples as well. Even some of our shopkeepers in Colombo are being kidnapped, but there I think it is the local police and army deserters who are doing that. Ours is a very complicated situation."

With that conversation fresh in my head, I had gone over to the Jaffna Library, where on a June night in 1981, the curator and several others stood behind some hastily erected police barricades and watched helplessly as the building burned to the ground. Ninety-seven thousand volumes and fifteen thousand manuscripts, some written on *ola* (palm) leaves, went up in smoke, along with the archives of the art historian Ananda Coomaraswamy and the Tamil historian Dr. Issac Tambiah. The library was rebuilt shortly after the fire, but as I wandered through it, I understood that despite donations from numerous countries and organizations, it houses merely the shell of the collection it once did.

In the afternoon I had biked over to the local branch of the Halo Trust, the organization responsible for mine clearance on the Jaffna Peninsula. It is run by a young man named Callum Peebles from Scotland. Something he said struck a chord. He confirmed that the mines up here are set by both sides. "People seem surprised," he told me, "but the LTTE has actually been very helpful in clearing away the mines. Why shouldn't they be? They have no interest in seeing their own people killed. But that sort of thing doesn't get reported in the press down south. The press is incredibly biased on both sides; it rarely reflects what is actually going on up here. And about your book. Please don't sensationalize what you have seen and what we have talked about. We have enough of it already. For me this place is a country of rumor."

I had told him about the rumors I'd heard in Colombo that people were living extravagantly up here.

"Show me somebody," he said.

Company had arrived. A team from the Swiss Embassy was here to do a site visit of the Jaffna branch of the Swiss Development Corporation. It had been a presence in Jaffna for twenty years, doing aid work. A lot of organizations had left; this one stayed. I was enjoying our time together over breakfast and dinner. They shared their muesli with me in the mornings.

Over vegetables and noodles one night I sat alone in the dining room with Emily Dickinson, wondering what she could possibly have to say to the students up here. I was going over some poems and thinking about the disconnect between the life Dickinson led and the lives to which people here had become accustomed. I mulled over her poetry and was lost in how circumspect and protected her life was. Today a student had told me that several years ago she was walking on campus and saw a woman in the distance kneeling down on the ground next to a body. She had a rifle in her hand and her arm was raised. There was a crowd around her. As the student got closer, she realized that it wasn't a gun but the arm of her husband, who was lying there on the ground, bleeding.

"We tried to get help, but there were no medics, no ambulances, nothing, as all essential services were shut down during the war. Ten minutes later this man died. He bled to death."

Even given the times, and the constraints, I wondered if part of me was not angry at Dickinson for not having lived differently, perhaps for not having lived larger. I settled on the poems "The soul selects her own society," "I heard a fly buzz when I died," "After great pain a formal feeling comes," "I never saw a moor, I never saw the sea," and "Tell all the truth but tell it slant." What, if anything, would Emily have to say to my Jaffna students? How would they read her? I went to bed that night pondering and listening to what I thought were shots being fired in the distance. A local Tamil told me that if you live here long enough you learn to distinguish between army shells and Tiger shells. I thought of the different ways that war sensitizes and desensitizes us. And I remembered the man who had made his way through the Russian classics during the war. There are people up here who have managed to live gracefully during times that have been anything but graceful.

The next day I spoke about flies buzzing and souls shutting doors. "What about the moor and the sea?" I asked my students. "Does anyone here know what a moor is?"

A student raised her hand. "Well, madam, I am like Emily Dickinson. I haven't seen the moor. I haven't really seen much. I haven't been out of Jaffna because of the situation here. But when you talk about it, I can imagine it."

I told them about the Caribbean poet Derek Walcott, who said that the right journey is always motionless. "What do you think he meant?"

"Maybe," said a very quiet voice, "that you don't need to go anyplace to see things and to feel things."

"Yes, that our imagination can take us places where we otherwise cannot go."

"Still, it's nice to travel," one of the young women said. The nuns smiled silently.

"Yes," I said. It was either this one word or a discourse on the politics of moving from north to south and vice versa in this country. I chose the one word.

We moved onto the next poem, "Tell all the truth but tell it slant." I decided to introduce it by talking about how radical Dickinson was for her time while living an almost hermitlike existence secluded in her father's house. I talked about the little ditties she wrote, all the poems that were discovered after her death, the quirkiness of her style, her habit of writing verse for various people on special occasions and lowering the poems down to the street in a basket. I was having trouble getting discussion going on this one, probably because I was uncomfortable with some of the things I was saying. This poem looked very different up here on the northern tip of this island than it had in Tucson, Arizona. Here people had been killed for telling the truth, slant or otherwise. I knew a Tamil journalist who had been beaten up and had both his legs broken by the LTTE for writing articles critical of them. He subsequently left the country.

After class a circle of students gathered around me in the courtyard—young women in *saris,* nuns in habits, two Muslim students. They were waiting for me to say something. I asked them if they liked Dickinson.

"Oh yes, very much, madam," came the reply. "But you didn't mention anything about her husband."

Of course, here women are married. And up here most marriages are still arranged. The idea of moving through life without a husband was, for the women here, completely alien.

"No, there was no husband. There were men with whom she had close relationships, men who influenced her enormously, but whether they were lovers we don't know. There was perhaps one woman. Perhaps a love relationship with a woman."

Raised eyebrows but not as high as I expected.

"What do you like about Dickinson?" I asked them.

"I like the way she speaks," one of the young women spoke up. "So simple but deep."

We were standing there, women talking about women. Another came forward. "You know, I am Sinhalese," she said. "I am from the south. My name is Darshini. Do you know some Sinhalese, madam?"

I bowed deeply to her and said a few sentences in Sinhalese. I was not sure I would have had the courage to come up here to study as she did. I told her that she was doing what people need to do in order to stop this war, and that I thought she was remarkable. The other girls agreed.

They asked me about my students in Arizona and what they were like. I told them that some are talented and hardworking but that many take their education for granted. I also told them that from what I had seen, the quality of instruction they receive up here is on a par with American universities. I spoke from the heart.

The bell had long since rung, and we all lingered until the last minute. I'd see them later for Woolf's *To the Lighthouse.* I'll never quite understand this, but something about Dickinson, who never knew war, never had her house bombed, and never, ever moved broke the ice between me and the students that day. It is one of the finer mysteries of literature.

The next morning I went down to the center of Jaffna to pick up a *chalwa* and to see the market area. I was also trying to sort through how I was going to teach *To the Lighthouse* to a class that had only the first ten pages of the novel in its possession. I took a three-wheeler into town and walked around to see what the stores might be selling. Central Jaffna, such as it is, is a lesson in wartime economics, whereby the vicissitudes of trade mirror those of war. In addition to the usual assortment of fruit vendors, most stores were stocked with the basics—tools, twine, cooking ware, the no-nonsense materials of a town trying to put itself back together. I turned up side streets that dissolved into alleys, past neglected mosques and a row of stalls where six or seven men were hard at work designing bicycle seat covers. I bought candy at the Jaffna version of Food City, the upscale market in Sri Lanka designed for the elite and the expats. Improbably, one had appeared here, though it had decidedly fallen on hard times. I wanted the candy to give as a present to the couple who had put me up for a few nights. I walked in to the strains of Matt Monroe singing "Have Yourself a Merry Little Christmas," an awkward nod to a world no one was living in here.

Time was when across the twenty-two miles separating India from Sri Lanka, ships came bearing wedding *saris* and *chalwas,* spices, incense, soap—and, beginning in 1983, arms to support the Tiger cause. Now anything that is imported from India comes first to Colombo and then by plane or vehicle up to Jaffna. That is how—legally, at least—things come in and out of the country. I remembered the man at the first Tiger checkpoint with his boxes full of *saris* from India and my neighbor commenting on the duty the man was going to have to pay on them. Illegally, things move in different ways. Contraband comes in and out north of Colombo off the coast of Wennappuwa in the Sinhalese part of the country. There is also the economics of scarcity. Prices are higher on the Jaffna Peninsula than in areas down south. Oranges in the Jaffna market are selling for 300 rupees ($3.00) apiece. I had tried to find some sandalwood oil that a friend in the States had brought me from India and was told by one of the merchants that they just don't import it anymore. "No one will buy it. Too much money," he said, gesturing up to the sky.

There is no tourism here, so no one is trying to make a living off of me. No one asks me where I am going. The paradox of Jaffna for me was and remains simply that here I had the illusion of breathing more freely and walked the streets with greater ease than down south.

I needed to make a stop at a bookstore to pick up a novel in Tamil for Velu. The shop was noticeably bereft of books. A young man was trying to help me find something appropriate for Velu while his cell phone was beeping with text messages. Mine began to beep as well. It was from a colleague, asking me where I was. The clerk in the store, busy with his own text messages, looked up and asked me if I was going far after I left the bookstore. A tractor-trailer carrying fifteen Sinhalese soldiers had just been hit by a claymore mine not far from the university. This was all anyone knew except that there were fatalities.

I text-messaged back that I had an appointment at a children's home in Thinakurivaly. Could I still bike over there? I typed.

"No, near blast," came the message. "Don't go."

"I think you should go back to the guesthouse at once," came another message from a friend. I needed no convincing. The man behind the counter was closing the bookstore. With Velu's book in hand, I grab a *tuk-tuk* and within ten minutes I was behind the locked gates of the guesthouse. The silence on the street was palpable. These killings were not, in Gerard's words, "normal murders." This was something else. The man at the desk shook his head and told me he hadn't seen anything like it since the late 1990s.

Another message from a colleague. "There has been a roundup."

At 5:00 the Swiss officers arrived back at the guesthouse without their SUV. I went out to meet them and noticed that this time they were with the head of the local office of the Swiss Development Corporation. The group seemed visibly shaken. The wife of one of the officers told me they had been passing the tractor-trailer at the very moment it had hit the claymore mine. The SUV with the Swiss in it was badly damaged, the driver ordered, rifle barrels pointed at his head, to take the wounded from the trailer to the military camp in what remained of the SUV. The vehicle managed to limp another kilometer, just enough to get it to the military camp. The men in the back seat, however, had already died. The Swiss officers, in the meantime, ran and hid on the grounds of a nearby house. Thanks to cell phones and the intervention of the head of the Swiss Development Corporation, they were finally rescued.

The Swiss stayed up late that night, needing to tell their story to each other and to others. Their driver was clearly in shock. He compulsively spun out his story again and again over the course of the evening, finding some comfort in the retelling. The next day the entire group flew out of Jaffna. Two weeks later, after twenty years in the north, the Swiss Development Corporation closed its offices and left.

Each day brought new violence. Moreover, as the outsider here, I was not adept at reading the danger signs around me. Some of this was undoubtedly due to the nature of this particular war, or postwar, as people were in the habit of calling it. The day after the incident involving the Swiss on Palali Road, the entire city closed down yet again for *hartal*. Our gate remained locked all day. The smell of acrid smoke had hung in the air already from early morning and hovered over the city all day. Toward sunset the gates were unlocked, and we began to mingle outside. One of the neighbors brought his German shepherd out; other people hugged their property lines, talking quietly to each other in their *sarongs* and housecoats. I decided to bike over to the university and inwardly cursed whoever it was who, today of all days, had decided to burn their garbage in the middle of the street. All the way down our lane, onto Temple Street, and past the Nallur Temple, I encountered fires strewn across the streets, the air noxious with the smell of burning tires piled onto palm branches and barbed wire mixed with shattered glass. I crossed them because I didn't know how to get around them. Only later did I learn that what I took for garbage were military barricades. I simply had not learned to decipher what everyone else could read living here.

Sadly, the people up north have become all too proficient as readers of war. A friend told me that he had learned to calibrate exactly how much time he had to get to his shelter before a bomb dropped or whether it was even necessary to seek shelter at all. When I heard a grenade going off one morning uncomfortably close, the man at the front desk told me it was over on Baker Street. "No reason to be alarmed," he said. I thanked him, and the first hint of a smile appeared on his face.

"You learn to calculate the distance by the sound," he explained. "Take yourself, for instance. Since you came to this country, your senses have been sharpened to the sound of birdsong. You like the birds up here, I think, no? You are always listening to birds. Our senses have gotten sharpened to the sounds of war."

The mood has changed over the past week. Gerard kept his promise to show *The Hours,* and on Saturday afternoon my students somehow managed to show up at the Alliance. I cycled past roadblocks and military now at full alert. Some stood at the end of the driveway leading up to the Alliance, watching each of us as we went in. Most of the students came that day, but with the news that the Muslim and Sinhalese students had left for home in the south, fearing the worst and worrying over their safety. I asked about Darshini, the Sinhalese girl with whom I had spoken the other day.

"She has just now left for the south, madam," came the answer.

The students brought their printouts of the first few pages of *To the Lighthouse.* They wanted to know how to read Woolf. They were puzzled by the dialogue, by the slow drift of the action. We sat and talked before the movie, and I shared some of my ideas about how to read the text. I told them that sometimes so much hangs on so little said. "Think of the first sentence, 'Yes, of course, if it's fine tomorrow.' That's what Mrs. Ramsay says, but then look at what Mr. Ramsay says on the next page. 'But it won't be fine.' So much of the action and feeling of the novel depends on these two sentences. They set the mood. They are the keys to these two characters."

We watched *The Hours* together. 1941—the war. We watched Nicole Kidman as Virginia Woolf write the final letter to Leonard and then drown herself in the river. We watched Julianna Moore trying to decide whether to live or commit suicide as she suffocates in a 1950s marriage in America. On a hotel bed she turns over the pages of Woolf's *Mrs. Dalloway*. Flashback to Woolf struggling, with the tip of her pencil in her mouth, over the first sentence of the novel, then announcing to Leonard that she has it: "Mrs. Dalloway said she would buy the flowers herself." Afterward we talked a little about the movie, about Woolf, about our lives.

"Madam, why did Woolf commit suicide?" asked one of the girls.

"I'm not sure there is a simple answer to that," I replied, remembering the high suicide rate in Sri Lanka, "but I think it was a combination of several things. She suffered from depression her entire life. I think she very much felt that she was a burden to her husband. Between novels her depression became worse. It was almost as if she held it at bay by writing. And then, of course, there was the war and the German bombing of England. It became too much; ending it became the only way out."

The talk shifted to what lay outside. They were concerned about me. "You don't know your way around here," one girl said. She was right.

We agreed to meet on Monday for more discussion of Woolf.

"Be careful going home," they said. The nuns looked particularly worried.

I never got to finish teaching Virginia Woolf to those students. Moving about became impossible over the next few days, as the violence moved in on the university. Even the Tamil students began to leave. My colleagues advised me to get out. I talked to Gerard about this. He said that at least for the time being he was going to stay and that he'd get out if need be. We said a lingering good-bye; I gave the Alliance dog, to which I had given the Russian name Zhuchka, a scratch, and thanked the caretaker, the lovely Tamil man who had watched all the movies the Alliance owned in a language he didn't understand.

Two weeks later Gerard wrote me in an e-mail that the man had gotten caught in crossfire when he went to the bank to get his salary check cashed and barely managed an escape through the back door.

At 6:00 the next morning, I checked in for the flight to Colombo in a shed in an abandoned field next to a church. Along with nuns, mothers and children, the wounded from the hospital, a Hindu priest, and several people who appeared to be Sinhalese, I stood in line waiting to be processed, checked, searched, and boarded onto the bus. We headed north to the Palali Airfield, which serves both military and civilian aircraft. Leaving Jaffna behind, the bus worked its way through the high-security zone. Miles of landscape with its foreground encased in barbed wire watched us miserably, as sick of the whole thing, I suspected, as we were. Hollowed-out buildings, some now occupied by the Sri Lankan Army, some long since abandoned, stared just as miserably out at us, their blasted-out walls adding nothing new to the same tired narrative that had been played out on these fields since 1983. I watched the winter visitors—kingfishers, bee-eaters, and some magpie robins—take flight over the morning haze, wondering to myself if war affects birds' migratory patterns.

At 10:30 Aero Lanka flight #760 took off from Palali. The seats around us had been laid flat so that a woman with her leg broken in two places could rest more comfortably. The young man next to me, a Sinhalese doctor who had received his medical degree in Russia and was currently working at the Point Pedro Hospital, told me that he couldn't do his job if he were dead and was flying back to Colombo until the worst was over to be with his wife and daughter. "The hospital," he went on, "probably could have been worse," not a comment that inspired confidence. The government was allowing medical supplies through because many of the casualties were Sri Lankan military. The hospital in Point Pedro had three doctors for over a hundred patients, with no surgical or diagnostic equipment. "This is why this woman is here with this leg," he explained. "They have no way to fix it."

The woman across the aisle listened in, and the two of us began to talk. She was in charge of an organization that provided prosthetic limbs to military and civilian casualties of the war. She had no intention of leaving Jaffna for good, just until "this" was over.

We landed at Ratmalana Airbase, fifteen kilometers south of Colombo, and were bused into the city along Galle Road. As we pulled out of the base, I noticed soldiers at work erecting barricades, sandbagging and encasing the entrance to the airfield in barbed wire, no doubt in response to recent events up north. We turned onto Galle Road and merged into the flow of traffic heading north past Majestic

City Shopping Center, past the new, Western-style coffeehouses, the fancy shopping mall at Crescat Center, and the Deli France, where a smattering of Sri Lankans and the usual gaggle of foreigners were busy with their croissants and coffee. I needed to make sense quietly of all that had happened and asked the bus driver to let me off at the Galle Face Hotel, where I managed to snag a room without a reservation. I wanted to stay there alone for the night. I called Nalini and told her I'd be over the next day. She told me that while I was gone there had been a new registration of Tamils in Colombo. The police had gone door to door in all the Tamil sections of the city, requiring each Tamil to register with the police. Mutto had had to register. It had all been fairly routine, "not like 1983." There were stories in the papers, she reported, of Tamils being taken from their houses in the middle of the night down to the police stations. There had been sporadic incidents of Tamils being beaten.

I took a bath and a nap and later in the day went down to the terrace by the sea and ordered a gin and tonic. I sat looking at the ocean as another day of heat heaved a sigh before it collapsed below the horizon. Three hundred and four kilometers north, the citizens of Jaffna were beginning to wander out onto the street from behind closed gates to speculate on what tomorrow might bring. As the ocean turned the color of quicksilver, I could make out the lights of the freighters lined up in the shipping lanes, waiting to unload their cargo in Colombo harbor.

CHAPTER 23

Going and Coming II

During my last months in Sri Lanka, Colombo lay moribund in the heat. I spent more and more time in the city to have better access to some of the people I still needed to see and some of the things I needed to do. In the mornings I would pack up my laptop and head for coffeehouses (a recent addition to Colombo), teahouses, anyplace with fans and, perchance, air-conditioning. I installed myself there for hours, drinking iced lattes (another new arrival in the capital), writing, listening to conversations at the tables next to me, and worrying about Noah.

Events punctuated the haze of heat. A friend from Jaffna had come down to Colombo to help organize his daughter's wedding. One morning he arrived at Nalini's along with his daughter to present me with an invitation to the event. He had traveled from Jaffna —with no small amount of effort—in order to deliver these invitations in person. "It's the custom," he told me. "We looked very long for a husband for my daughter," he continued. "It was a lot of work." The daughter sat at the table, blushing. I gathered things were working out well with the fiancé, whom she had met just two weeks ago.

I knew that I wouldn't be able to attend the wedding, though. Noah needed me. I needed him. The time to go home was approaching.

In those last weeks Nalini saw that I was becoming demoralized by the heat. Mostly we sat immobilized, listening to the click of the fans. For my part, I was trying to put something together on bird life here for the book I was writing.

"Just go down to Sinharaja," Nalini suggested. "You can listen to birdsong and you'll be cooler."

She was right. I was trying to write about birds while breathing in bus fumes. And so, with my bird book, a journal, and a pair of binoculars I headed south and inland.

Tucked deep into the southwest part of the island, the Sinharaja Forest Reserve was declared a National World Heritage site by UNESCO in 1990. For centuries, the area was protected by its inaccessibility. It is still difficult to access and is blissfully off the tourist route. When people began using the western part of the forest for logging in the early 1970s, scientists and environmentalists got together and lobbied against the logging. By the late 1970s, it had been banned entirely, and Sinharaja became a research station. There are 118 different kinds of trees here, many endemic to the island. Naturalists have counted as many as 147 bird species and 262 vertebrate species, 70 of which are native to Sri Lanka. For a forest as populated as this one (leopards, civets, wild boar, purple-faced leaf monkeys, several species of shrews, squirrels, amphibians, and invertebrates), it is only the birds that I heard. Only when I wrote it all down in my journal did the place feel crowded.

Nimal and Savi Gunatilleke have been working here as resident naturalists since 1978, studying and researching the flora and fauna of the rainforest. For most of the year, this is their home. It is a place they study, and a place they protect. A primitive dormitory type structure sits above the river and houses those who come here on educational trips. From its balcony I watched life move slowly in the waters below. In the mornings Nimal was out on the balcony deep into his reading, binoculars draped over his neck. It was E. O. Wilson's memoirs, *Naturalist,* that he was working on during my stay. I had brought down with me W. H. Auden's *Letters from Iceland,* perhaps an odd book to read in the midst of tropical jungle. And yet, something in it resonated deeply within me. Auden says at one point that he doesn't know whether to write about the island in prose or in poetry. Six thousand four hundred miles to the south, I was asking the same question. I looked up; Savi had come out from the kitchen to join us. We smiled and dipped back into our books.

On my first morning Nimal walked up the hill with a group of us to the research station. In his late fifties or early sixties, he walked with the energy of someone much younger and with unequivocal enthusiasm for what he did. "Look at that canopy of trees." He pointed to the very top of a hill, much higher than the one we were climbing. "We have reason to believe that every tree up there is specific and unique to this island. They occur no place else in the world." As we walked he would point to one bush, and then another. "There is nothing here that cannot be used for something. So much of this forest can be used for medicinal purposes. The local villagers use the woody climber here as aspirin. The *hwen bowitiya* is used against jaundice and hepatitis. The roofs of their small houses are made from the leaves of some of these trees."

I thought as we made our way up the hill about what I had heard about the increasing garbage problem on the island. If you live your life with no plastic aspirin bottles, no zip lock bags; if you take from the trees and plants what you need; if you grow what you eat, you will produce no waste, the naturalists here tell us. One had only to travel around the island to sense the truth of this. In Loku Menike's village there is almost no garbage produced. The only refuse I ever saw was in front of the small *kade* where they sell packaged goods and sodas in glass bottles. In Kandy things were very different. Our street was lined with garbage. People brought it out from their homes and dumped it—plastic bottles, tin cans, food scraps, everything—and set fire to it, hoping it would burn, which it didn't. Instead thick smoke rose into the air, and scavenger dogs were left to pick at what remained.

"What about the villagers in this area?" I asked Nimal. "What kind of relationship do you have with them?"

He smiled. "A very good one. We bring them here to educate them, and we also train them to be guides and naturalists here. It provides many with a living and an appreciation of the importance of this rainforest. Everybody wins."

Later that day Nimal and Savi pointed out a paradise flycatcher, blue magpies, barbets, brown-breasted flycatchers, a crested serpent eagle, and a bee-eater. They knew how to identify them visually, but almost thirty years in the rainforest had also taught them to identify almost anything by its song.

"Some of these birds are being studied," Savi told me later, "because there are different species here that are flying together."

"Is that so unusual?" I asked.

"Yes, certainly. When you look at the sky and see birds flying in groups, that group is made up of just one species. But here it is all different species that are flying together. Not all of them, but some of them. And it is not just the birds but mammals. The squirrels, the monkeys, and the mouse deer are all moving together in flocks and herds."

"Do you know why they are doing this?" I asked her.

"We think it is for their mutual benefit and protection. When all these different species fly together, they make a big noise that disturbs the insects. So the insects come out of their burrows, and it is easier to find them. So really the birds and mammals become more efficient this way. They protect each another."

Later that evening we sat and talked on the porch overlooking the river. The mosquitoes had risen and then settled in for the night, but small flies were landing on every available surface as we listened to the sounds of the river below.

"These just appeared since the tsunami," noted Savi, swatting one away. "They're tiny little flies. They're new here, so we are calling them 'tsunami flies.'"

When the flies had finally dispersed, I decided to take a walk down to the river.

"Watch out for snakes," warned Savi as I headed off into the darkness "The cobras and pythons like to come out and lie on the road at night because it's warm. Don't step on them."

"Message received," I said, grabbing my flashlight. The birds had tucked themselves into the trees for the night. Whatever was hunting in the forest was doing it silently.

The next morning I tied my *sarong* around me and stepped into the river. Two monitor lizards surveyed me from several yards away

as I floated downstream on my back and looked up at flame and aca-
cia trees in the forest canopy. One of the workers on the hill above
me yelled down: "If snake drops from tree, don't bite it! Ones who
don't drop from tree, you can bite those." I waved, smiled to myself,
did a little flutter kick, and paddled on.

Later I said my good-byes to this lovely couple who had made
this rainforest their life's work. They were just two among the many
I had met here who had refused to let the political maelstrom in-
terfere with the work they knew to be important. Books had been
written, land salvaged and saved—people had simply refused to give
up the work that had sustained them. I was humbled by what I saw.

I headed back up to Colombo and points north for my farewells.
It was time to go home. Over the next week good-byes lingered
and stretched as I went up and down the mountain. Kandy was the
first stop. I was trying to see if I could help Champika resolve the
problem of thirty square feet of space, enough to give him and Chamilla some privacy. He came to get me at the train station and took
me to his family's house, where a pile of sand had been delivered to
their door. His mother had prepared a lunch of curries for all of us.
Champika and I stood outside for awhile, and he showed me the part
of the hill where he was intending to build the room. He measured
it out with his feet. Money for the wedding was out of the question.
They would go down to the town clerk's office and get the marriage
registered with a few witnesses. We went inside and waited on chairs
covered in plastic until lunch was ready. His sister came in to greet
me. I asked her what she was doing now. "Not working now," she
told me.

"No jobs," said Champika.

We ate our curry in silence as the mother watched to see if I had
made progress since I was last there in mixing the curries with my
hands. My habits, how I ate my food, my skin and its freckles, everything about me held for Champika's mother and now for his fiancée
the same interest it had when we had first arrived in 2001.

Later that day Champika took me down the hill to Kush and
Nandana's. I gave him what I could so that he could make some
headway on the room. Dubai remained a dream, as did his hopes

for a van. He would call, and we would talk several more times before our final good-bye, the last as I was in the customs line at the airport.

I spent a few days at Kush and Nandana's so as to be able to visit with them as well as Velu and Latha. During the days I sat with Latha as she prepared the meals, smiling to myself as I realized that I still watched her shredding the coconut and cooking the curries with the same interest I did in 2001. We talked about bad husbands, her daughter, my son, wet laundry, and our lives. She gave me a going-away recipe for eggplant curry.

One night Nandana and I sat at the kitchen table and talked. I hadn't really had a good visit with either him or Kush since I had returned from Jaffna. Their lives were hugely busy, in a way that seemed almost American to me. But I knew that Nandana in particular wanted to find out more about life up north. I told him what I'd seen in Jaffna and what I thought about it. "Remember," I warned him, "this is just one pair of eyes."

There was a silence. And then he said something I had never heard him say before: "You know, I have been working for twenty years, as has Kush, to make this country better, to do something for it. And in all that time I haven't seen any improvement. It is no better than it was. Nothing has changed. This was to be the next Singapore. Look at the mess we've made of it."

On my last day at Mahamaya Mawatha, Velu asked me when I was coming again.

"I hope soon," I told him, though I wasn't sure.

"Can you bring me next time a really good watch?"

Latha, too, seemed eager for my return. She wanted a cell phone and some clothes.

Later that night I packed my things to the aroma of chili and garlic, which breathed from my pores, and folded my clothes to the clicking of the fan overhead. Relationships, I thought, laying my clothes in the bag, were given form centuries before I ever set foot here. Differences had been deeply etched since the first Europeans set foot on these shores, looking for the spice that would keep food from rotting back home. The British presence only dug them in deeper. I could live here forever. I could take up residence in a village. I could become fluent in Sinhalese. I could grow cinnamon trees and dress in *saris,* but I would never be part of Velu, Latha, and Loku Menike's world. Nor they of mine. I was the emissary, the residue of British colonialism that brought largess and with it power. Champika once said to me, "You will be white lady, I will be black man. No future for black man. No problem for you." And who were they for me? They were the people who had led me by the hand through this culture. And they were also the subjects of my book. Were they, I wondered, any the less on display for me than I was for them?

I spent my last few days on the mountain with Udaya and Aruni in Peradeniya. On the last night we did what we always used to do, which was to sit on the front stoop and listen to the evening *dharma* over the PA system from the village below. Achala was inside still studying for his A levels, with the statue of Buddha watching over him on the dining-room table. I could tell from his face that this was torture. This was not where he wanted to be. I wasn't sure the Buddha wanted to be there either.

"You know, you have a lot we don't have," said Udaya, sensing my mood. "You have garbage pickup, for example."

"Well, most of the time," I countered.

"You have things that work. Things get done when they are supposed to get done. Your telephones work. You don't have power outages every day. Your bathrooms are clean. You don't feel like you're entering a swimming pool every time you go to use the toilet. But I'll tell you. I love visiting America, but I could never live there forever."

"Why not?" I asked him, though I knew the answer already.

"You don't have mystery, and ghosts, and elephants. I'd miss that."

I went upstairs for the last time, tucked the corners of my mosquito netting in, and listened to the *dharma* until late. I thought about what Udaya had said about the ghosts and the elephants and remembered the story about the lone elephant down on the southern shore that, according to popular accounts, had made its way down to the beach between the second and third tsunami and stood looking out to sea. Scientists disputed it, but the people held fast to it.

Dulip came to get me the next morning. We loaded my duffle bags into his van and made stops in and around Kandy before heading down to Colombo. Pictures were taken, flowers, buds, and seeds were given me in the hopes that I would plant some of Sri Lanka in my desert garden in Tucson.

"Can we give you a small package to send to our daughter?" Kanchuka's parents had asked me. She was now studying for the Ph.D. in comparative literature at the University of Massachusetts, Amherst, and slogging through northeast winters. And so, as my last stop before I left the mountain, I went by the Dharmasiris to pick up a package of good Ceylon tea, some Dr. Johnson's tooth powder, a package of ayurvedic herbs, her mother's toffee, and a small sack of *kottamalli,* or coriander, which, when fried or boiled, promised to head off winter flu in Massachusetts. Small touches of a home profoundly missed.

Hours later, our local peregrinations over, Dulip and I began our journey down into Colombo: past the village with the corn sellers on the road, past the cashew ladies at Cadjugama, the rambutan sellers, the plastic beach toy man with inflatable Snoopies, rabbits, and rocket launchers. We passed the pineapple ladies, the clay pot ladies, the wicker villager, and maneuvered our way through towns whose once-white buildings had turned a grayish green from years of jungle mildew implanted on their walls. Toward evening, stuck in gridlock in a town called Heap of Milk Rice (Kiribathgoda) outside of Colombo, we pulled over to eat our rambutan fruit. Dulip managed to sprint across the gridlock and reemerged with hot *samosas.*

"Don't eat too many of these," he warned me, pointing at the rambutans. "They're heaty."

I laughed, needing no explanation this time about the impenetrable distinction between heaty and cool. And so I put the rest of the fruit back in a bag, and we set off on the last leg of our descent into the pre-monsoon heat of Colombo.

Dulip left me off at Nalini's. He had over the past eight months taken me places he had not wanted to go. He understood things about the shifting boundaries of war that I could not always comprehend. He had been born to it. We stood outside. I wanted him to understand how much I valued what he had done. I bowed deeply to him.

I sat with Nalini and Nimal until late at night. Things had changed in Colombo. Just days before, a Tamil member of Parliament, a man much respected for his intelligence, sensitivity, and ability to see beyond partisan politics, had been assassinated by the LTTE in his home in Colombo. It had come as no surprise; he had been on the LTTE's hit list for years, viewed as a traitor to the Tamil cause because of his willingness to work with the central government. He had foreseen his own death.

"I don't know if there will ever be peace in this land." Nalini sat, ruminating.

"Is it peace?" I said. "Is it peace after everyone's dead, and there is one broom left to sweep up the fragments of this country with?"

We had asked these questions every day since the time we became friends.

The next morning I had a few errands to run and one more good-bye to say, this to Udaya and Aruni's daughter Atulya. She worked in the center of Colombo at the British Council, not far from where the recent blasts had been going off.

"Listen, I want you to stay off buses, okay?" I told her.

"It's been like this forever," she assured me. "There's nothing special about the violence now. We go on about our business as we always have. This is what war is like over here."

I had one last thing to do before my flight that night and flagged down a *tuk-tuk* to take me to the photocopying shop.

"Going and coming, madam?" asked the three-wheel driver.

"Yes, going and coming."

My last conversation in my last *tuk-tuk* ride was much like other conversations I had had over the years in a trishaw in Colombo. It began like this:

"What country are you from, madam?"

And when I told the driver America, he said, "Sri Lanka good, madam, no?"

Usually I said yes, but on this last morning, something prompted me to a slightly different answer: "Well, sometimes. Some things are good. Some things are not so good."

Mostly, I think, the drivers understand me, but sometimes they don't. More often, I think, it's a question that remains unanswered in their own minds, regardless of what I say and what they can or cannot understand. They ask me perhaps more out of a need to get confirmation of the beauty and validity of a country in which they themselves have come to have increasing doubts.

On this last morning we passed the storefront of Atlas Van Lines, where I had waited in the rain for the bus to Jaffna several months back. It had been replaced by a clothing shop, the manager of Atlas having been assassinated in front of the store two weeks earlier. The murder generated the usual rumors and finger-pointing. The government blamed the Tigers, the Tigers the government. There was another version, given me by a Sri Lankan journalist, possibly the more accurate one—that the manager was a Tiger front man and had been killed by Sri Lankan intelligence. Three months after I returned home to the United States, someone called me to tell me that my Internet café in Jaffna had been torched. They didn't know if there were survivors.

I left in the middle of the night for the airport. The taxi moved along dark streets lit by the sparkle of water from a midnight rain. I watched from the window while my mind did its own dance with the images and fragments of conversations from the past months, some merging with memories of our life in the hills that year after 9/11. Singing geckos and curries, children in their whites merged with soldiers in body bags and posters of kids in Tiger uniform with their throats slashed. I thought of children running to the shore, squealing, on the day of the tsunami and remembered a *dharma* I had once heard a Buddhist nun preach. "Lemmings," she said, "run straight into the sea and never look back. That is how they die. We run like lemmings straight towards our own death yet act like we are not doing it."

I thought of a sea with wooden spoons and *saris* floating in it, and the mangoes of Jaffna.

"When you can taste the mangoes again, you will know that the war is over," I remembered Udaya saying.

The airport that night was its usual maelstrom. Someone's village was outside on the sidewalk, waiting. The taxi fell into the security lines for military inspection, which had tightened considerably in Colombo since December.

I grabbed my bags, my satchel of tea that Nalini and Nimal had given me the day before, and lingered a second on the platform between traffic. I breathed in the mingled smells of jet fuel and jasmine, and thought about the birds of Sinharaja.

"Going and coming?" the taxi driver asked me.

"No," I answered. "Just going."

And I left for home.

Velu, his granddaughter, and our pup, Samba, outside our house in Kandy. In the background, a profusion of bulat.

People move about the sand-swept streets of Jaffna with ease now. In May 2009 the civil war in Sri Lanka ended. The monomaniacal leader of the Tigers, who had managed to deflect and defeat the Sri Lankan military for twenty-six years, had, in the final days before his capture, been forced onto an isolated spit of land in the northeast where, according to reports, he had been killed while attempting to flee in an ambulance. But there was no real way to verify this, nor any other news coming from the war zone, since reporters had been barred from that area. This had become a war without witnesses.

"Is it Prabhakaran?" I wrote to Nalini, as the leader's photograph circulated over the Internet, showing him lying with his eyes wide open, seemingly surprised by his own death. "Even we aren't sure," came the response by return e-mail. The Tamil news services throughout the world denied it, claiming that Prabhakaran had escaped and was safe and well. With each day, however, the news became more certain. The Tamil press finally acknowledged the death of their beloved leader. In the days following, Colombo was awash in jubilation, parades, demonstrations, and the like. An effigy of Prabhakaran was paraded down the streets of the capital. In the south, where many of the Sri Lankan soldiers came from, the joy was almost frenzied.

Nalini wrote that Sri Lankan flags were flying over Tamil businesses in Colombo 6. "I can't tell you more because these days we are not going out." Others wrote: "We are just keeping our heads down and going on about our business." "We don't know what is going to happen. We feel that we should not say anything."

What happened in Sri Lanka in May was the culmination of a political promise to wipe out the Tigers made by President Rajapakse during his campaign for the presidency in 2005. It was also the result of an unprecedented push by the Sri Lankan military into the northeast in a final assault upon the Tamil Tigers, during which thousands of civilians were caught in its cross fire. Buddhist monks regularly offered *poojas* for the soldiers leaving for the front and tied *pirith* strings of blessings around their wrists. I heard of a monk who was preparing 1,500 amulets, each with a piece of *pirith* thread on it, to be sent to the government troops in the war zone.

The war on the battlefield is over now. The Sinhalese soldiers who did not die in its last bloody encounter have returned with blessings tied to their wrists. As for the northeast, the bodies of the Tamils who died have been cremated. Those who survived, some 300,000 of them, have now become internally displaced persons and languish in refugee camps. The death toll among civilians is unknown. Some of the camps house as many as 45,000 people; the smaller ones, 7,000 to 10,000. Sometimes the population shifts slightly as people are reunited with their families and placed in the same camp. Other times the displaced are identified as Tiger cadres and shifted to a special camp, so as to isolate them from the rest of the civilian population. The old Tamil=Tiger equation is primarily what keeps people in these camps. It has haunted the country since the mid-1970s and continues to do so in the aftermath of the war. The assumption on the part of the government and the military—that the Tamils in the north are, by extension, Tigers—means that persons in the camps must be vetted and cleared before being released. The process, it is estimated, will take up to two years. In the meantime, journalists and aid workers report that basic food and sanitation needs are being met, and that the children are attending school in the camps. The wife of a friend went up to the area recently and reported that in one camp a sixteen-year-old girl came up to her and began to talk. She said she had completed her O-level examinations.

When my friend's wife asked her if she wanted to continue her studies, the girl shook her head and said, "I just want out of here," pointing to the gate.

The streets of Colombo operate more or less normally these days, as they have throughout the war, with the cacophony of bus and *tuk-tuk* sounds heralding the start of another day. And yet Nalini writes, "Everything has changed. You would not recognize it now. Pennants hang on street corners with the larger-than-life images of the president on them. More and more frequently one hears [President Rajapakse] exhorted as Maha Raja or 'great king.'" "I thought we stamped the cult of personality out with Prabhakaran," writes another friend. "Now we have it all over again."

Amidst the maddening throng of traffic one can sometimes see unmarked white vans making their way down the roads. Sometimes at night, sometimes in broad daylight, they stop, pull someone over, throw them into the van, and disappear. In such a way have abductions been managed over the past several years. In the main the disappeared have been journalists who have dared to speak out against the government or the military, but others have vanished too. Since President Rajapakse took office in 2005, sixteen journalists have been assassinated. Dozens have been forced to flee, fearing for their lives. Yet others are imprisoned. On January 8, 2009, Lasantha Wikramatunga, editor-in-chief of the *Sunday Leader,* was killed on his way to work, shot to death by eight gunmen on motorcycles. He had foreseen his fate. The Sunday after his murder his article "And Then They Came for Me" was printed in his own newspaper. In it he had written, "Countless journalists have been harassed, threatened and killed. It has been my honor to belong to all those categories and now especially the last. When finally I am killed it will be the government that kills me."

I spend my time half a world away, wondering and ruminating over whether peace, real peace, will ever come to this island. What happened here in May felt too much like a Sinhalese victory, a Buddhist victory. I thought of the *pirith* threads that for centuries have tied this country together in a graceful interweaving of cultures and traditions. I do not know anymore if these threads can hold. I know that military victory cannot erase a century's worth of grievances of the Tamil people, and that ideas do not easily get snuffed out on a battlefield. I still wait for the government to address these grievances. But I also know that much of the violence of the past decade might well have been avoided had the LTTE taken part in serious negotiations and discussion offered them by President Kumaratunga and again during the cease-fire in 2002. In refusing a more peaceful solution the LTTE almost certainly orchestrated its own downfall.

The people who graced the pages of this book, as well as my life in Sri Lanka, are well, all except Mutto, who was diagnosed with cancer recently. He lies in a hospital in central Colombo. Nalini and her family are with him daily. "We are all praying to the gods," she told me. "He spent his life serving other people their tea and their meals. How can what has happened to him be right?"

I smile when I read the e-mails from friends telling me that people are once again eating Jaffna mangoes in the south. Udaya had been right. War's end has brought commerce to north and south, and with it the sweet fruit of the Jaffna mango. But mostly these days I remember something someone said to me in 2002. "We are in postwar, not in peace," he said. "Therein lies the difference."

ACKNOWLEDGMENTS

This book is blessed in debts. Tissa Jayatilika of the U.S. Sri Lankan Fulbright Commission made my first trip to the island possible. My students Tanya, Kanchuka, Nirosha, Rozmin, Sumudu, and Vihara taught me even as I taught them. My colleagues in the English department at Peradeniya, in particular Thiru Kandiah and Nihal Fernando, patiently helped me make sense of the world in which I found myself. Special thanks to Nayomini Padeniya for her help. Kush and Nandana Kariyaperruma, Velu, Latha, Loku Menike, Champika Prasanne, and Dulip Ruwan looked after us with patience, grace, and unending good humor. My deep thanks to Jean Arasanayagam, C. M. Madduma Bandara, the Chandrasekeras, Kapila Dahanayake, Chandra De Silva, the late Rev. Warakave Dhammaloka of the Natha Devala Temple in Kandy, K. Devarajah, Prithiviraj Fernando of the Centre for Conservation and Research, Fr. Superior W. Fernando and Brother Anthony Crooz of the Adisham Monastery in Haputale, Sam Gunaratne, Sunil Gunasekera, Nimal and Savi Gunatilleke, Ashley Halpé, Steve and Felicia Holgate, Firiyal Ismail, Dr. "Katu," Anthony Newman, Mr. W.K.B.N. Preme of the Bureau of Geology and Mines, Fr. Martin Quéré, o.m.i., of the National Seminary in Ampitiya, Callum Peebles at the Halo Trust, Jaffna, Monica Rani, Gerard Robouchon of the Alliance Française in Jaffna, Merete Scheller, Rukman Senanayake, the staff at Project Galle and at Thinakkural Rest, Mr. S. Thanabaalasinham of the Jaffna Library,

Ambikai Vamadevan, S. N. Wickramaratne, and Venerable B Shantal Wimala.

In the United States and Canada, I am indebted to Stuart Weinstein of the Pacific Tsunami Warning Center, who patiently explained to me the science of tsunamis; Paula Dunbar of the National Oceanic and Atmospheric Administration (NOAA); Manoranjan Selliah; and Mary Wiens of the Canadian Broadcast Company. To my friends and colleagues who believed in this project: Susan Aiken, who listened long ago to the first chapters; Matt Rotando, who brought his poetic ear and eye and his love of the island to early versions of the manuscript; and Naomi Sokoloff, who, with many more important things on her mind, read and listened to the final chapters. Al Babbitt, Laura Briggs, Richard Eaton, Phyllis Eisenberg, Ann Harkins, Barbara Kingsolver, Kate Kuhns, Georgia Maas, Eileen Meehan, Dan Peters, Del Phillips, Marty Reubin, Kristy Schmidt, Laura Schnapps, Aurelie Sheehan, Jacqueline Wales, David Yarnelle, and the late Jean Zukowski-Faust reached out in innumerable ways. And Kenny Cargill, George Gutsche, and Romy Taylor at the University of Arizona all bought me time when I most needed it.

Sometimes good things coalesce at just the right moment in one's life. My editor at Beacon, Helene Atwan, guided this manuscript toward completion with graceful hand and unerring eye at the same moment as the Ucross Foundation in Ucross, Wyoming, provided me with peace of place to do the final stitching together of this story. I watched deer watching me and listened to the ice flows on the creek stretch and contract as I wrote about a small island half a world away.

There are debts I cannot repay except perhaps to tell this story as honestly as I can. The current situation in Sri Lanka sadly prevents me from freely acknowledging some of the people both in Sri Lanka, Canada, and the United States who shared their stories with me. For security reasons some of the names in this book have thus been changed. I carry their stories in my heart and hope for the day when I can thank them openly.

A great debt, one arising out of love, is to Udaya Meddegama and his family—Aruni, Indu, Achala, and Atulya—who welcomed us into their home and hearts and tirelessly led me by the hand through their culture. *Godak pin.* And to Jon Pearce, who carries the island inside of him, as I do. And finally to my son, Noah, intrepid traveler, who shared so much of this even when he would rather have been doing so much else.

A list of works cited in this volume may be found on the book's page on the Beacon Press Web site.